Aquatic Sports
Medicine
1991

Aquatic Sports Medicine 1991

Editor

J.M. CAMERON

1991
FARRAND PRESS
LONDON

FARRAND PRESS
50, Ferry Street,
Isle of Dogs,
London E14 3DT, U.K.

ISBN 1850830258

Aquatic Sports Medicine 1991

A catalogue record for this title
is available from the British Library

Typeset in Times 10 on 12pt by the Publisher.
Printed on Ref. P paper by Page Brothers, Norwich.

Preface

And He shall spread forth His hands in the midst of them, as he that swimmeth spreadeth forth his hands to swim.

Isaiah 25: 11

In September 1989, London was the venue of the VIIIth World FINA Medical Congress of Aquatic Sports. Many World authorities on a wide range of such subjects attended and offered contributions. It is from these that this text has been compiled using a common standard of editing and English. It is my sincere hope that with my editorial pen I have not changed the sense of any of the excellent contributions, for that, one can be assured, was not the intention.

The task of scanning all the contributions and redrafting required considerable assistance, especially from my secretary, Miss Lisa Micallef and Mr David Meeks of the Computer Centre at The London Hospital Medical College: to both go my sincere thanks. Whilst expressing my thanks I must acknowledge the considerable support I have received from my wife, daughter and dog, even when working into the small hours. They and my publisher Farrand Press, a helpful cheery crew, have all been generous in their expertise.

One has attempted, in compiling the text, to group the contributions around particular topics – if this has been unsuccessful, I apologise. I have in most cases retained the personal touch of all the contributions and trust that no-one will be dissatisfied with the final result.

J. M. Cameron
1991

Contributors

Alarcon, N. Brosystan Institute, Sport and Aerobic Activities Research Institute, Rosario, Argentina

Arredondo, S.M. US Swimming International Center for Aquatic Research, Olympic Training Center, Colorado Springs, Colorado, USA

Avlonitou, E. Hellenic Sports Research Institute, 37 Kifissias Ave, 15123 Maroussi, Athens, Greece

Barzdukas, A. US Swimming International Center for Aquatic Research, Olympic Training Center, Colorado Springs, Colorado, USA

Beckett, A.H. IOC Medical Committee; c/o British Olympic Association, Church Row, 1 Wandsworth Plain, London, SW18 1EH, England

Beerman, S.B. RLSS Canada, 191, Church St, Toronto, Ontario, Canada

Bermudez, C. Brosystan Institute, Sport and Aerobic Activities Research Institute, Rosario, Argentina

Beyer, H. Judge of the Criminal Court, Kunhardtstrasse 5, D-2000 Hamburg 20, Germany

Bodnár, Ä. Hungarian Water Polo Association; Head, Department of Surgery, Korányi Frigyes and Sándor Hospital-Polyclinic, Budapest, Alsó erdösor str. 7, 1074 - Hungary

Bonifazi M. Istituto di Fisiologia Umana, Università di Siena, I-53100 Siena, and Centro Studi F.I.N., Via Laterina, 8, Roma, Italy.

Cade, R. Department of Physiology, University of Florida, Gainesville, Florida 32610, USA

Cameron, J.M. The London Hospital Medical College, London E1 2AD, England

Carli, G. Istituto di Fisiologia Umana, Università di Siena, I-53100 Siena, Italy

Chatard, J.C. Laboratoire de Physiologie, GIP Exercise, Faculté de Médecine de Saint-Etienne, 42650 Saint Jean-Bonnefonds, France

Childs, A. Department of Physiotherapy, Guy's Hospital, St Thomas' Street, London SE1 9RT, England

Collomp, C. Laboratoire de Physiologie, GIP Exercise, Faculté de

Médecine de Saint-Etienne, 42650 Saint Jean-Bonnefonds, France

Cooke, L.E. Senior Lecturer in Physiology, Chester College of Higher Education, Cheyney Road, Chester CH1 4BJ, England

Cosolito, P. Brosystan Institute, Sport and Aerobic Activities Research Institute, Rosario, Argentina

Costill, D.L. Distinguished Professor of Exercise Science; Director, Human Performance Laboratory, Ball State University, Muncie, Indiana, USA

Cristea, E. Sports Policlinic and Faculty of Medicine, Calea Dudesti 102, sect. 3, Bucharest, Rumania

Cuthbert, M.F.H. Medical Adviser, Royal Life Saving Society, Mountbatten House, Studley, Warwickshire, England

D'Acquisto, L.J. US Swimming Sports Science Research Co-ordinator, International Center for Aquatic Research, Olympic Training Center, Colorado Springs, Colorado, USA

Dal Monte, A. Coni Institute of Sports Science, Via Dei Campi Sportivi, 46, 00197 Roma, Italy

Daniels, J.T. US Swimming International Center for Aquatic Research, Olympic Training Center, Colorado Springs, Colorado, USA

Di Cave, P. Coni Institute of Sports Science, Via Dei Campi Sportivi, 46, 00197 Roma, Italy

Dinu, V. Sports Policlinic and Faculty of Medicine, Calea Dudesti 102, sect. 3, Bucharest, Rumania,

Dragăn, I.Gh. Sports Policlinic and Faculty of Medicine, Calea Dudesti 102, sect. 3, Bucharest, Rumania,

Dufficy, F. Legal Adviser – SCASA, c/o Cameron, Markby and Hewitt, Septre Court, 40 Tower Hill, London EC3N 4BB, England

Faina, M. Coni Institute of Sports Science, Via Dei Campi Sportivi, 46, 00197 Roma, Italy

Galasso, C. Brosystan Institute, Sport and Aerobic Activities Research Institute, Rosario, Argentina

Gallozzi, C. Coni Institute of Sports Science, Via Dei Campi Sportivi, 46, 00197 Roma, Italy

Garratt, L.P. GB and ASA Olympic Coach, The Flat, Beck House, Moorlands Road, Skelton, Yorkshire YO3 6XZ, England

Gerrard, D.F. Fitness Assessment Laboratory, University of Otago, Dunedin, New Zealand

Gribaudo, F. Brosystan Institute, Sport and Aerobic Activities Research Institute, Rosario, Argentina

Goode, A.W. Asst. Director, Surgical Unit, Department of Surgery, The

London Hospital, London E1 2AD, England

Guidi, G. Coni Institute of Sports Science, Via Dei Campi Sportivi, 46, 00197 Roma, Italy

Handley, A.J. Medical Adviser, Royal Life Saving Society, Mountbatten House, Studley, Warwickshire, England

Hardy, C.A. Department of Physical Education and Sports Science, University of Technology, Loughborough, Leics LE11 3TU, England

Hartung, G.H. Aquatic Research Laboratory, University of Hawaii, Honolulu, Hawaii, 96822, USA

Henderson, R., QC, 2 Harcourt Bldgs, Temple, London EC4Y 9DB, England

Herrara, J. Blanco, Calle 35 no. 1403 e/26 y La Torre, Apt. no. 1 Nuevo Vedado, c. Habana, Cuba

Hollings, S.C. University of Auckland Fitness Assessment Laboratory, Auckland, New Zealand

Holmberg, S. US Swimming International Center for Aquatic Research, Olympic Training Center, Colorado Springs, Colorado, USA

Hommen, N. Department of Physiology, University of Florida, Gainesville, Florida 32610, USA

Horiuchi, M. Laboratory for Exercise Physiology, Biomechanics and Sports Sciences, Faculty of Education, University of Tokyo, 7-3-1, Hongo, Bunkyo, Tokyo, 113, Japan.

Jegier, A. Department of Sports Medicine, Institute of International Medicine, Medical Academy, 90-532 Lódz, Poland

Kaas, P. Aqua System A/S, Box 275, 7400 Herning, Denmark

Kimura, S. Laboratory for Exercise Physiology, Biomechanics and Sports Sciences, Faculty of Education, University of Tokyo, 7-3-1, Hongo, Bunkyo, Tokyo, 113, Japan.

Kipke, L. Nachtigallenweg 13, Waldsteinberg X 7521, Germany

Kuński, H. Department of Sports Medicine, Institute of International Medicine, Medical Academy, 90-532 Lódź, Poland

Künstlinger, U. Institute of Aquatic Sports, Deutsche Sporthochschule Köln, D-5000 Cologne 41, Carl-Dien-Weg, Germany

Lally, D.A. Aquatic Research Laboratory, University of Hawaii, Honolulu, Hawaii, 96822, USA

Lawrence, M. US Swimming International Center for Aquatic Research, Olympic Training Center, Colorado Springs, Colorado, USA

Macdonald, I. Professor and Head of Department of Physiology, United Medical and Dental Schools, Guy's Hospital, St Thomas' Street, London SE1 9RT, England

Macdonald, R. Chief Superintendent Physiotherapist, Sports Injury Clinic, Crystal Palace National Sports Centre, Norwood, London SE 19 2BD, England

Mackay, W. Department of Physiology, United Medical and Dental Schools, Guy's Hospital, St Thomas' Street, London SE1 9RT, England

Maes, K.E. Aquatic Research Laboratory, University of Hawaii, Honolulu, Hawaii, 96822, USA

Maglischo, C. Laboratoire de Physiologie, GIP Exercise, Faculté de Médecine de Saint-Etienne, 42650 Saint Jean-Bonnefonds, France

Maglischo, E. Laboratoire de Physiologie, GIP Exercise, Faculté de Médecine de Saint-Etienne, 42650 Saint Jean-Bonnefonds, France

Martelli, G. Istituto di Fisiologia Umana, Università di Siena, I-53100 Siena, Italy

Marugo, L. Centro Studi F.I.N., Roma, Italy

Maslankiewicz, A. Department of Sports Medicine, Institute of International Medicine, Medical Academy, 90-532 Lódź, Poland

Mazza, J.C. Brosystan Institute, Sport and Aerobic Activities Research Institute, Rosario, Argentina

McConnell, A.K. Department of Human Sciences, University of Technology, Loughborough, Leicester, LE11 3TU, England

Miller, K. US Swimming International Center for Aquatic Research, Olympic Training Center, Colorado Springs, Colorado, USA

Mohora, M. Sports Policlinic and Faculty of Medicine, Calea Dudesti 102, sect. 3, Bucharest, Rumania,

Mutoh, Y. Associate Professor, Laboratory for Exercise Physiology, Biomechanics and Sports Sciences, Faculty of Education, University of Tokyo, 7-3-1, Hongo, Bunkyo, Tokyo, 113, Japan.

Orr, J.S. Director, Professor Medical Physics, University of London, Royal Postgraduate Medical School Hammersmith Hospital, London England

Pavlou, K.N. Sports Research Institute, 37 Kifissias Ave, 15123 Maroussi, Athens, Greece

Pavlik, G. Hungarian Swimming Federation, Budapest, Árpád fejedelem u.8. 1023 - Hungary

Ploesteanu, E. Sports Policlinic and Faculty of Medicine, Calea Dudesti 102, sect. 3, Bucharest, Rumania

Prins, J.H. Aquatic Research Laboratory, University of Hawaii, Honolulu, Hawaii, 96822, USA

Privette, M. Department of Physiology, University of Florida,

Gainesville, Florida 32610, USA

Rakus, E. Department of Sports Medicine, Institute of International Medicine, Medical Academy, 90-532 Lódz, Poland

Reese, R. US Swimming International Center for Aquatic Research, Olympic Training Center, Colorado Springs, Colorado, USA

Richardson, A.B. US Swimming Sports Medicine Council, Colorado Springs, Colorado, USA; Professor of Orthopaedics, John A. Burns School of Medicine, Honolulu, Hawaii, USA

Robson, G.J. University of Auckland Fitness Assessment Laboratory, Auckland, New Zealand

Rohn, T. Institute of Aquatic Sports, Deutsche Sporthochschule Köln, D-5000 Cologne 41, Carl-Dien-Weg, Germany

Rouard, A.H. Centre de Recherche d'Innovation sur le Sport, Lyon, France

Sanders, J.E. Executive Director, Australian Diving Association Inc. Perth, W. Australia

Sardella, F. Coni Institute of Sports Science, Via Dei Campi Sportivi, 46, 00197 Roma, Italy

Saini, G. Centro Studi F.I.N., Distiluto di Fisiologia Univerita di Umana, Siena Roma, Italy

Sgouraki, E. Sports Research Institute, 37 Kifissias Ave, 15123 Maroussi, Athens, Greece

Sims, B.V. Senior Tutor, Royal Life Saving Society, Mountbatten House, Studley, Warwickshire, England

Skipka, W. Institute of Aquatic Sports, Deutsche Sporthochschule Köln, D-5000 Cologne 41, Carl-Dien-Weg, Germany

Snode, C. Director, Crystal Palace Diving Institute, Crystal Palace National Sports Centre, Norwood, London SE19 2BD, England

Stephenson, J.W. Senior Consultant ENT Surgeon, Beckenham Hospital, Beckenham, Kent, England England

Strescu, V. Sports Policlinic and Faculty of Medicine, Calea Dudesti 102, sect. 3, Bucharest, Rumania,

Telander, T. Director, US Swimming International Center for Aquatic Research, Olympic Training Center, Colorado Springs, Colorado, USA

Troup, J.P. International Center for Aquatic Research, Olympic Training Center, Colorado Springs, Colorado, USA

Tsopanakis, A. Sports Research Institute, 37 Kifissias Ave, 15123 Maroussi, Athens, Greece

Uno, J. Aquatic Research Laboratory, University of Hawaii, Honolulu,

Hawaii, 96822, USA

Walker, M. Borough Council, Bromley Civic Centre, Rochester Avenue, Bromley, Kent BR1 3UH, England

Wielki, Cz. Professor, Faculty of Medicine, UCL, L-la-N, Beukenlaan 13, B-3030 Heverlee, Belgium

Zimmermann, E. Institute of Aquatic Sports, Deutsche Sporthochschule Köln, D-5000 Cologne 41, Carl-Dien-Weg, Germany

Contents

CONTENTS

CONTENTS

CONTENTS

Nota bene

Every care has been taken to ensure that drug dosages in this book are correct. Inevitably, however, there may still be errors that have evaded the most rigorous proof reading. Since moreover, new information on indications, dosages and side-effects is continually appearing, readers are advised to consult current information provided by drug manufacturers and licensing authorities before acting on the information in this book.

Part 1
Nutrition, Diet and Performance

1. The Importance of Nutrition for Optimal Swimming Training and Competition

D. L. COSTILL

ASIDE FROM THE LIMITS imposed by heredity and the physical improvements associated with training, no single factor plays a more important role in optimizing performance than diet. Despite the wealth of published information dealing with "proper nutrition," few efforts have been made to describe the nutritional needs and optimal dietary regimen for the swimmer. That is not to say that the topic of nutrition has not been considered important by coaches and swimmers. Like all other athletes, swimmers are always on the alert for the "magic food" that will make them winners. Unfortunately, most efforts to manipulate diet have been prompted by suggestions from more successful performers, poorly designed research studies, invalid commercial advertising claims and the misinterpretation of facts relating to the energy needs of the swimmer.

In their quest for success, most swimmers are willing to try any dietary regimen or nutritional supplement. The following discussion will take an objective look at the body's nutrient needs and present the more recent research findings that have direct bearing on swimming, training and performance.

Nutrient status of muscle

The energy used for all cellular operations is derived from the splitting of a powerful chemical compound known as adenosine triphosphate, (ATP). The energy stored in the ATP molecule is obtained from such fuels as carbohydrates (sugars), fats and protein. The energy needed to make the muscle fibers shorten cannot be obtained directly from fuels like sugar and fat, since they release only small quantities of energy when they are broken down. Instead, each cell uses the energy stored in ATP as the immediate energy for its operation. Nevertheless, without the availability of carbohydrates and fats, the muscle cannot maintain adequate levels of ATP. Since the mid-1930s we have known that both carbohydrate and fat contribute the primary energy for endurance exercise (Christensen and Hansen, 1939a). Though protein may contribute 6 to 9% of the energy during long periods of exercise lasting several hours, it is not a major energy source in competitive swimming events. Rather, carbohydrate stored in the muscles as glycogen is the primary fuel used during exhaustive swimming.

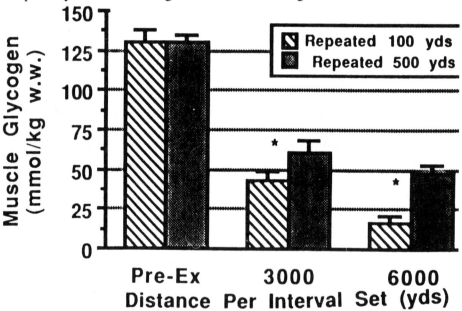

FIG. 1. Effects of interval-training on muscle glycogen utilization during repeated 100 and 500 yd front crawl swims. Note that muscle glycogen was more depleted after the 100 yd intervals than when the swimmers performed intermittent 500 yd swims.

As shown in Fig. 1, swimmers experience a dramatic depletion of arm muscle glycogen during an interval training session of 6000 yd (5486 m) (Costill *et al.*, 1988a). The histological examination of muscle sections following the training sessions revealed that nearly all the muscle fibers were empty of glycogen. In light of the muscle's reliance on glycogen for energy, it is surprising that the swimmers were able to maintain a steady swimming pace during the final phase of the training. In any event, these data clearly demonstrate the exhaustive nature of such interval training, and the greater rate of glycogen use during repeated 100 yd swims than during a similar volume of work performed in repeated 500 yd bouts. This difference in the rate of muscle glycogen use appears to be related to the relative intensity of swimming, since the swimmers were able to perform each of the 100 yd swims approximately 7% faster than during the 500 yd repetitions.

Measurements of muscle glycogen use from selected muscle fibers have been used to estimate the recruitment pattern used during exercise. Gollnick *et al.* (1985) have shown that type I fibers provide most of the force development during low-intensity, aerobic activities. As the muscle tension requirement increases at faster swimming speeds, the type II fibers are added to the pool of contracting fibers to increase the force of contraction. During high intensity sprint swimming, therefore, both the type I and II fibers in the posterior deltoid muscle contribute equally to the force production, becoming depleted of glycogen to about the same degree.

Since swimmers often train twice each day, covering more than 5000 m in each session, it is interesting to note that muscle glycogen resynthesis is incomplete when they are allowed only 6-8 h of recovery and a light carbohydrate meal between the training sessions (Fig. 2). Recent studies have shown that muscle glycogen depletion and the inability to resynthesize muscle glycogen between training sessions may be the primary cause for chronic fatigue in swimmers (Costill *et al.*, 1988*b*).

The amount of energy derived from this carbohydrate source is, of course, dependent on a number of factors including swimming speed, physical conditioning, environmental temperature, and the pre-exercise diet (Christensen and Hansen, 1939*b*; Fink *et al.*, 1979). Depletion of muscle glycogen has been shown to limit performance during swimming training, but there is less evidence to suggest that performance in swimming events lasting less than a few minutes will be impaired by low muscle glycogen levels.

Blood glucose also serves as a major contributor to the carbohydrate pool. At rest, the uptake of glucose accounts for less than 10 per cent of the total energy used by muscle (Anres *et al.*, 1956). During steady swimming, however, the net glucose uptake by the leg muscles may in-

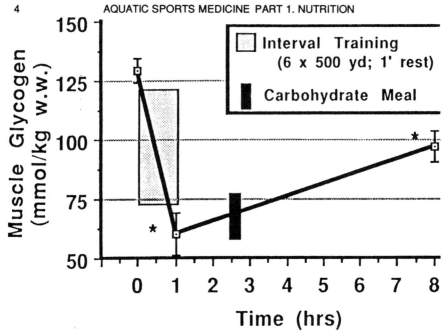

FIG. 2. Depletion and repletion of muscle glycogen during the interval training and in the 8 hours of recovery after the training session.

crease 10 to 20 times the resting level (Wahren *et al.*, 1971). As the duration of exercise is extended, the fraction of energy derived from blood glucose grows and may account for 75 to 90 per cent of the muscle's carbohydrate use (Wahren *et al.*, 1971). This large drain on blood glucose necessitates a concomitant increase in liver glucose output to lessen the risk of hypoglycemia (low blood sugar). Since the liver is the major contributor of glucose to blood, the increased demands by muscular activity rapidly reduce liver glycogen stores. During several hours of hard training, the swimmer's liver glycogen may be nearly emptied (Wahren, 1966; Felig, 1973). As a result, swimmers who train in multiple sessions each day and do not consume a carbohydrate rich diet may experience low blood glucose (hypoglycemic) (Levine, 1924).

Thus, optimal swimming performance is strongly influenced by the availability of carbohydrate. Nutrition plays a central role in both the storage and use of these fuels. Though the body's fat stores exceed the amount needed for even the longest swimming events, carbohydrate (glycogen) reserves in the liver and muscles are limited and may not be able to accommodate the requirements of training sessions lasting 2 to 4h. Competitive swimmers must, therefore, consume a diet rich in carbohydrate to replace tissue glycogen used during training and to promote glycogen storage prior to competition.

Dietary carbohydrates and training

Early studies demonstrated that when men ate a diet containing a normal amount of carbohydrates, about 55 per cent of total calories, their muscles stored approximately 100 millimoles of glycogen per kilogram of muscle (mmol/kg) (Bergström and Hultman, 1966). Diets low in carbohydrate, less than 15 per cent of calories, resulted in storage of only 53 mmol/kg, whereas a rich carbohydrate diet produced a muscle glycogen content of 205 mmol/kg. When these subjects were asked to exercise to exhaustion at 75% VO_2 max, their exercise times were proportional to the amount of glycogen present in the muscles before the test (Table 1). Thus, carbohydrate in the diet clearly has a direct influence on muscle glycogen stores and the swimmer's ability to train and compete.

TABLE 1. *Effects of dietary carbohydrate on muscle glycogen stores and endurance performance.*

CHO Intake g/24 h)	Glycogen Content (mmol/kg muscle)	Exercise Time to Exhaustion (min)
100 g	53 mmol/kg	57 min
280 g	100 mmol/kg	114 min
500 g	205 mmol/kg	167 min

Studies from Scandinavia in the mid-1960s indicated that muscle glycogen was restored to muscle within 24 h after exhaustive exercise if athletes ate a rich carbohydrate diet (Bergström and Hultman, 1966). Continuing this diet for two additional days elevated the glycogen to twice the pre-exercise level. More recent studies have shown that glycogen replacement and storage is not so simple. We have observed that 7 days after a marathon race in which muscle glycogen dropped from 196 to 26 mmol/kg, replacement processes had restored the glycogen to only 125 mmol/kg (Sherman *et al.*, 1983). We have recorded similarly slow glycogen restorage after exhaustive swimming training.

This delayed recovery of muscle glycogen seems to be more characteristic of running than swimming. Although the cause has not been fully explained, the muscle trauma which occurs in running may inhibit the mechanisms normally responsible for the uptake and storage of glucose by the muscle. Swimmers may experience the same delayed response if they develop muscle soreness as a consequence of weight training.

We have observed that when runners trained heavily and ate low carbohydrate diets (40 per cent of total calories), they had a day-to-day decline in muscle glycogen. When the same subjects ate high carbohydrate diets (70 per cent of calories) of equal caloric content, muscle glycogen replacement was nearly complete within the 22 h separating the training bouts. The runners perceived the training as much less difficult when they ate the high-carbohydrate diet.

When swimmers eat only as much food as *ad libitum,* they often underestimate their caloric needs and fail to consume enough carbohydrate to compensate for that used during training or competition. This discrepancy between glycogen use and carbohydrate intake may explain, in part, why some swimmers become chronically fatigued and need 48 h or longer completely to restore muscle glycogen (Piehl, 1974). Swimmers who train exhaustively on successive days must consume a diet rich in carbohydrates to reduce the heavy, tired feeling associated with a deficit in muscle glycogen .

It has been suggested that various types of carbohydrates (i.e. fructose, glucose, maltodextrin, etc.) may produce different rates and degrees of glycogen formation. Tests of this idea, however, are inconclusive. We studied six men who were fed diets principally composed of either simple sugars or starches (70 per cent of calories) for 2 days following exhaustive exercise (Costill *et al.*, 1981). No significant difference in muscle glycogen formation was found between the two diets, although there was a trend toward greater glycogen storage when the men consumed starch. Recent studies, on the other hand, have shown that simple carbohydrates facilitate glycogen storage to a greater extent than do complex carbohydrates (Roberts *et al.*, 1985). In light of these conflicting reports, the preferential use of either simple or complex carbohydrates for muscle glycogen replacement is unclear.

Diet before competition

In the preceding discussion we have established that different diets can markedly influence muscle glycogen stores and that endurance performance depends in part on the glycogen content at the onset of exercise. Based on muscle biopsy studies in the mid-1960s, a plan was proposed to help swimmers store the maximum amount of glycogen possible, a process known as glycogen loading (Bergström *et al.* 1967). It has been proposed that endurance athletes (i.e. runners) prepare for competition by completing an exhaustive training run 7 days before the event. For the following 3 days, these individuals are directed to eat fat and protein almost exclusively to deprive the muscles of carbohydrate and elevate glycogen synthetase. The athlete should then eat a rich carbohydrate diet for the remaining days. The intensity and volume of training during the 6-day period should be markedly reduced to prevent additional consumption of muscle glycogen and to maximize liver and muscle glycogen reserves. While this regimen has been shown to elevate muscle glycogen to twice the normal level, from 100 to 200 mmol/kg w.w., it is somewhat impractical and unnecessary for the competitive swimmer. During the 3 days of low carbohydrate intake, swimmers generally find it difficult to train, are often unable to perform mental tasks, are irritable, and show the usual signs of low blood sugar. In addition, exhaustive "depletion" exercise performed 7 days before the competition is of little training value and may impair glycogen storage rather than enhance it. In addition, it should be noted that extremely high muscle glycogen levels are not essential for competitive swimming, since muscle glycogen is seldom the cause of fatigue and exhaustion.

The pre-competition meal should be taken 2 to 3 hours before the race and should contain few fats and proteins since they digest slowly and do not provide fuels that are readily used during the event. A light carbohydrate meal of cereal, toast, and juice should be eaten since it digests quickly and will leave a minimum of residue in the stomach. To this point, it would appear that carbohydrates can do no harm; they replace muscle and liver glycogen, maintain blood glucose, and provide the primary fuel for endurance performance. The one time that the swimmer should not consume carbohydrates is during the final 30 to 60 min before a long hard run. As early as 1939, studies showed that such feedings temporarily elevate blood glucose and insulin (Christensen and Hansen, 1939*a*; Böje, 1940). Since insulin transports glucose out of the blood and into the body tissues, elevated blood insulin at the beginning of exercise results in a rapid uptake of glucose by the muscles with a sudden drop in the sugar content of the blood. Blood glucose declines rapidly within the first 15 min of exercise when sugar is consumed 45 min before exercise (Costill *et al.*, 1977; Foster *et al.*, 1979). Elevated blood glucose and insulin levels at the onset of exercise also tend to suppress the liver's normal release of glucose, making it difficult for the body quickly to readjust the glucose after it has fallen to the low levels seen at 15 to 45 min of exercise. The key here is to ingest a light carbohydrate meal roughly two hours before exercise so that blood insulin and glucose have adequate time to return to normal levels.

Dietary supplements

Athletes are always looking for an edge, something that will give them an advantage. Since the difference between winning and losing can often be measured in fractions of a second, no athlete wants to feel that they did not try everything possible to achieve their best performance. Manipulating the diet and taking extra quantities of various vitamins and minerals seem to be relatively harmless methods to make the body work at its best. But do these efforts really help?

Vitamins are organic substances necessary for growth and cellular function. Though some vitamins can be produced by the body and others stored in the body fat, most must be consumed in the diet. Vitamins C and B-complex, for example, are water soluble, cannot be stored, and must be constantly replenished in the foods we eat. The fat-soluble vitamins (A, D, E, and K) are stored in the liver and fatty tissue of the body and can accumulate during a period of excess intake for use at times when they may not be readily available. Unfortunately, there is no simple way to judge vitamin levels, until someone becomes vitamin deficient, at which time they exhibit unpleasant symptoms of extreme vitamin deficiency. The characteristic sores and loss of vision associated with a deficiency in vitamin B2 (riboflavin), for example, are a rare event in our society. Treatment with foods and tablets containing the essential vitamins generally eliminates the symptoms.

A recent survey by Jang et al. (1987) of swimmers' diets demonstrated that, on average, the intake of vitamins was equal to or greater than the recommended daily allowance (RDA). Individually, however, some number of the swimmers were eating diets containing less than the RDA for vitamins B6, B12, pantothenic acid, and folic acid. When we consider that the levels needed of these vitamins vary in proportion to the number of calories consumed in the diet, things looked even worse. Some of the swimmers were taking in less than 50 per cent of the recommended amount of these vitamins, based on the number of calories they were eating. One explanation for the low levels may be that some of the swimmers were vegetarians or ate diets low in such animal products as meats, cheese, milk, and eggs, which are the principal sources of B6, B12, and panothenic acid. Even though some swimmers consumed low levels of certain B vitamins, none of the swimmers exhibited any symptoms of vitamin-B deficiencies, such as anemia or unusual fatigue. Despite such assurances, some of the swimmers were taking vitamin supplements, containing two to five times that recommended by the RDA.

Over the past 40 years a variety of attempts has been made to resolve the question of whether vitamins taken in doses greater than the RDA will enhance performance and produce better health. To state that the research findings showed no benefits of vitamin supplementation would be inaccurate and somewhat misleading. There have been studies that found increased endurance with megadoses of vitamins C, E, and B-complex, but there are far more studies demonstrating that vitamins in excess of the RDA will not improve performance in either strength or endurance activities. Experts generally agree that popping vitamins will not make up for a lack of talent or training or give one an edge over the competition. As a matter of fact, too much of a good thing can be harmful. Extremely large doses of vitamins A and D may produce some undesirable effects. Overdoses of vitamin A, for example, may cause a loss of appetite, loss of hair, enlargement of the liver and spleen, swelling over the long bones, and general irritability – scarcely ideal conditions for a good swimmer. We have never seen these symptoms, however, even in athletes taking two to three times the RDA for these vitamins.

All in all, it appears that the RDA values for the various vitamins are about optimal for normal body operations, though possibly on the conservative side. Certainly, there is no convincing evidence to prove that vitamin pills taken to supplement a "balanced diet" will improve endurance or swimming performance.

Minerals are the second most widely used diet supplements by athletes. Iron, for example, is an essential component of hemoglobin, the oxygen-carrying component of blood, and of myoglobin, the oxygen-transporting pigment of muscle. Since iron deficiency anemia is known to impair endurance performance, it is important to distinguish between true anemia and the plasma volume dilution associated with repeated days of training in warm weather. Training tends to increase the volume of plasma more than the number of red blood cells, producing a drop in hemoglobin concentration with no apparent effect on oxygen transport or endurance.

Several studies have reported that between 36 and 82 per cent of female swimmers are anemic or iron deficient (Plowman and McSwegin, 1974; Clement and Asmundson, 1982). In light of this high frequency of iron deficiency in females, it seems logical to suggest that they include iron-rich foods in their diets. Iron supplementation should be directed by a physician, since prolonged administration of iron can cause an iron overload, a potentially serious condition (Bunch, 1980).

Conclusion

The preceding discussion has made it clear that proper nutrition can play an important role during training and swimming performance. The key to success is the availability of carbohydrates for muscle energy, though fat serves as an alternative fuel source and contributes to the energy pool during the long training sessions. Muscle glycogen stores depend on a rich carbohydrate diet, though a complement of all the basic food groups, vitamins, and minerals is essential for peak performance. Repeated days of intense training can result in a slow recovery of muscle glycogen, leading to a chronic state of fatigue. Periods of reduced training and diets supplemented with carbohydrate foods promote good training and the adaptations needed for improvement.

Finally, swimmers who consume balanced diets have little need for vitamin and mineral supplements. Though there is some evidence to show that female swimmers may develop an iron deficiency, it is inaccurate to generalize that all swimmers should supplement their diets with this mineral. While some swimmers may take less than the RDA for specific vitamins, symptoms of vitamin deficiencies have not been reported.

References

Anres, R., Cader, G. and Zierler, K.L. (1956). The quantitatively minor role of carbohydrate in oxidative metabolism by skeletal muscle in intact man in the basal state. Measurements of oxygen and glucose uptake and carbon dioxide and lactate production in the forearm. *Journal of Clinical Investigations*, 35, 671-682.

Bergström, J. and Hultman, E. (1966). The effect of exercise on muscle glycogen and electrolytes in normals. *Scandinavian Journal of Clinical Laboratory Investigation*, 18, 16-20.

Bergström, J., Hermansen, L. and Hultman, E. (1967). Diet, muscle glycogen and physical performance. *Acta Physiologica Scandinavica*, 71, 140-150.

Böje, O. (1940). Arbeitshypoglykamie nach Glukoseeingabe. *Scandinavian*

Archives of Physiology, **82**, 308-312.

Bunch, T.W.(1980). Blood test abnormalities in runners. *Mayo Clinics Proceedings,* **55**, 113-117.

Christensen, E.H. and Hansen, O. (1939*a*). Zur Methodik der Respiratorischen Quotient-Bestimmungen in Ruhe und bei Arbeit. *Scandinavian Archives of Physiology*, **81**, 137-143.

Christensen, E.H. and Hansen, O. (1939*b*). Arbeitsfähigkeit und Ernährung. *Scandinavian Archives of Physiology*, **81**, 160-171.

Clement, D.B. and Asmundson, R.C.(1982). Nutritional intake and hematologic parameters in endurance runners. *Physology of Sports Medicine,* **10**, 37-43.

Costill, D.L., Coyle, E., Dalsky, G., Evans, W., Fink, W. and Hoopes, D. (1977). Effects of elevated plasma FFA and insulin on muscle glycogen usage during exercise. *Journal of Applied Physiology*, **43**, 695-699.

Costill, D.L., Sherman, M., Fink, W., Maresh, C., Witten, M. and Miller, J. (1981). The role of dietary carbohydrates in muscle glycogen resynthesis after strenuous running. *American Journal of Clinical Nutrients*, **34**, 1831-1836.

Costill, D.L., Hinrichs, D., Fink, W.J. and Hoopes, D. (1988*a*). Muscle glycogen depletion during swimming interval training. *Journal of Swimming Research*, **4**, 15-18.

Costill, D.L., Flynn, M.G., Kirwan, J.P., Houmard, J.A., Mitchell, J.B., Thomas, R. and Park, S.H. (1988*b*). Effects of repeated days of intensified training on muscle glycogen and swimming performance. *Medical Science of Sports Exercise*, **20**, 249-254.

Felig, P.(1973). The glucose-alanine cycle. *Metabolism*, **22**, 179-207.

Fink, W.J., Costill, D.L. and Van Handel, P.J. (1975). Leg muscle metabolism during exercise in the heat and cold. *European Journal of Applied Physiology*, **34**, 183-190.

Foster, C.C., Costill, D.L. and Fink, W.J. (1979). Effects of pre-exercise feedings on endurance performance. *Medical Science of Sports*, **11**, 1-5.

Gollnick, P.D.(1985). Metabolism of substrates: Energy substrate metabolism during exercise and as modified by training. *Federation Proceedings*, **44**, 353-357.

Jang, K.T., Flynn, M.G., Costill, D.L., Kirwan, J.P., Houmard, J.A., Mitchell, J.B. and D'Acquisto, L.J. (1987). Energy balance in competitive swimmers and runners. *Journal of Swimming Research*, **3**, ˙9-23.

Levine, S.A., Gordon, B. and Drick, C.L. (1924). Some changes in the chemical constituents of the blood following a marathon race. *Journal of the American Medical Association*, **82**, 1778-1779.

Piehl, K. (1974). Time course for refilling of glycogen stores in human muscle fibers following exercise-induced glycogen depletion. *Acta Physiologica Scandinavica*, **90**, 297-302.

Plowman, S.A. and McSwegin, P.C. (1981). The effects of iron supplementation on female cross country runners. *Journal of Sports Medicine and Physical Fitness*, **21**, 407-416.

Roberts, K.M., Noble, E.G., Hayden, D.B. and Taylor, A.W. (1985). The effect of simple and complex carbohydrate diets on skeletal muscle glycogen and lipoprotein lipase of marathon runners. *Clinical Physiology*, **5**, 41.

Sherman, W.M., Costill, D.L., Fink, W.J., Armstrong, L.E. and Hagerman, F.C. (1983). The marathon: Recovery from acute biochemical alterations. *Biochemistry and Exercise*, **13**, 312-317.

Wahren, J. (1966). Quantitative aspects of blood flow and oxygen uptake in the forearm during rhythmic exercise. *Acta Physiologica Scandinavica*, **67**, 92.

Wahren, J., Felig, P. and Ahlborg, G. (1971). Glucose metabolism during exercise in man. *Journal of Clinical Investigation*, **50**, 2715-2725.

2. Nutrient Requirements of Adolescent Swimmers

I. MACDONALD

ADOLESCENCE IS THE TERM used to describe the period between childhood and adulthood and is obviously a time of considerable change, both physical and emotional. It is a time when the food and eating habits of the home tend to be discarded because more time is spent away from the home – this is especially true in those who are training for sport – and it often allows the young person the opportunity to develop their coming independence by rejecting family habits. It is the age group with the highest incidence of vegetarianism, and this is especially so in young women. Another factor that may give rise to anxiety over the nutritional well-being of these young men and women is the modern tendency for lifestyles to become informal which means a greater resort to snack meals.

Physical changes

In this age group dramatic physical changes take place. The second growth spurt occurs at this time, the first is in early life; at the peak of the adolescent growth spurt, the rate of growth is equivalent to that in early infancy. Changes in growth at this age contribute to a doubling of body mass and to 15% of final adult height. The peak velocity of increase in height is about 10 cm (4 in.) per year in boys and occurs between 12.2-15.2 years. For girls the increase in growth velocity is slightly less and occurs earlier, between 10.2-12.2 years. The height of boys in this spurt increases by about 20 cm (8 in.) whereas the girls increase by about half as much. This means that boys have greater demands on nutrients.

Another factor that has nutritional implications is that the age at which a child matures has become progressively earlier during the past 100 years – perhaps due to improved nutrients and a reduction in disease.

During the growth spurt males have a very rapid gain in their body tissue and in the mineral skeleton so that there are increased needs for protein, iron, calcium and zinc. Girls have a smaller increase in lean body tissue, but a greater increase in adipose tissue and, overall, their nutrient needs are less. If the energy needs of this age group are not met the growth spurt may be delayed or damaged. (The dramatic increase in the height of Japanese children after World War II compared to before is a classic example of what inadequate energy intake at this age can do). Nutrient requirements are much more clearly associated with physiological rather than chronological age.

Energy requirements

The major components of the energy requirements of the body are (1) maintenance of the body at rest, (2) those of growth and (3) those of physical activity.

The amount of energy required for growth is significantly small compared with that required to maintain the basal metabolic state. It has been calculated that at the peak of the growth spurt the tissue gain for males is satisfied by 66 calories and for females by 123 calories per day (Dwyer, 1980). Thus the energy requirements for growth for an adolescent constitute only a small percentage of the total energy intake.

There has been a marked fall in energy requirements in the last 40 years due to decreased physical activity among adolescents because of cars, television, and the popularity of sedentary pursuits during leisure time. This does not apply to swimmers in training. A recent UK survey reported that only 5.8% of children did not watch TV at all the previous day and 20% watched for more than 2 h a day (Balding, 1988).

What about energy requirements for adolescent swimmers and how do they differ from the requirements for non-swimmers? It is very difficult to estimate the precise energy cost of swimming because this depends on the skill of the swimmer, the type of stroke, body drag and buoyancy (Costill, 1988).

The single competitive swimming event itself, though expensive in energy, does not constitute a large proportion to the daily energy expenditure. In adults, studies with highly skilled swimmers have shown that about 250 kcal/km are expended when swimming the crawl, and this is one of the most economical forms of swimming (Costill, 1988). However in training energy expenditure is about 17-50 kcal/kg body weight per session. This, in combination with the energy expenditure of ordinary living (30-35 kcal/kg BW/day adds up to a total of about 50-85 kcal/kg BW/day) (Costill, 1988).

TABLE 1. *Daily increments in body content due to growth.*

		Average for period 10 - 20 yr (mg)	At peak of growth spurt (mg)
Calcium	M	210	400
	F	110	240
Iron	M	0.57	1.1
	F	0.23	0.9
Nitrogen	M	320	610 (3.8g protein)
	F	160	360 (2.2g protein)

Rees and Mahan, 1988

In what form should the increased need for energy be consumed? It is not easy, in practical terms, when the diet is low in fat, to consume large amounts of dietary energy, and especially during training, when the time available for eating is limited by academic as well as training demands. This means that fat in the diet is necessary. Fat contains more than twice the amount of nutrient energy of carbohydrates and protein. It is therefore a compact source of dietary energy. The problems of dietary fat, and especially saturated fat do not apply to the adolescent, so long as the dietary habits needed at this time do not continue when adolescence and active training are over. A common cause of overweight, leading to obesity, is the persistence of an eating pattern that is no longer required, as, for example, in the increase of weight seen in many women after pregnancy.

The question of the pre-competition energy intake is not a problem unless the event lasts more than 60 min (e.g. cycling, marathon) and there is a report (Singer and Neeves, 1968) that in a study on a 200 yd freestyle swim, the performance was not affected by the time interval between eating and swimming. Carbohydrate loading, favoured by marathoners, is of no relevance unless the event is of long duration, when it would be of value.

Protein

Dietary protein is closest in composition to that of skeletal muscle and it is assumed that dietary protein therefore builds up muscles. This is not true, as protein cannot be stored in the body and any excess intake is broken down and used as energy or stored as energy, namely adipose tissue. Nevertheless without adequate protein intake muscles cannot develop to their full capacity – as witness the thin spindly legs and arms of malnourished Third World children. The World Health Organisation in 1985 recommended, for 10-12-year-old boys and girls, 1.0 g protein/ kg BW/day with this level falling to 0.9 g for boys and 0.8 g for girls aged 16-18 years. What about physically active adolescent swimmers? There are some who advise intakes above those recommended by WHO during training in order to maintain muscle mass. However, it should be remembered that with increased physical activity there will be an increased calorie intake so there is going to be increased protein intake, if the person takes a "mixed" diet.

Contrary to the teaching of 10 or more years ago there is some evidence to support the view that an increase in muscle activity, as in sport, does require an increase in protein intake apart from the very slight increase required to build up muscle mass brought about by training. This increase in need is academically interesting but practically there can be very few if any adolescents in competitive swimming whose time would be improved by increasing their protein intake. However there is one case that concerns protein intake, and this seems to be more relevant to girls than boys, and that is the tendency for young people to be either strict vegetarians (vegan) or those who will eat milk and eggs but no other forms of animal protein, the so-called "ovolacto vegetarians". These adolescents need to be specially careful to select the correct combinations of grains and legumes to ensure they get a correct mix of essential amino acids.

Calcium

Approximately 45% of the adult skeleton is laid down during

adolescence although peak bone mass may not be attained until the third decade of life. Retention of calcium in adolescence averages 160 mg/day, but at the peak of the growth spurt it is estimated to be about 200 mg/day in girls and 300 mg/day in boys (Greenwood and Richardson, 1979). Failure to lay down adequate calcium in bone during adolescence and early adult life may be a risk factor for osteoporosis in later life. Although bone mass continues to increase in early adulthood, it is uncertain whether severe defects in adolescence can be compensated for. A problem found in female adolescents and relating to calcium and bones is the onset of menarche. When comparing girls who undertook a fair amount of athletic activity with sedentary controls it was noted that the onset of menstruation was delayed in the active group by a mean of nearly 1 year. The bone density was lower in those girls with infrequent menstruation and they were found to have higher intakes of dietary fibre (Lloyd et al., 1987). Dietary fibre as bran can impede calcium absorption so perhaps a word of warning to adolescent swimmers about their fibre intake?

Iron

Another nutrient with special reference to female adolescents is iron though even males require iron because of the increase in lean body mass, blood volume and haemoglobin. Everybody has heard of "sports anaemia", and the first observations (Yoshimura, 1970) were reported in swimmers in whom an iron and protein deficiency was detected, and it was postulated that there was a greater loss through the faeces, sweat and urine as a result of traumatic microhaemolysis in active muscles as well as reduced iron absorption from the gut. Some scientific studies carried out at the European Swimming Championships in Rome in 1983 suggested that "sports anaemia" may not occur in swimmers. The swimmers (mean age = 19.2 years) were of international level and had been swimming for at least 6 consecutive years. The controls were healthy persons practising sports such as golf, sailing, horse-riding. The results showed that athletes such as swimmers practising aerobic sports possess an iron pool which is greater than normal. The exception seems to be in long-distance runners whose iron pool is below normal, presumably because of recurrent traumatic microhaemolysis (Pelliccia and Di Nucci, 1987).

Vitamins

A mention must be made of vitamins because this is expected and because in some countries vitamin supplementation seems routine. There is very little evidence of any lack of vitamins in swimmers as a group and in fact one report stated that riboflavin supplements had no influence on swimming performance (Tremblay *et al.*, 1984).

Are dietary supplements, including vitamins, needed? With the possible exception of iron, nutrient supplements alone cannot improve swimming performance. While vitamins, mineral and protein are essential, eating a varied diet will give adolescent swimmers the nutrients they need. For insurance some individuals like to take a supplement. They should take only a single multi-vitamin and mineral tablet containing the recommended daily allowance. Vitamins and minerals do not supply energy and "more" is no better. A recent double-blind study was unable to demonstrate any effect on performance of a 3 month course of multi-vitamins and minerals in trained athletes (Weight *et al.*, 1988). Protein supplements are never needed by healthy individuals and do not boost athletic performance.

In those adolescent swimmers who are vegans some supplementation may be of value, for example vitamin B12, needed for vegans of all ages. Because of the high demand of calcium in adolescence and because plant sources of calcium are relatively poorly absorbed, calcium supplements may also be necessary. Iron and zinc intakes may also be marginal in adolescent vegans. Another problem with active adolescents is that, because of the bulky nature of the vegan diet, it may be difficult to consume enough energy to supply their relatively high needs.

Food habits of adolescents

The food habits of adolescents reflect the weakening influence of the family at this age, the young person's increasing social involvement with those of his/her age, his or her concern about their appearance and the high needs for energy. Thus they turn to outlets where the food supplied is eaten while standing up or taken away and where there is no need for a knife and fork or plate to consume the food. These so-called "take-away" foods are not a new phenomenon: there were take-away food shops in Pompeii and throughout medieval Europe. The Earl of Sandwich, who gave his name to a common form of "take-away" food, lived 1718-1792.

There is a considerable opinion that "fast foods", "take-away" and "junk food" are undesirable and nutritionally unsound. This implies that these foods are poor sources of nutrients and also that those who consume them eat little else. Both these implications appear to be incorrect. Fast foods often provide a third of the recommended daily allowance for all major nutrients and average about 660 kcal (Greecher and Shannon, 1977). A "large beef burger", a serving of french fries and a chocolate milk shake provide 40% of the daily energy requirement, and a higher percentage of protein, thiamine, riboflavin, calcium and iron. Vitamin A is on the low side.

Do adolescents in fact consume mainly fast food, snacks, etc? Studies reported over 10 years ago in the USA and Sweden indicate that about 15% of the daily energy intake came from snacks (McGandy *et al.*, 1972; Samuelsson, 1971). A more up-to-date study from Australia indicates that, in high school students, over 25% of daily energy and 18% of daily protein intake came from snacks (Truswell and Darnton-Hill, 1981). It seems the consumption of snacking and /or fast foods may be on the increase, but, it still is a small proportion of the daily intake. Perhaps the problems with snacking, etc, in adolescents is not under-nutrient but over-nutrition. For adolescent swimmers with little time for family meals due to training schedules, snacks are necessary, but they must not be confectionery only.

References

Balding, J. (1988). "Young People in 1987". UK Health Education Authority, Schools Health Education Unit.

Costill, D.L. (1988). Carbohydrates for exercise. Dietary demands for optimal performance. *International Journal of Sports Medicine, 9*, 1.

Dwyer, J. (1980). Nutrients and requirements of adolescence. Nutrition in Adolescence. *Naringsforskining.* Suppl. 18.

Greecher, C. P. and Shannon, B. (1977). Impact of fast food meals on nutrient intake of two groups. *Journal of American Dietetic Association, 70*, 368

Greenwood, C.T. and Richardson, D.P. (1979). Nutrition during adolescence, *World Review on Nutrient and Diet, 33*, 1.

Lloyd, T. Buchanan, J.R. ,Bitzer, S. *et al.* (1987). Interrelationships of diet, athletic activity, menstrual status and bone density in collegiate women. *American Journal of Clinical Nutrients, 46*, 1.

McGandy, R.B., Hall, B., Ford, C. *et al.* (1972). Dietary regulation of blood cholesterol in adolescent males. *American Journal of Clinical Nutrients, 25*, 61.

Pelliccia, A. and Di Nucci, G.B. (1987). Anaemia in swimmers: fact or fiction. *International Journal of Sports Medicine, 8*, 227.

Rees, J.M. and Mahan, L.K. (1988). Nutrition in adolescence. *In* "Nutrition throughout the Life Cycle". (Eds S.R. Williams and B.S. Worthington-Roberts). Mosby.

Samuelsson, G. (1971). An epidemiological study of child health and nutrition in a northern Swedish county. *Acta Paediatrica Scandinavica*, Supplement 214.

Singer, R.N. and Neeves R.E. (1968). Effect of food consumption on 200 yard freestyle swim performance. *Research Quarterly*, **39**, 355

Tremblay, A. Boilard, F., Breton M.F. *et al.* (1984). The effect of a riboflavin supplementation on the nutritional status and performance of elite swimmers. *Nutrient Research*, **4**, 201.

Truswell, A.S. and Darnton-Hill, I. (1981). Food habits of adolescents. *Nutrient Review*, **39**, 73.

Weight, L.M. Noakes, T.D., Labadarios, D. *et al.* (1988). Vitamin and mineral status of trained athletes including the effects of supplementation. *American Journal of Clinical Nutrients*, **47**, 186.

Yoshimura, H. (1970). Anaemia during physical training (sports anaemia). *Nutrient Review*, **28**, 251.

3. Nutrient Intake of Synchro and Other Swimmers

M. WALKER, W. MACKAY and I. MACDONALD

THE DIETARY INTAKES of 18 synchro and 13 male swimmers were assessed using the 3 day diary method, where one of the days was at the week-end. The daily intake of 14 dietary components was carried out using a computer programmed with values from the 4th Edition of McCance and Widdowson.

The cut-off value chosen was 80% of the Recommended Daily Allowance (RDA) set by the UK or USA. Though the RDA is intended for communities and not individuals it was felt that a nutrient intake below 80% of this level in an individual might cause concern.

Of the men swimmers, six were butterfly and three freestyle, with two medley, one backstroke and one breaststroke competitors training for the national team. There was a short-fall in some nutrients with 30% of the men below the 80% RDA in one nutrient and two below this cut-off in six nutrients.   The commonest nutrient with reduced intake was vitamin A followed by total folic acid and pyridoxine. In no nutrient was the group mean intake below the 80% RDA.

On the other hand the synchro swimmers, who, training for the national team appeared to have a poor nutrient intake. Forty per cent of the females were below the cut-off in 10 of the nutrients monitored, with one girl below the 80% RDA cut-off in 13 of the 14 nutrients assessed.

As in the men, the vitamin A intake seemed to be inadequate in girls, but three-quarters of the synchro swimmers had a limited intake of zinc, vitamin B6, energy, magnesium and iron. The mean intake of the whole synchro group was below 80% RDA in energy, iron, vitamin A, total folate and zinc.

There was some clinical evidence to support these findings in the Body Mass Index which was below the normal value (20-25) in nearly half the synchro group and 14 of the 18 were below 21, whereas in the male swimmers only three of the 13 had a BMI below 20.

Thus it seems, bearing in mind the limitations of this type of survey, men competitive swimmers probably have a nutrient intake that is adequate. The synchro swimmers, on the other hand, have a very poor nutrient intake.

We are grateful to the swimmers for their co-operation and to Professor J.M. Cameron for his help.

Part 2
Medical Problems Peculiar to Swimming

4. Hyperventilation in Synchronized Swimmers: Consequences and Treatment

A.K. McCONNELL

SYNCHRONIZED SWIMMERS ARE a unique group of athletes. The ability strictly to control their breathing is one of the most important skills these athletes must develop. Without this skill the swimmer will hyperventilate; this is a common problem amongst novices. The first detectable symptoms may be a tingling of the fingers and toes which increases in intensity. This is accompanied by a feeling of dizziness and detachment. As the symptoms intensify, the swimmers fingers extend and the thumbs and wrists flex in an uncontrolled spasm (tetany). It is at this point that an attentive coach will remove the swimmer from the pool. Typically, the symptoms subside within 5 or 10 min. However, upon re-entering the pool they will recur, but this time more quickly than in the first attack.

All these symptoms are caused by a low body carbon dioxide (CO_2) content. A fine balance exists between metabolic rate, ventilation and body CO_2 stores. If ventilation exceeds the level required to clear the metabolically produced CO_2 (VCO_2) from the body, the body CO_2 stores begin to "wash-out". Under these conditions, an individual is said to be hyperventilating. Although the synchronized swimmer is performing vigorous exercise, it is wrong to think that VCO_2 will necessarily be high. The intensity and duration of the exercise bouts performed by the synchronized swimmer dictate that the predominant metabolic pathway is anaerobic (without oxygen). Unlike aerobic (with oxygen) exercise, anaerobic exercise does not produce CO_2. Thus, although the swimmer is working very hard, little CO_2 is produced. This makes synchronized swimmers particularly vulnerable to the effects of hyperventilation.

Hyperventilation eventually leads to almost complete emptying the body CO_2 stores. The time required for this process depends upon the severity of the hyperventilation, but it is typically about 10 min. Low arterial CO_2 content ($PaCO_2$) causes a reduction of brain and coronary blood flows; the former causing the feelings of dizziness and detachment. Low $PaCO_2$ also leads to an increase in the excitability of nerves and muscles. This increase in excitability is responsible for the tingling (paraesthesia) and tetany of the extremities. By the time that these symptoms occur, the body CO_2 stores are already very low; complete replenishment of these stores requires hours. For this reason, once the symptoms have occurred, it is advisable to abandon the training session since the symptoms will almost certainly recur upon re-entering of the pool. It is important that swimmers are familiar with the symptoms of hyperventilation. In severe cases hyperventilation can lead to complete spasm of major muscle groups and unconsciousness; this is clearly life threatening to an individual immersed in water. At the first sign of any of these symptoms, the swimmer must be removed from the pool.

Recovery of the CO_2 stores may be accelerated by re-breathing from a bag (until the swimmer experiences the sensation that breathing is being "driven"), or by light exercise, cycling, for example, but not swimming. In the interests of safety, both of these activities should be supervised.

---

5. Medical Care of Olympic Swimming Team

Y. MUTOH, S. KIMURA and M. HORIUCHI

THE AUTHORS WERE TEAM physicians and trainers of Japan's swimming team in the Seoul Olympic Games (the group comprised 30 swimmers (14-27 years old, 19.4 years old in average) and 13 officials), during a period of about 100 days from the beginning of the intensive training camp until the end of the competitions.

Their main activities consisted of medical care, education on drug problems and investigations from the view point of sports medicine.

This paper reports and examines the activities of the medical staff of the Olympic Swimming Team.

Medical care of the swimmers

A total of 140 cases with 142 diseases were treated, including gastrointestinal disorders (30.3%), upper respiratory tract infections (22.5%), trauma, dermal disorders, arthralgia (9.2%) and others as shown in Table 1.

TABLE 1. *Breakdown of the injuries and diseases treated.*

1. Gastrointestinal disorders	43	cases	(30.3%)
2. Upper respiratory tract infections	32	cases	(22.5%)
3. Trauma	13	cases	(9.2%)
4. Dermal disorders	13	cases	(9.2%)
5. Arthralgia	13	cases	(9.2%)
6. Headache	6	cases	(4.2%)
7. Eye disorders	5	cases	(3.5%)
8. Menstrual disorders	5	cases	(3.5%)
9. Neck pain, lumbago	4	cases	(2.8%)
10. Others	8	cases	(5.6%)
	142	cases	(100%)

The most common illness was the gastrointestinal disorders as predicated. Since the intensive training camp in Japan, swimmers had been told repeatedly to avoid drinking raw water and eating raw vegetables and ice-creams. Some swimmers suffered from travellers' diarrhoea during the intensive training camp in Seoul in August1988, a month before the competitions. This bitter experience made the swimmers and coaches more careful during the Games. It is reported that the prophylactic use of norfloxacin and pepto-bismol before and during the Games helped the US Olympic swim team members stave off travellers' diarrhoea.

This was in contrast with the team's experience at the 1986 World championships in Madrid, where 90% of the swimmers had severe diarrhoea and emergency shipments of disphenoxylate with atropine (Lomotil) and Pepto-bismol had to be flown in (Nash, 1988). Though we did not give the medicines to Japanese swimmers for the prophylaxis of travellers' diarrhoea, there was no case with such a severe diarrhoea that it affected individual swimming performance. However, a couple of female swimmers suffered from terrible constipation before and during the Games. We had to treat some swimmers with an enema in the hospital in Tokyo and the athletes' village in Seoul, and saw that constipation in the female athlete was difficult to treat. It was considered that the female swimmers especially should be instructed to have a regular habit of defaecation each day.

As it was cooler in the early morning and in the evening in Seoul than in Tokyo, there were many swimmers who complained of sore throat. We recognized this at the time of the intensive training camp in Seoul before the Games. Gargle medicines and throat lozenges were given to every swimmer during the Games. This treatment was useful.

Even very well trained swimmers, if they sustain injuries immediately before the Games, cannot do their best in competition. There were many swimmers who could not swim at their best because of unexpected significant injuries due to tension and excitement of international competition. We experienced 13 cases with injuries, including four cases during the stay in the athletes' village. The atmosphere peculiar to the Olympic Games and fatigue due to a long-period training may contribute injuries of swimmers.

There were several cases with foot problems such as shoe sore and callus caused by new shoes. It is necessary to make sure that the shoes supplied must fit the size and shape of the feet of the swimmers. Well-fitted swimmers should take their own shoes when they go abroad to participate in the Games, and swimmers should be careful not to wear shoes without socks shortly after swimming. The places of treatment for these cases comprised lodgings (62.1%), swimming pool (31.4%) and others (6.4%). There were more cases treated on the occasion of taking meals, moving, gathering for the team meeting than cases treated when swimmers visited the doctor's room to seek for medical attention. It became known that team medical staff should accompany the swimmers as often as they could.

Survey of the medicine used and doping control

The results of the study on the medicines used by swimmers showed that 63% of the team used some kind of medicine. Nourishing tonic drinks, digestive drugs, vitamins and supplements were taken to relieve fatigue, to increase mental concentration, to eliminate gastrointestinal disorders, and to increase vitality.

TABLE 2. *Results of the survey of medicines used by swimmers.*

Number of swimmers who used medicines (19/30)	63%
Reasons for using medicines	
To alleviate fatigue	31.8%
To increase mental concentration	22.7%
To cure gastrointestinal disorders	18.2%
To supply with nutrition	9.1%
To cure diseases	9.1%
To increase vitality	4.5%
To relieve pain during menstruation	4.5%
	99.9%
Where to get medicines	
Coaches and other persons	44.4%
Pharmacy	38.9%
Physicians	16.7%
	100 %
Kinds of medicines	
Nourishing tonic drinks	
Digestive drugs (including Chinese herbal medicine, Kanpo-yaku)	
Vitamins	
Supplements	
Pain killers	
Colds medicines	

Although about 40% of swimmers who used medicines purchased them at the pharmacy, the similar numbers were given medicines by coaches and others. Some types of these medicines contain IOC banned substances such as caffeine, ephedrine and its derivatives. Inadvertent or innocent use of medications containing these substances can result in a positive test for banned substances (Voy, 1988). In fact, recently, a young Japanese skier suffering from a cold was disqualified as a result of using a cold medicine without the knowledge of its banned status. During the intensive training camp, advice was given to the swimmers not to take medicines carelessly.

On the questionnaire concerning drug control, 10% of the swimmers responded that they did not know how the drug control would be performed. However, all the swimmers knew that the athletes who used the banned drugs would be disqualified. The results of the drug tests on four Japanese swimmers were all negative.

For all that Ben Johnson, a short-lived gold medalist, was disqualified for using the steroid stanozolol, some fear that his winning may actually encourage steroid use among young athletes (Nash,1988). On the other hand, Janet Evans, who won three gold medals, showed the world that despite a short stature and slender build, victories can be achieved; her victories were achieved through appropriate scientific non artificial training methods. Similarly Daichi Suzuki, the only Japanese gold medalist, proved that if a Japanese swimmer with small body build trains himself or herself intelligently and appropriately, he or she can improve performance without drugs.

Conclusion

As Hanneman says, cooperation is very important between swimmer, coach, trainer, physician and masseur prior to planning the long-term training in order to preserve the health of the swimmers and reach best training results as a single unit (Hanneman, 1988).

Especially in the case of international competition such as the Olympic Games, from the view point of the medical care of the team, it is particularly necessary to prevent and treat early gastrointestinal disorders, upper respiratory tract infections and trauma. Furthermore, education in the danger of abusing drugs from an ethical and medical point of view should be stressed.

References

Hanneman, D. (1988). Relationship between athlete, physician, trainer and coach. *In* "The Olympic Book of Sports Medicine". Vol.I of Encyclopedia of Sports Medicine, International Olympic Committee Publication, (Eds A. Dirix, H.G. Knuttgen and K. Tittel), pp.563-565. Blackwell Scientific Publications, London.

Nash, H.L. (1988) Reflections on the medical aspect of 1988 Olympic Summer Games. *Physical Sports Medicine*, **16**, 118-127.

Voy, R.G.(1988). Doping and doping control – clinical aspects of the doping classes. *In* "The Olympic Book of Sports Medicine". Vol.I of Encyclopedia of Sports Medicine, International Olympic Committee Publication, (Eds A. Dirix, H.G. Knuttgen and K. Tittel), pp. 659-668. Blackwell Scientific Publications, London.

6. Swimmer's Shoulder: Arthroscopic Treatment – Case Reports of two Cases of Differing Aetiology

A. B. RICHARDSON

TRADITIONALLY, SWIMMER'S SHOULDER has been defined as a manifestation of Impingement Syndrome of the shoulder. This condition was described by Charles Neer as diffuse pain about the shoulder as a result of constant abrasion of the rotator cuff tendons against the undersurface of the acromion. This condition is common to all sports requiring overhead motion, and is most commonly associated with American baseball pitchers.

Shoulder pain in swimmers is usually associated with freestyle, backstroke, or butterfly, use of hand paddles, over-zealous weight training and the hand-entry phase of the front crawl stroke. It is felt to be more common in sprint swimmers and in those aquatic athletes who have been involved in competitive swimming for more than 8 years. Some 60-70% of competitive swimmers will experience pain at some time during their careers.

Conservation treatment of Swimmer's Shoulder Syndrome includes anti-inflammatory medications, ice packing, alteration of stroke techniques, and a rotator cuff strengthening program.

Surgical treatment has consisted of decompression of the sub-acromial space, by excising the sub-acromial bursa and the coraco-acromial ligament and removing the undersurface of the acromion (acromioplasty).

More recently, the role of instability of the shoulder in Impingement Syndrome has been recognized. We now know that sub-clinical instability predisposes the shoulder to upward movement of the humeral head resulting in impingement pain that may be recalcitrant to standard conservative and surgical techniques for treatment of swimmer's shoulder.

The majority of frank dislocations of the shoulder joint is anterior.

Joint capsule laxity, and sub-clinical multidirectional instability of the shoulder, are, however, common in those sports which emphasize flexibility. In these cases, simple surgical decompression of the subacromial space may be inadequate in dealing with the pain and discomfort of swimmer's shoulder.

The following two case histories demonstrate the ends of the spectrum of shoulder pain in competitive swimmers:

Case 1

D. H., a 21-year-old Oriental female college competitive swimmer with a 2 year history of progressive pain diffusely about both shoulders associated with swimming practice. She had no specific injuries, was primarily a butterfly swimmer, but swam most practice sessions freestyle. Although she had used hand paddles in the past, she had discontinued their use with the onset of pain. She had done weight training, including the swim bench, on a regular basis which had aggravated the pain.

Once the pain started, she was placed on a regimen of rotator cuff exercises, non-steroidal anti-inflammatory medications, ice packing, and she received one corticosteroid injection in each subacromial bursa.

Because of persistent bilateral shoulder pain, she underwent an arthroscopic decompression of the right shoulder in December 1987, and a similar procedure on the left shoulder in February 1988. Her post-operative course was uneventful and she has been able to return to competitive swimming without further pain in either shoulder.

Case 2

L.L., an 18-year-old Caucasian female college-level competitive swimmer with complaints of bilateral diffuse shoulder pain associated with practice and competition. With the onset of pain, she had been treated with ice packing, rest, non-steroidal, antiflammatory medications, and rotator cuff exercises. She had received two corticosteroid injections per shoulder.

Because of persistent pain, she underwent an arthroscopic decompression of the left shoulder in October 1987, followed by a similar procedure on the right in November 1987. Post-operatively, her course was characterized by initial decrease in pain, but recurrence of her pain with return to light swimming, especially on the right side.

In addition, she complained of the shoulder "coming out of place", especially posteriorly and inferiorly. Examination of the shoulder at this time was consistent with posterior, inferior, and anterior instability of the shoulder. She underwent a capsular shift procedure for multi-directional instability of the shoulder in June of 1989 and is presently recovering.

Discussion

Clearly, the histories and physical examinations of both these swimmers were similar. Both had persistent shoulder pain associated with competitive swimming. Both had conservative care, including corticosteroid injections. Both had bilateral arthroscopic decompressions of their shoulders. Yet the first patient was able rapidly to return to her athletic activities, while the second patient had immediate recurrence of pain with return even to light swimming. The difference lay in the underlying condition of the shoulders of the second swimmer, sub-clinical instability, which allowed continued impingement of her humeral head against the acromion.

Fortunately, most swimmers who experience pain about their shoulders do not require surgical intervention. In the past, surgical procedures have been aimed at decompressing the area of impingement between the humeral head and the overlying acromion. This has included simple section of the coraco-acromial ligament, acromioplasty, and/or resection of the subacromial bursa.

Instability of the shoulder, particularly multi-directional instability which allows superior migration of the humeral head in the glenoid, may render standard surgical approaches ineffectual.

Further, surgical approaches to purely anterior instability of the shoulder are inappropriate for multi-directional instability. A procedure which addresses the global laxity of the joint capsule must be used to correct this problem.

If, by history and examination, this sub-clinical instability can be identified, the goal of surgery must be to stabilize the gleno-humeral joint, thereby preventing the upward movement of the humeral head and the pain of swimmer's shoulder.

7. Studies on the Antioxidant Effects of Selenium on Top Swimmers

I. DRAGĂN, V. DINU, M. MOHORA, E. CRISTEA, E. PLOESTEANU and V. STRESCU

Introduction

LIPID PEROXIDATION (self-maintained) represents an active metabolic process, which takes place under the influence of free radicals derived from oxygen (FRDO). The excess of peroxidations can act noxiously upon cellular membranes and genetical apparatus (peroxidation of lipids and nucleic acids). The body is provided with some protective systems against peroxidation, for instance haemodynamic ones, some antioxidant factors (alphatocopherol, selenium, etc.), some enzymes (catalysis, superoxiddismutasis, SOD, glutathionperoxidasis, GPx), etc., (Abstracts, 1988). Endurance exercise, for instance swimming longer than 70 min, promotes an excess of peroxidation, which sometimes overpasses the physiological protective systems, becoming a limiting factor of muscular output. Selenium seems to be one of the protective factors against toxicity of the O_2 inside the biological medium; it enters in the composition of glutathionperoxidasis (4 atoms), enzyme which associates the antioxidant effects of the -SH radicals and selenium, catalysing the break-up of many peroxides (Rostruck et al., 1972). Vitamin E seems to play a potentialization role upon selenium, lack of these two factors underlies some pathological troubles (Combs and Scott, 1977). For man 50-150 µg selenium/day seems to be sufficient and this quantity is provided in a normal diet (Food and Nutrition Board, 1980). Long-term ingestion of high quantities of selenium (2000-3000 µg/day) can induce some toxic troubles (Nutrition Review, 1976). In a former study (Dragăn et al., 1988) we showed some antioxidant effects of selenium (a single dose of 150 µg or 3 weeks treatment of 100 µg selenium daily) on rowers and weight-lifters. Our present trial, performed on a group of swimmers (endurance exercise), tried also to illustrate these antioxidant effects of selenium.

Material and method

Thirty-three top swimmers (16 girls and 17 boys), ranging in age from 13 to 25 years, participated in this study. The subjects had a controlled programme of training (9-10 training sessions of 2 h each, weekly); controlled food and under medical supervision. A prospective double-blind placebo-controlled trial of selenium (50 μg as dried yeast, produced by Cantasium, London) was carried out in these swimmers, in two distinct stages:

Stage 1: the subjects were randomized into two groups, group A ($n= 17$) and group B ($n= 16$). One morning, on basal conditions and 2 h later (after 150 μg selenium or placebo administration and 2 h hard training) we recorded the following biochemical parameters: lipid peroxides (by determining the MDA, malondialdehyde, using the method of Jose and Slater (1972), which gives normal values from 60 to 184 μmol/dl); nonproteic-SH (essential glutathion), by using a colorimetric method (Sedlak and Lynsday, 1968), which gives normal values from 39 to 115 μmol/dl; blood lactate by using an enzymatic micromethod (Bergmeyer and Bernt, 1970), which gives normal values from 0.63 to 2.44 mmol/l. One week later (during which time the athletes continued their progamme) we repeated the trial applying the cross-over method (group A received placebo and group B selenium, single dose + 2 h hard training).

Stage 2: 16 swimmers out of these 33 (selected by draw) were also randomized into two groups, group A ($n = 7$) and group B ($n = 9$). The above biochemical parameters were recorded initially at rest, after 14 days of treatment (placebo or 100 μg selenium/day, before the morning training) and again after another 14 days of treatment, when applying the cross-over method (group A received selenium and group B placebo); all tests were recorded at rest, in the morning and the training sessions continued as mentioned above (in the afternoon, prior to the tests, there was no programme of training). During both trials (acute and chronic) no side-effects were mentioned and the swimmers did not use other medication. Statistical analyses were carried out using Student's "t" test.

Results and discussion

The results obtained are presented in Tables 1 and 2.

TABLE 1. *Change of some biochemical parameters induced by a single dose of 150 μg selenium (or placebo) + 2 h of hard training.*

| | Group A (n = 17) | | |
	Basal conditions	Selenium + Effort	Placebo + Effort
Peroxides (μmol/dl)	117.1 ± 24.1	170.44 ± 24.3	196.0 ± 31.5
		$p < 0.05$	$p = $ n.s.
Nonproteic-SH (μmol/dl)	56.15 ± 14.95	51.87 ± 12.56	56.35 ± 12.1
Blood lactate (mmol/l)	4.61 ± 0.84	3.59 ± 0.78	3.85 ± 1.2
		$p < 0.05$	$p = $ n.s.

| | Group B (n = 16) | | |
	On rest (initially)	Placebo + Effort	Selenium + Effort
Peroxides	159.56 ± 32.7	184.63 ± 30.7	164.3 ± 30.5
		$p = $ n.s. $\quad p = $ n.s.	
SH (nonproteic)	58.36 ± 10.9	56.35 ± 12.1	58.75 ± 9.7
Blood lactate	5.29 ± 1.01	3.85 ± 1.2	3.21 ± 0.79
		$p < 0.05$ $\quad p = $ n.s.	

Compared with the previous study (Dragǎn *et al.*, 1988), when after a single dose of selenium + 2 h hard training, the lipid peroxides decreased significantly (under placebo they increased significantly), in our present trial stage 1, the changes of the biochemical parameters were not significant, both under selenium and placebo single dosage + 2 h hard training (Table 1). The same was noted when we applied the "crossover" method. In stage 2 of the trial (Table 2) a significant decrease of lipid peroxides was noted under selenium treatment ($p < 0.01$), on group A, whose subjects came after 14 days of placebo, when lipid peroxides had increased significantly ($p < 0.02$); on group B, which started with selenium; a light decrease of the lipid peroxides (not significant) was noted and later under placebo a light increase of lipid peroxides (possibly due to the post-action of selenium). Regarding the nonproteic -SH, we noticed a significant increase under selenium treatment ($p < 0.05$), on group A, whose subjects received initially placebo, while on group B, which started with selenium, the increase of the -SH radicals was significant ($p < 0.05$) followed by a significant decrease under placebo. Regarding blood lactate we cannot explain our results because we lack the initial values (anyway significant increase was noticed both under selenium treatment and under placebo, but a little lower increase under

TABLE 2. *Changes of some biochemical parameters, induced by selenium or placebo treatment (2 weeks, 100 μg daily).*

| | Group A (n = 7) | | |
	Initially	2 weeks placebo	2 weeks selenium
Peroxides (MDA) (μmol/dl)	198.85 ± 28.7	232.57 ± 31.3	114.37 ± 23.6
		$p < 0.02$	$p < 0.01$
Nonproteic-SH (μmol/dl)	46.38 ± 10.1	47.12 ± 12.3	67.65 ± 16.8
		$p = $ n.s.	$p < 0.05$
Blood lactate	–	3.18 ± 0.81	4.31 ± 0.94
		$p < 0.05$	

| | Group B (n = 9) | | |
	Initially	2 weeks selenium	2 weeks placebo
Peroxides	192.4 ± 28.1	186.6 ± 29.0	198.7 ± 30.5
		$p = $ n.s.	$p = $ n.s.
Nonproteic-SH	48.0 ± 91.1	66.7 ± 12.4	47.97 ± 11.0
		$p < 0.05$	$p < 0.05$
Blood lactate		3.08 ± 0.71	5.15 ± 1.0
			$p < 0.05$

selenium). The intensification of the oxidative metabolism increases the flow of electrons in the respiratory chain and the possibility of incomplete reduction of oxygen to reactive species: O_2, H_2O_2, OH (in presence of free iron) which would result especially in the redox cycle of the ubiquinone. Studies performed on animals exercising endurance have proved a dramatically high increase in the number of mitochondria, this biogenesis contributing to the excessive formation of superoxide anion, which is probably decomposed by the SOD (superoxid-dismutasis), enzyme activated by the increase of O_2, according to the reaction: $2O_2 + 2H^+ \rightarrow H_2O_2 + O_2$ (Kelvin et al., 1981). Hydrogen peroxide formed excessively overpasses the possibility of GPx (glutathionperoxidasis), selenium-dependent and cumulates. Recent studies have demonstrated some inhibitory level of substratum, 1,3 diphosphoglycerate $\rightarrow$ 3, phosphoglycerate and ATP-synthetasis). The decrease of the ATP induces the increase of cytosolic Ca^{++}, which produces the conversion of XD (xanthindehydrogenasis) to XO (xanthinoxidasis). Another source of free radicals could result from the action of mono-amine-oxidases (MAO) upon cathecolamines liberated excessively during endurance exercise. The overpass of the antioxidant protective systems, among which GPx allows the reactive species of O_2

to combine with biological molecules, including polyunsaturated fat acids, produces a real "oxidative stress" expressed by the increase of the lipid peroxides (Kelvin *et al.*, 1982). The administration of selenium reduces significantly the level of peroxides, even under the initial values (group A, Table 2, from 232 to 114 μmol/dl) probably by the increase of GPx activity, antioxidant selenium-enzyme which breaks up lipid peroxides. The influence of selenium might be also explained by the potentialization of vitamin E activity, knowing that deficiency of selenium can be made up by a supplement of selenium and *mutatis mutandis* selenium; increases the concentration of vitamin E in the skeletal muscles and liver of rats performing endurance exercise (Packer, 1984). In subjects under exercise which received selenium for 14 days, this effect seems to maintain in time. Surprisingly, in the group treated by selenium we noticed an increase of the nonproteic-SH (essential glutathion), specific nucleophile substratum of GPx, which might signify a restoration of the redox disequilibrium disturbed by exercise (Dinu *et al.*, 1988). Although we do not know its exact role, the presence of selenium protein in muscles (different from GPx) and sensitive to the deficiency of selenium is probably not happening.

Conclusion

1   A single dose of 150 μg selenium orally followed by 2 hours of endurance exercise (swimming) induced contradictory effects upon some biochemical parameters (lipid peroxide, nonproteic -SH, blood lactate); the same aspects were recorded when applying cross-over method; these results were different from those of a previous trial (Dragăn *et al.*, 1988).

2   Beneficial effects of 2 weeks treatment by selenium (100 μg daily) were noticed (decrease of lipid peroxides, increase of nonproteic -SH) compared to placebo; when crossing over the subjects the same beneficial effects appeared only under selenium treatment.

3   Our results and those of the previous study (Dragăn *et al.*, 1988) support the idea of the benefit of selenium (protective effect against peroxidation) in endurance performers, a fact which would recommend a daily supplementation by 100-150 μg selenium during hard training (2-3 weeks) in order to support the biological preparation for competition, by attenuating the effects of excessive peroxidation, and so facilitating the extra demand of sport and maybe the energetic output at the molecular level.

References

Abstracts of the symposium "Drugs and Exercise". (1988). Romanian Sports Medicine Society, May 12, Bucharest.

Abstracts of the symposium "Carnitine in Elite Athletes". (1988). Chieti, July 7.

Bergmeyer, H.H. and Bernt, E. (1970). "Methoden der enzymatischen Analyse". Berlin, p. 1057.

Bishop, C.J. (1966). *Laboratory and Clinical Medicine*, **68**, 149.

Combs, G.F. and Scott, M. L. (1977). *Bioscience*, **27**, 467.

Davies, K.J.A., Packer, L, and Brooks, G, (1981). Biochemical adaptation of mitochondrial muscle and whole animal respiration to endurance training. *Archives of Biochemistry and Biophysiology*, **209** (2), 539-541.

Davies, K.J. A. and Packer, L., (1982). Free radicals tissue damage produced by exercise. *Biochemical and Biophysical Research Communications* **107** (4), 1198.

Dinu, V. (1981). Lipid peroxidation in atherosclerosis. *In* "Studies and Researches of Biochemistry". pp.161-166.

Dinu, V., Mohora, M. and Cristea, E., (1988). Role of selenium in the redox equilibrium restoration. *In* "5th Symposium on Biochemistry." Bucharest. May 13th.

Diplock, A.T. (1984). Vitamin E, selenium and free radicals. *Medicine and Biology*, **62**, 78-80.

Dragăn, I., Ploesteanu, E., Cristea, E., Mohora, M., Dinu, V. and Stroescu, V. (1988). Studies on selenium in top athletes. *Rev. Roum. Morphol. Embryol. Physiology*, **25**, (4) 187-190.

Dragăn, I. *et al.* (1986). Studies concerning acute and chronic effects of l-carnitine in elite athletes. Free communication at the XXIII World Congress of FIMS, Brisbane, 20-26 September.

Food and Nutrition Board. Recommended Dietary Allowances, IX-th. Edition, (1980). National Academy of Science, Washington, D.C.

Garrison, R. H. Jr. and Somer, E. (1985). "The Nutrition Desk Reference". Klats Publishing, Inc., New Canaan, Conneticut, USA.

Jose, P.J. and Slater, R.F. (1972). *Biochemical Journal*, 128-141. *Nutrition Review* (1976). **34**, 347.

Olinescu, R. (1982). "Peroxidation in Biochemy and Biology". Scientific and Encyclopaedic Editure, Bucharest.

Packer, L., (1984). Vitamin E, physical exercise and tissue damage in animals. *Medicine and Biology*, **62**, 105.

Petkau, A. (1981). Free radicals involvement in physiological and biochemical processes. *Canadian Journal of Physiology and Pharmacology*, **60** (1), 25-38.

Rostruck, J.T., Pope, A.L., Ganthier, H.E. and Hoekstra, W.G. (1972). *Science*, **179**, 588.

Sedlak, J. and Lynsday, R. (1968). *Analytical Biochemistry*, **25**, 192.

Stroescu, V. (Ed.) (1988). Bazele farmacologice ale practicii medicale. Medicala, I.II. The V-th Symposium on Biochemistry, Bucharest, May 13, 1988.

8. E N T Problems

J.W. STEPHENSON

I AM NOT A SCIENTIFIC EXPERT, well primed with statistics and references, but a working Ear, Nose and Throat Surgeon who has had an interest in otitis externa for many years. In recent years I have been encouraged to help look after swimmers by my good friend, Professor Cameron.

The effects of water on the ear

Ear wax is not true wax, but consists of fatty alcohols, and is not water repellant, but is water-soluble to a degree. The swimmer, who spends several hours a day in training, seldom has wax in his ears. Protection is therefore lost. Drying of the ears with towel or tissue may produce slight excoriations, and precipitate otitis externa.

Otitis externa is primarily an allergic type of reaction rather than an infection, although, of course, infection may supervene. This view is supported by the speed with which the condition is controlled by steroids or astringents, as opposed to antibiotics alone. Unless there is a perforation of the drum, water has no direct effect on the middle-ear, apart from damage by grossly excessive pressure. Needless to say a person with a perforated drum should not risk infection due to immersion, if it can be avoided. There is a widespread tendency to insert grommets in the treatment of "glue-ear" or serious otitis media. This carries a risk, sometimes serious. Although some authorities encourage swimming with grommets, I am very uneasy and usually advise my patients to avoid water in the ears.

It is possible to avoid the use of grommets in the great majority of cases, although the alternative non-surgical treatment is fairly prolonged and requires supervision. However it does allow children to swim without the risks attached to grommets. The protection given by ear-plugs is questionable: from the studies I have seen, many ear-plugs leak at depths of only 2 - 3 ft and even the most effective are unreliable at 10 ft. This supports my concern regarding grommets. In addition, some surgeons use long shafted grommets, and, as is shown in some papers, ear-plugs may be driven into the canal by pressure and onto the grommet. Divers are of course subject to considerable pressure.

PROTECTION OF THE EXTERNAL CANAL

The ideal protection is of course to remove the swimmer from water until treatment is complete. Competitive pressures, however, make this impossible.

As I have said, ear-plugs are limited. Their effectiveness depends on the individual, his meatal anatomy, and the sensible choice and use of ear-plugs. Ear-plugs may also make it difficult to hear instructions from trainers.

Regular use of almond or olive oil will give limited protection. Some swimmers use a light grease such as white vaseline, but it is difficult to reach the deep meatus. Self-induced damage to the canal or drum by the use of Q-tips or cotton-wool buds is unfortunately quite common.

Some veteran swimmers have discovered bizarre methods of protection, such as the use of alcohol. In some cases, where surgical spirit has proved unobtainable, they use whisky from the duty-free shops when travelling abroad!

TREATMENT OF OTITIS EXTERNA

As might be expected, otitis externa is relatively common amongst swimmers. The object of treatment is to control the eczematous reaction as rapidly as possible.

There are two main approaches – the modern standard treatment is by means of antibiotic – steroid drops and systemic antibiotics. The other is with non-steroidal, non-antibiotic anti-inflammatory preparations. I find that the antibiotic-steroidal drops are often slow and less effective, and are much more often associated with recurrence. The use of systemic antibiotics is useless in most cases, and may be dangerous. Some non-steroidal anti-inflammatory agents which exert a steroid-like effect are effective. Many years ago liquorice extract was hailed as a great discovery, but was extremely messy, like the old icthyol and glycerine.

The most acceptable and effective material is simple peppermint oil as an aqueous suspension. Combined with an astringent such as aluminium acetate 2% it is extremely rapid and effective. Unfortunately the original old Guy's Hospital formula of aluminium acetotartrate 2%, lead subacetate 2% and aqua menthol. pip. is no longer obtainable in England. If anyone knows where we can buy lead subacetate - please let me know!

Treatment is two or three drops twice a day for 1-2 weeks. At that stage most ears can be left to dry out for a week, and then a daily drop of almond oil instilled until evidence of wax is seen, at which point a weekly oiling is carried out.

In swimmers, more frequent oiling is advisable, and total protection of the ears during the period of active treatment may be necessary. Where there is pressure of competition, which makes it impossible to stop training, it has proved possible to use adcortyl-in-orabase thinned with liquid paraffin, and allow swimming to continue provided regular treatment is undertaken. Where a meatal furuncle is present, with severe meatal oedema, 5-6 min strip of ribbon gauze, cut longitudinally to about 5 cm, soaked in the aluminium acetate/peppermint water solution, and gently inserted into the meatus with a ring probe, and moistened with solution every hour for 12 to 18 h, will almost invariably open up the meatus for the use of drops in the normal way.

Some resistant cases will grow manilia, and/or, aspergillus on culture. In such cases Peveryl or Canestan solution can be used for a few days as drops, and then treatment with aluminium acetate drops resumed. In many simple fungal infections, the old formula of 1:1000 mercuric perchloride is extremely effective.

Sometimes, although very rarely in competitive swimmers, wax becomes soaked with water, swells and produces obstruction. Needless to say it is wise to be sure there is no risk of syringing a perforated drum. The safest, and certainly most effective means of syringing is with a Eustachian Catheter on a Higginson's type of syringe-pump. If the jet is directed at the meatal roof, even the most reluctant foreign body will be safely ejected. I have never had or heard of damage due to this method.

Effects of water on the nose and sinuses

Since various forms of allergic rhinitis are becoming so common in succeeding generations – the present estimate is about 93% in the 0-10 year old at present – it is not surprising that swimmers, who are predominantly young, suffer accordingly.

Congestion with catarrh and "sinus headaches" are common. In my experience of nearly 40 years, true sinusitis is rare. Antibiotics, therefore, have little place in treatment. Many people have an irregular septum which exacerbates the congestion. The side-effects of congestion are to cause blockage of the Eustachian tubes and thus the whole range of problems from intermittent deafness to "glue-ear" and otitis media.

It is not logical to plunge straight in and carry out myringotomies and insert grommets when the primary cause is nasal congestion, which should receive attention.

Clinically, the nasal mucosa may appear as the dark congested tissue of the vasomotor or "non-specific" rhinitis, or the pale mauve congestion of the specific type. Since treatment is similar, the question is largely academic.

It is worth noting that many factors causing rhinitis, apart from viral infection, are not protein or even metallic, but may be abstract as in cold, heat, emotion, sunlight and so forth. This implies vast gaps in our areas into research as to the causes of allergic rhinitis.

MEDICAL TREATMENT

This consists mainly of a combination of antihistamines and decongestants. Care must be taken when prescribing, that substances which are not acceptable in competitive swimming are not given, and reference to the list of recommended drugs is essential.

The problem with medication in this condition is that it is very long-term and may produce unacceptable side-effects.

SURGICAL TREATMENT

If a course of several weeks of medical treatment indicates improvement, it is a further indication that surgical treatment would be not only more effective, but hopefully life-long.

Correction of the deviated septum is simple, rapid and effective. I have not found that alternatives such as septoplasty have any advantage, and in fact have had to carry out sub-mucous resection on many such patients subsequently.

The treatment of the rhinitis is based on the production of fibrosis within the grossly hypertrophic submucosal tissue. This is produced by a pattern of diathermy strokes in the submucosal layer, which creates a mesh of fibrosis which subsequently contracts. This produces reduction in bulk, reduction of hyperaemia and reduction of surface sensitivity.

The inferior turbinates are so treated, but similar treatment of the middle turbinates should be avoided in view of the danger of orbital oedema. Pin-point low intensity coagulation of the margins of the middle turbinates may be sufficient, but surgical "trimming" may be necessary.

Patients who are particularly prone to the typical "sinus headaches" respond very well to simple intra-nasal antrostomies where there is no evidence of actual sinus infection. Such patients suffer no pain, external swelling or bruising, and are admitted for one day only. After-care is important however, in order to prevent adhesions.

Nasal polypii may be removed under local anaesthesia in the clinic, although they are frequently associated with deviated septums which prevent access. Such patients require admission for septal resection, submucosal diathermy and polypectomy, but subsequent polypii are usually easy to remove in the clinic. Experience has shown that interference with the ethmoids and frontals is often the precursor of long and unpleasant problems and should be avoided if possible.

Effects of water on the throat

It has always struck me how frequently we read that this or that athlete was struck down by tonsillitis and forced to withdraw from competition. This raises questions:

First, is it really tonsillitis or merely sore throat associated with other conditions such as catarrh, allergic rhinitis and so on. Tonsillitis is well defined in signs and symptoms, and in my experience many patients are diagnosed as having tonsillitis who have sore throats but not the other signs of tonsillar infection. Such sore throats are often related to rhinitis, colds, etc. which produce a hyperaemic pharyngitis. Response to a course of nonsoluble aspirin gargles and antihistamines is often effective in these cases.

In the age-group of most swimmers the peritonsillar abscess or quinsy is fairly common. Immediate treatment by "hot-tonsillectomy" under antibiotic cover is often dramatic, or the tonsils may be removed after 6-8 weeks.

A further cause of discomfort in the rather older patient may be due to tonsillar concretions, caused by the extrusion of detritus from large tonsillar crypts, and accompanied by pain, discomfort, and halitosis. Tonsillectomy may be necessary to relieve the condition. Glandular fever is also a condition of this age-group. If there is no preceding history of tonsillitis it is reasonable to see if further infections occur before deciding on tonsillectomy.

My impression is that the nature of glandular fever has been changing in recent years. Conversion of the Monospot test is later, and the disease is often more severe and prolonged. Bizarre blood counts sometimes cause great anxiety that one may be missing an unusual presentation of leukaemia.

One encouraging aspect of a correctly assessed patient for tonsillectomy is that there is often a significant increase in performance and general wellbeing in competition 2 or 3 months after operation.

With regard to tonsillitis in sportsmen it seems that, to some extent, the incidence relates to the level at which they perform. Thus at national and international levels it seems to be more frequent.

Such competition entails much long-distance travel. It is acknowledged that one of the problems of long-distance flying is dehydration. Provision of alcoholic drinks does nothing to help the situation.

There does seem to be an association between dehydration and tonsillitis, especially when related to intense physical exertion. Perhaps counselling about this problem might be helpful to competitors.

I have met and treated many athletes; swimmers seem to be a class apart. I have rarely seen the high-strung hypochondriacs common in other sports. The swimmers have been happy genuine people. I do not think you could work with a better group.   Finally, I would like to thank Professor Cameron, who, over the years, has fed me information, patients, and occasionally his favourite malt whisky.

Part 3
Physiological and Biological Aspects of Training and Stress

9. Medical Sport Diagnostics using the Lactate Test

L. KIPKE

TRAINING ACTIVITIES IN SPORTS aim to produce sport – specific adaptations. These are of physiological, psychological, and morphological character. We have to distinguish between external aspects of training loads, i.e. amount, intensity, frequency or type; and internal ones, i.e. physiological, biochemical, and morphological response reactions. These aspects are both closely interrelated and assessed as measured by most varied means and methods. During the last 30 years, enormous development in competitive swimming, those coaches and scientists engaged in that sport have ever better managed to define the most relevant factors of performance (like endurance, strength, technique and many others) to measure them, to evaluate their weight and to draw conclusions therefrom for further training activities.

Assessing internal loads seems always to be rather difficult whereas the external factors, like kilometres, amount, intensity (as measured by velocity), frequency and type of loads can be registered by the coach in his personal documentation. The registration of values which express internal loads and the task to inter-correlate them is a wide field of sport science with many sub-disciplines, where remarkable progress has been achieved during the last few decades.

Performance diagnostics has the task continuously to control the dynamics of internal demands in close relation to external loads as given by external sport-methodical measures and to assess the accordance between aims and objectives of training activities and their biological implementation. In doing so, major performance factors should be registered in as much detail as possible to lead to performance assessments from which conclusions can be drawn for further training activities. It seems also to be possible to deduce therefrom certain individual standards that can be used as guidelines and should be achieved by related means and methods during a given training period.

It is, of course, not possible to analyze all those factors which have contributed to a swimming result from only one performance diagnostic test. One is forced to restrict oneself to a minimum. From sport medical points of view we have always to answer the question how the aerobic and anaerobic-lactacide energy metabolisms have been used and how they could be optimized by training activities. Swimming has been included into the endurance type sport categories, with varying importance of the aerobic or anaerobic – after introducing the 50 m distances also the alactacide – energy metabolisms, according to the distance swum.

For the assessment of the aerobic or anaerobic capacities biological data are at our disposal, such as oxygen uptake or lactate concentration in blood. As early as in 1977 the problems have been reported (Kipke, 1977) that are connected with the assessment of the oxygen uptake during sport specific loads. Since oxygen uptake can, however, not be tested continuously under swimming specific conditions, the assessment of lactate concentrations in blood are the main point of performance diagnostics in swimming today. The ability to measure blood lactate concentrations micro-methodically has enabled comprehensive and practical analysis of the alactacide and lactacide energy disposal in the skeletal muscle. This can be applied and further developed for training control and diagnostics under actual training conditions.

Everywhere in modern swimming training experts recognize that about 50 to 65 % of the total training session is performed in the aerobic range, about 15 to 25 % in the so-called transitory or developmental range and only some 20% at maximum speed. There are various terms in various countries, having the same meaning, however. In the GDR the term "basic endurance I" is applied for loads below 4 mmol/l blood lactate. This is termed "aerobic training" in the USA while the term "basic endurance II" of the GDR is called "overload range" in the US, the latter at a lactate range from 4 to 8 mmol/l. It was, therefore, necessary to define these training ranges to be able to control training activities.

Hereafter some experience will be presented which was collected when lactate assessments were made in GDR swimming training over about 15 years with top-class swimmers. Two basic forms of application should be distinguished at the beginning:

1   Lactate assessments are made to define the intensities of single or serial loads. Lactate analyses have been made following given or "classic" training series from the athletes' blood to facilitate the definition of training loads and biologically to evaluate the effects of the training procedures. Following a training task of × 200 m performed within the basic endurance range II or over-load range, respectively, where lactate values of 6 mmol/l were to be reached, we could, e.g. test whether the velocity set for that task was correct or not. Accordingly, the level could be defined to which mechanisms of energy disposal had been used (aerobic-alactacide or anaerobic-lactacide) and how they should be registered in the training documentation.

We set the aerobic/anaerobic threshold empirically at 4.0 mmol/l, well knowing that there have been findings which do not coincide with it, but there are also studies which call for a definition of the individual threshold whenever individual aspects are to be investigated (Keul *et al.*, 1979).

Such procedures require great efforts during practice causing trouble in the daily training activities, so that athletes and coaches cannot recognize them as routine methods.

Our experience shows the test can successfully assess intensities in swimming training; it has been accepted by practice and proven to be supportive.

2   A second application of performance diagnostics in swimming training by lactate assessment is the analysis of the lactate-performance curve. The function between performance and lactate concentration in blood (Pansold *et al.*, 1982) by the exponential function $y = a \times b^{ex}$ can be found using a step test as performed in all the spiro-ergometric investigations at various load levels. At least four different levels should be selected provoking lactate concentrations in the swimmers of about 2 mmol/l, one between 2 and 4 mmol/l, one between 4 and 8 mmol/l and one maximum effort (Fig 1). This will be achieved in most cases if the athletes swim at 70, 80, 90 or 100 % of their actual capacity. Such loads must, however, be individually tested.

Three characteristic data are provided by these lactate performance curves from which qualitative conclusions can be drawn for training programs. Relations between levels, aerobic capacities, strength poten-

tials or athletic techniques as levels of the anaerobic-lactacide energy
supply can be deduced therefrom (Fig. 2).

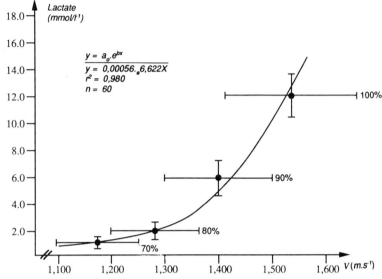

FIG. 1. Four different levels are selected, namely, about 2 mmol/l; one between
2 and 4 mmol/l; one between 4 and 8 mmol/l and one maximum effort.

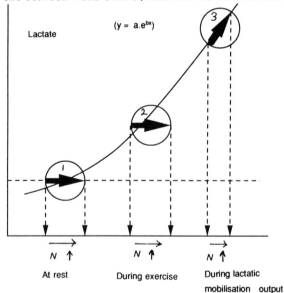

FIG. 2. The lactate performance curve provides three characteristic areas of data.

Value 1: Performance at lactate 4.0 mmol/l has often been termed aerobic capacity. We know very well that this is an abstract term and will always depend on test procedures. It has, however, been shown during practical work that a shifting of the lactate performance curve along the line 4 mmol/l lactate to the right means an increase of aerobic capacity. (Performances at lactate concentrations of 2 mmol/l are termed aerobic threshold, of 4 mmol/l anaerobic threshold, assuming that the aerobic anaerobic transitional range is located between the two limiting values.)

Value 2 considers the sport-specific strength:time relations which are characterized by changing strength or technical components of the athletes. The dynamics of increase of lactate:performance curves (shown by the exponential B) dictate how maximum lactate levels correspond with aerobic capacities (lactate at 4.0 mmol/l) and, thereafter also, with the performance achieved at maximum lactate level.

Value 3, expressing maximum loads and their blood lactate concentrations, reflects then, in the case presented, the aerobic capacity while we have to recognize that there are also other procedures to assess anaerobic capacity.

Applying the lactate:performance curve has been shown to be practical and informative for sports practice and a decisive means in sport medical performance diagnostics. According to Pansold et al. (1982) there are several variants to typify these possibilities (Fig. 3) reflecting the performance progress as follows:

Case 1 (b) can be retraced upon an improved aerobic capacity and increased performance factors (strength, speed, endurance).

Case 2 (c) shows an improved aerobic capacity and strength or technique at higher mobilizational level.

Case 3 (d) shows stagnating aerobic capacity but an increase of strength or improved technique at higher mobilizational levels.

Case 4 (e) shows the same at further lowered capacity.

Case 5 (f) only an improvement or the anaerobic mobilizational capacity.

Lactate performance curves should, therefore, be applied in the following three points:

1 Using the lactate performance curve graded training ranges can be defined by means of lactate. The ranges used for many years: compensation (0-2), stabilization or economization (2-4), and development (lactate 4-6) coincide with the terms introduced quite recently: aerobic threshold, anaerobic transition (Keul et al., 1979) to a far-reaching extent.

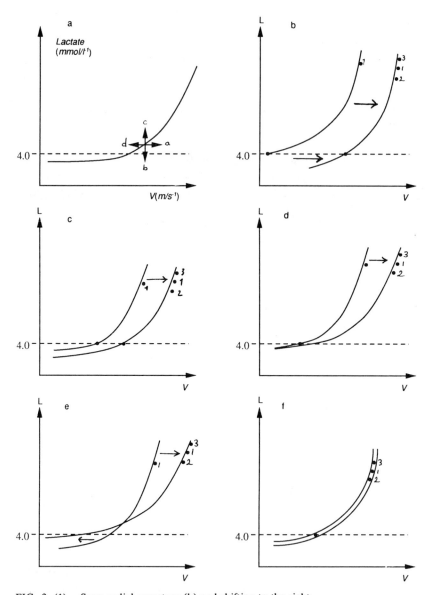

FIG. 3. (1)   Same radial curvature (b) and shifting to the right
       (2)   Shifting to the right and decline of exponential relations lactate velocity (c)
       (3)   Decline of function without shifting to the right (d)
       (4)   Decline of function and shifting to the left (e) in the lower part of the curve.
       (5)   No shifting to the right but higher maximum lactate values.

2   It is possible to gain data on prognostic performances to be used at competitive distances on the basis of individual measurement results by individually testing lactate concentrations after maximum loads.

3   Recommendations are possible therefrom on how to program training activities further, regarding the proportions of anaerobic/ aerobic levels or strength/endurance.

Considering lactate performance relations we should not assume that an individual performance curve would keep its stable form and the training process automatically effect the required parallel shifting to the right, i.e. aerobic and maximum performance increases at the same time. This is why lactate performance relations should continuously be analyzed after shorter or longer periods or after given training stages with certain specific training aims or objectives to draw conclusions therefrom for the further programming of training activities.

For short-time training assessments lactate performance curves are a valuable support for the coach to define training stages and to prepare a prognosis for competitions to be held during the near future because it is a training stimulus in itself, can be performed during the training session and costs no additional time which must be taken from the time available for training.

Thus, the application of lactate analysis in swimming, enables an athlete or trainer to harmonize training methods aims and objectives with their biological implementation, as well as the inter-relation between internal and external loads.   The experience of the physician and that of the coach plays as decisive a role as does their good cooperation.

References

Keul, J., Simon, G., Berg, A., Dickhuth, H.H., Goerttler, I. and Kübel, R. (1979), Bestimmung der individuellen anaeroben Schwelle zur Leistungsbewertung und Trainingsgestaltung, *Deutsche Zeitschrift für Sportmedizin*, **7**, 212-218.

Kipke, L. (1977). Dynamics of oxygen intake during step-by-step loading in a swimming flume. *In* "Swimming Medicine IV". University Park Press, pp. 137-142.

Pansold, B., Roth, W., Masart, E., Zinner, J. und Gabriel, B. (1982). Die Laktatleistungskurve – ein Grundprinzip sportmedizinischer Leistungs-diagnostik. *Medizin und Sport, Berlin* **22**, (4), 107-112.

Pessenhofer, H., Schwaberger, G. and Schmidt, P., (1981). Zur Bestimmung des individuellen aerob-anaeroben Überganges. *Deutsche Zeitschrift für Sportmedizin,* **32**, 15-17.

Stegmann, H. and Kindermann, W. (1981). Bestimmung der individuellen anaeroben Schwelle bei unterschiedlich Ausdauer Trainierenden auf Grund des Verhaltens der Laktat-Kinetik während der Arbeits- und Erholungsphase. *Deutsche Zeitschrift für Sportmedizin,* **32,** 213-221.

10. Blood Lactate Accumulation in Top Level Swimmers after Competitions

M. BONIFAZI, G. MARTELLI, L. MARUGO, F. SARDELLA, G. SAINI and G. CARLI

Introduction

THE MEASUREMENT OF BLOOD lactate levels is commonly utilized as a practical tool to estimate the amount of energy derived from anaerobic glycolysis during exercise (Margaria *et al.*, 1971; Di Prampero *et al.*, 1978) In swimming, as in other disciplines, trials of different intensities are utilized to determine individual blood lactate-velocity relationships (Mader *et al.*, 1980). The lactate level recorded after competition could represent the most important value to define this relationship at high lactate levels. It was the aim of the present study to evaluate the significance of blood lactates collected after competitions and the importance of the analysis of the individual blood lactate-swimming velocity relationship in connection with the performance in top level swimmers. We were interested in establishing:

1   the mean values of blood lactates after competitions and possible differences between men and women;

2   possible correlations between blood lactates and swimming velocities in competitions;

3   possible correlations between swimming velocities corresponding to 4 mmol/l lactate value and swimming velocities in freestyle events;

4   whether it is possible to estimate the velocity in swimming competitions by the analysis of the individual lactate-velocity relationships, knowing the lactate value after competition.

Material and methods

In 203 top level Italian swimmers (116 males and 87 females; age: 15-26 years) capillary blood samples (n = 421, 237 males and 184 females), 20 µl each, were collected from the ear lobe 5 min after the end of competitions and lactate levels were determined with a Roche Lactate Analyzer mod. A 640. The trials took place in a 25m swimming pool during the "European Cup" (1985 and 1986) and the Italian Championships (1986 and 1987). All performances were within the 1984 compulsory time to participate at the Italian Championships. To determine the possible relationship between blood lactate and swimming velocities in all events, the best performance of each athlete and the corresponding lactate value were utilized.

In some of the athletes (n = 42, 25 males and 17 females) performing freestyle competitions, supplementary blood samples were collected also in test sessions within 3 weeks before or after the 1987 Italian Championships. Tests were performed in a 25 m pool on 400 m distances to determine the swimming velocity at 4 mmol/l lactate (V_4), according to Mader's methods (1980), and this velocity was chosen as a criterion of aerobic capacity for swimmers (Mader *et al.*, 1976, 1980; Heck *et al.*, 1985). The possible relationships between individual V_4 and corresponding velocity of the best performances were determined for every freestyle event.

In another subgroup of swimmers (n = 23, 13 males and 10 females) blood samples were collected after two submaximal training trials in the same distance and stroke of the competition. This test was performed, in each athlete, the day after the 1987 Italian Championships to determine the individual blood lactate-swimming velocity relationship. From this relationship, the estimated competition velocity was assessed by extrapolation at the lactate value collected in the same event after competition.

Results and discussion

(a) BLOOD LACTATES AFTER COMPETITIONS

The mean values of swimming velocities and blood lactates after competitions in all events are shown in Table 1. All male velocities were significantly higher than females ($p < 0.01$), while in five events the mean lactate values were lower in females than in males (Fig. 1).

TABLE 1. *Competition velocities (m/s) and Lactates (mmol/l) in all events (mean values ± s.d.).*

Event	Male Velocity	Male Lactate	Female Velocity	Female Lactate
50 FS	2.139 ± 0.043	10.40 ± 2.59 (13)	1.852 ± 0.033	9.98 ± 2.01 (14)
100 FS	1.946 ± 0.029	11.84 ± 2.38 (28)	1.718 ± 0.031	9.95 ± 1.68 (23)
200 FS	1.775 ± 0.031	12.35 ± 2.62 (24)	1.599 ± 0.028	8.35 ± 1.97 (19)
400 FS	1.696 ± 0.038	11.16 ± 3.06 (24)	1.550 ± 0.022	8.80 ± 2.21 (18)
1500/800 FS	1.601 ± 0.034	6.45 ± 2.92 (14)	1.522 ± 0.016	7.17 ± 2.40 (9)
100 BK	1.705 ± 0.030	11.17 ± 2.09 (14)	1.551 ± 0.031	11.32 ± 2.11 (12)
200 BK	1.588 ± 0.036	12.04 ± 2.83 (15)	1.442 ± 0.035	10.06 ± 1.86 (14)
100 BR	1.571 ± 0.041	10.15 ± 2.46 (17)	1.396 ± 0.024	10.05 ± 2.68 (12)
200 BR	1.437 ± 0.033	10.75 ± 2.27 (19)	1.287 ± 0.022	9.06 ± 1.57 (13)
100 FLY	1.773 ± 0.033	10.04 ± 1.84 (17)	1.600 ± 0.033	9.29 ± 1.84 (10)
200 FLY	1.611 ± 0.017	11.17 ± 3.19 (6)	1.458 ± 0.027	11.11 ± 2.40 (14)
200 IM	1.595 ± 0.035	11.63 ± 2.37 (18)	1.417 ± 0.033	9.76 ± 1.99 (10)
400 IM	1.506 ± 0.037	12.46 ± 3.07 (18)	1.349 ± 0.021	10.44 ± 2.86 (16)

Key: FS = freestyle; BK = backstroke; BR = breaststroke; FLY = butterfly; I.M. = individual medley. (): number of swimmers for each event. Comparison of blood lactates after competitions: Student "t" test for unpaired data (* $p < 0.05$, ** $p < 0.01$): Males: 50 FS vs 200 FS *; 1500 FS vs all other competitions **; 100 FLY vs 200 BK, 200 I.M. *, 100 FS, 200 FS, 400 I.M .* *; 100 BR vs 100 FS, 200 BK *: 200 FS, 400 I . M . **. Females: 200 FS vs 50 FS, 200 BK, 200 BR, 200 I.M. *, 100 FS, 100 BK, 200 FLY **; 800 FS vs all other competitions except 200 FS **; 100 BK vs 100 FS, 100 FLY *, 200 BR **; 200 FLY vs 200 BR *, 400 FS **.

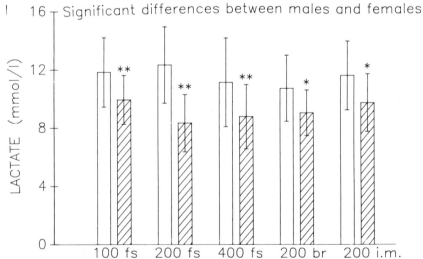

FIG. 1. Legend see Table 1. Males: blank box. Females: shaded box. Statistical analysis: Student "t" test for unpaired data: * $p < 0.05$, ** $p < 0.01$.

Sexual differences in blood lactates after maximal efforts have previously been described (Komi and Karlsson, 1978; Jacobs and Tesch, 1981; Karlsson *et al.*, 1981; Jacobs *et al.*, 1983). Compared to males, females show an inborn "glycogen sparing" metabolic profile (Karisson and Jacobs, 1982), less pronounced glycolytic activity in skeletal muscles (Komi and Karlsson, 1978; Karisson *et al.*, 1981), higher capacities for lactate oxidation (Komi and Karlsson, 1978) and a smaller active muscle mass to blood volume ratio (Shephard, 1982).

(b) CORRELATIONS BETWEEN BLOOD LACTATES AND SWIMMING

Positive linear correlations between lactate values after competitions and corresponding swimming velocities were found only in freestyle events: 200 m men (Fig. 2) and 200, 400 and 800 m women (Table 2). These results show that males, to excel in 200 m freestyle, should be able to utilize lactate mechanisms as confirmed by the high mean lactate value after this competition. In females, on the other hand, this correlation was obtained not only in 200 m, but also in 400 and 800 m freestyle. Our female swimmers, however, were aerobically trained to compete in all three distances. It is likely that the athletes able to sprint in the last 50m by using a higher frequency of leg strokes were faster in all three events with higher levels of lactate accumulation. It is suggested, therefore, that anaerobic training should be performed also in female swimmers competing in longer distances.

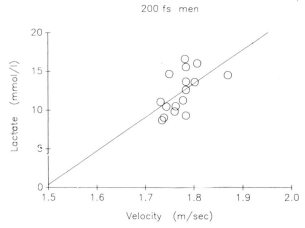

FIG. 2. Positive linear correlation between blood after the competition and corresponding swimming velocities in 200 m freestyle men (see also Table 2).

TABLE 2. *Significant correlations between blood and swimming velocities in freestyle events.*

Event	n	Equation	r	p
200 m men	16	y = 43.55 × -64.96	0.57	**
200 m women	7	y = 44.47 × -63.06	0.70	*
400 m women	9	y = 58.04 × -80.79	0.67	*
800 m women	6	y = 125.12 × -183.89	0.90	**

Statistical analysis: Pearson's correlation test (1-tail): $* p < 0.05$, $** p < 0.01$.

(c) CORRELATIONS BETWEEN V_4S AND SWIMMING VELOCITIES IN FREESTYLE COMPETITIONS

Individual V_4s and swimming velocities in freestyle events were positively correlated in men in 200 (Fig.3), 400 and 1500 m and in women in 400 and 800 m (Table 3). These findings suggest that all swimmers should develop their aerobic capacities in order to improve their performances in longer distances, where the aerobic mechanisms play a major role. It has to be underlined that the best female swimmers in our group show high V_4 and lactate values, thus suggesting that, in females, the aerobic training does not affect lactate mechanisms.

TABLE 3. *Significant correlations between V_4 and swimming velocities in freestyle events.*

Event	n	Equation	r	p
200 m men	11	y = 0.753 × + 0.267	0.72	**
400 m men	11	y = 0.910 × + 0.031	0.87	**
1500 m men	9	y = 1.337 × - 0.081	0.86	**
400 m women	8	y = 0.894 × + 0.081	0.86	**
800 m women	6	y = 1.539 × - 0.875	0.84	*

Statistical analysis: Pearson's correlation test (1-tail): $* p < 0.05$, $** p < 0.01$.

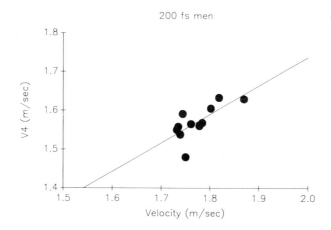

FIG. 3. Positive linear correlation between individual V_4s and swimming velocities in 200 m freestyle men (see also Table 3).

(d) CORRELATION BETWEEN ESTIMATED VELOCITIES AND MEASURED VELOCITIES

In the subgroup of 23 swimmers a linear positive correlation between estimated and actual measured velocities in competitions was found ($y = 1.009 \times -0.003$, $r = 0.98$). These results confirm that it is possible to estimate the velocity corresponding to the lactate after competition, by determining the individual blood lactate-swimming velocity relationship in the same distance after submaximal work load (Elliot and Haber, 1983).

Conclusion

In conclusion results confirm that blood lactate values in swimmers may be a useful indication of individual aptitudes and may aid the efficient planning of training.

References

Di Prampero, P.E., Pendergast, D.R., Wilson,D.W. and Rennie, D.W. (1978). Blood lactic acid concentrations in high velocity swimming. *In* "Swimming Medicine IV". (Eds B.Eriksson and B. Furberg), pp. 249-261. University Park Press, Baltimore.
Elliot, M. and Haber, P. (1983). Estimation of the peak performance in the 100

meter breast stroke on the basis of serum lactate measurement during two submaximal test heats at different velocities. *In* "Biomechanics and Medicine in Swimming". (Eds P. Hollander, A. Huijing, P.A. and G. De Groot), pp. 335-335. Human Kinetics, Champaign.

Heck, H., Mader, A., Hess, G., Mucke, S., Muller, P. and Hollmann, W. (1985). Justification of the 4 mmol/l lactate threshold. *International Journal of Sports Medicine*, **6**, 117-130.

Jacobs, I. and Tesch, P. A. (1981). Short time maximal muscular performance: relation to muscle lactate and fibre type in female. *In* "Woman and Sport". (Eds J. Borms, M. Hebbelinck and A. Venerando), pp. 125-132. Karger, Basel.

Jacobs, I., Tesch, P.A., Bar-Or, O., Karlsson, J. and Dotan, R. (1983). Lactate in human skeletal muscle after 10 and 30s of supramaximal exercise. *Journal of Applied Physiology*, **55**, 365-367.

Karlsson, J. and Jacobs, I. (1982). Onset of blood lactate accumulation during muscular exercise as a threshold concept. I. Theoretical consideration. *International Journal of Sports Medicine*, **3**, 190-201.

Karlsson, J., Sjodin, B., Jacobs, I. and Kaiser, P. (1981). Relevance of muscle fibre type to fatigue in short intense and prolonged exercise in man. *In* "Human Muscle Fatigue Physiological Mechanisms". pp. 59-74. Pitman Medical, London.

Komi, P.V. and Karlsson, J. (1978). Skeletal muscle fibre types, enzyme activities and physical performance in young males and females. *Acta Physiologica Scandinavica*, **103**, 210-218.

Mader, A., Liessen, H., Heck, H., Philippi, H., Rost, R., Schurch, P. and Hollmann, W. (1976). Zur Beurteilung der sportartspezifischen Ausdauerleitungsfahigkeit im Labar. *Sportarzt und Sportmedizin*, **27**, 80-89.

Mader, A., Madsen, O. and Hollmann, W. (1980). Zur Beurteilung der lactaziden Energie Bereitstellung fur Trainings und Wettkampfleistungen im Sportschwimmen. *Leitungssport*, **10**, 263-408.

Margaria, R., Aghemo, P. and Sassi, G. (1971). Lactic acid production in supramaximal exercise. *Pflügers Archiv*, **3**, 152-161.

Pacine, P., Klenk, H.O. and Kochsiek, K. (1975). Rapid lactate determination with an electrochemical enzymatic sensor: clinical usability and comparative measurements. *Journal of Clinical Chemistry and Clinical Biochemistry*, **13**, 533-539.

Shephard, P.J. (1982). "Physiology and Biochemistry of Exercise". Praeger, New York.

11. Effect of Work Intensity and Duration on Lactate Accumulation

J.P. TROUP, S.M. ARREDONDO, T. TELANDER and M. LAWRENCE

TESTING AND EVALUATION of athletes requires careful interpretation used accurately by the coach. Over the last decade, the use of blood lactate profiles has been helpful in evaluating the training status of the athlete. However, logistical and methodological problems exist that make the lactate test impractical for use in a workout situation. The purpose of this project, therefore, was (1) to determine the effective use of non-steady state test swims in comparison with steady state test swims for determination of the lactate response, (2) to establish the lactate response to varying intensities of work, (3) to determine an appropriate and acceptable test distance and intensity, (4) to establish time points for collection and analysis of lactate values, and (5) to evaluate possible interpretations and limitations of the lactate test as a single test in the field.

Methods

Twelve national and world class swimmers (six male, six female) participated in this study. The project took place during a 6 week period in the middle of a 16 week training season. During this time, the volume and intensity of work did not change.

At the start of the study, a swimming economy test was administered for determination of training paces. Blood lactate was determined from a finger-tip sample following each sub-max economy swim.

The study was divided into the following phases:

1   Comparison of a 3×200 m test swim to a 3×400 m test swim.

2   Measurement of lactate response to continuous swimming at each of six prescribed intensities.

Blood lactate analysis was done using the *ANALOX* automated analyzer. A two way analysis of variance was used to determine statistical significance at the $p < .05$ level.

Results and discussion

No significant difference was found in the lactate profiles between the 200 and 400 m test swims at velocities between 1.2 and 1.5 m/sec. The 400 m test did not result in a production of large lactate values making it a non-specific test for the majority of swimming distances.

The lactate response during continuous swimming at 90% of VO_2 max revealed no difference in lactate production during 30 min of swimming. At 100% VO_2 max lactate rose to a significant value at 2 min of work, but did not increase up to 20 min of work. At intensities of 112 and 118% of VO_2 max lactate reached a peak at 2 min of work and further increased during recovery up to 2 min of rest. In summary, these data suggest that a 200 m test distance can effectively be used to monitor the lactate response to a given workload. Overall, the 200 m distance may be more effective as a time, all out effort and a corresponding high lactate value will result.

12. Blood Lactate Responses After Competition

D. GERRARD on behalf of S.C. HOLLINGS and G.J. ROBSON

Introduction

IT IS BECOMING INCREASINGLY important in all sports to regulate duration and intensity of training. In swimming, training at velocities that are too slow means that a swimmer is unable to stimulate the aerobic system sufficiently, while training at too high a velocity means the swimmer places too much emphasis on the anaerobic system (Maglischo, 1982). Achieving the balance between the aerobic and anaerobic aspects of training becomes the coach's dilemma.

For several years now the rates of accumulation of blood lactate at various swimming velocities have been studied to determine optimum training speed (Mader *et al.*, 1976; Madsen, 1983; Olbrecht *et al.*, 1985; Madsen and Lohberg, 1987). The two-speed test of Mader and co-workers (Mader *et al.*, 1976), based on the fact that there is a practically linear increase in lactate concentration (above 2 mmol/l) in relation to velocity has enabled coaches to determine an individual training regime for each swimmer. The two-speed Mader test is often repeated every 4 to 6 weeks as a monitor of improvement in aerobic capacity and to establish new training velocities (Madsen, 1983; Maglischo, 1982, 1985). An improvement in aerobic capacity is indicated by a "right shift" in the lactate line on a velocity-lactate graph.

It has been suggested that for practical reasons many physiological studies of elite athletes (including blood lactate profiles) are conducted at training camps (Foster *et al.*, 1988). Quite often athlete assessment is determined by logistic and coaching concerns rather than a planned experimental protocol. In this environment an acute increase in training may in fact lead to errors in interpretation and application of the results obtained. Our study aimed to investigate a similar phenomenon – the effects of a competition on swimmers, in order to determine whether the acute stress imposed on the body in this situation had any effect on the lactate profiles of these athletes.

Methods

Ten New Zealand class swimmers were used as subjects in this study. Their individual endurance capacity was measured using the two-speed test of Mader *et al.* (1976). The swimmers were instructed to swim two 400 m freestyle trials – the first at about 80% of their maximum and the second, after a 20 min break, at a speed very close to their maximum. Fingertip blood samples (25 ml) were taken from each swimmer 1, 3, 5 and 7 min after each swim and lactate content was measured on a Lactic Acid Analyzer (Model 23L, Yellow Springs Instrument Co., Yellow Springs, Ohio, USA).

The velocity associated with a particular blood lactate value (e.g. 4 mmol/l (V_4)) is often used to compare changes in each individual's aerobic capacity. If this V_4 value increases then there is reckoned to be an increase in aerobic capacity; similarly if V_4 decreases then a detraining effect is seen. The swimming speed in metres per second (m/s) required to elicit a lactic acid concentration of 4 mmol/l (V_4) was determined by graphing swimming velocity against lactate concentration. Using simple linear regression V_4 was determined for each swimmer.

Seven of the swimmers performed three Mader Tests over a period of 2 months – the other three swimmers performed two Mader Tests 1 month apart. Nine of the 10 swimmers took part in a competition 2 to 3 days before either the second or third Mader Test.

Results

The results from each swimmer are presented below including the number of races swum in the competition and the percentage change in the V_4 value between the V_4 obtained after competition and that obtained from the previous test. Values underlined are those obtained 2-3 days after a competition. A negative relationship was shown between the number of races swum in competition and percentage change in V_4 value of post competition Mader Test and the previous test ($r = -0.69$, $p < 0.05$). In effect this means the more races swum in competition, the greater the probability is for the lactate line to move to the left when compared with the previous Mader Test.

Of the 10 swimmers studied only two, D.F. and R.T., undertook any type of tapering training towards the competition. All the other swimmers carried out normal distance training designed to increase aerobic capacity. Evidence of this is seen by an increase in V_4 values in all swimmers who undertook three tests (except A.M.) between their two non-competition Mader Tests.

Swimmer	TEST 1	TEST 2	TEST 3	No. of Races	% Change
D.F.	1.549	1.574	1.578	6	+ 0.25
R.T.	1.510	1.532	1.571	2	+ 2.87
J.M.	1.478	1.520	1.486	10	- 2.24
J.H.	1.398	1.438	1.409	12	- 2.02
M.C.	1.452	1.450	-	6	0.00
K.A.	1.374	1.333	1.387	8	- 2.98
G.K.	1.441	1.407	1.449	8	- 2.36
J.Mc.	1.372	1.362	-	8	- 0.73
A.M.	1.458	1.470	1.454	6	+ 0.82
K.H.	1.369	1.376	-	0	+ 0.51

Discussion

A recent paper (Prins *et al.*, 1988) has studied lactate profiles on swimmers over two successive swimming seasons. They have reported monthly variations in the total number of subjects whose lactate curves shifted in either direction, although they note a significantly higher number of subjects show a "right shift" in the lactate curve during the period of the swimming season where major emphasis is placed on building an aerobic base. A similar trend was also seen by Sharp *et al.* (1984) who reported that the greatest degree of "right shift" occurred during the first two months of the season. Since all our subjects were involved in building an aerobic base throughout the testing period by distance training, it is safe to assume we would expecting a "right shift" in their graphs. Prins *et al.* (1988) suggest their findings illustrate a variability amongst swimmers in both aerobic and anaerobic adaptations to training during a season.

The two individuals in our study who had tapered their training (D.F. and R.T.) still showed a "right shift" in their lactate curves. Costill *et al.* (1985) found essentially no change in lactate kinetics with 14 days of taper although with a 4 week taper there was essentially a "left shift" in the lactate profile, a result consistent with the work of Van Handel *et al.* (1988) with 20 days of taper. Our subjects used only a 2 week taper and this, together with 2 weeks aerobic conditioning prior to the taper and the limited volume of competition explains these results.

Performance is affected by overtraining (Harre, 1986). Therefore the structure of rest following fatiguing workloads is very important for recovery. It has been noted by Russian sport scientists that where fatigue is developed rapidly (e.g. competition) there is residual excitation afterwards. This residual excitation slows down recovery (Yessis, 1986). Kipke (1985) states that decreased performance after training and competitive efforts can be due to (1) loss of energy sources (ATP, creatine phosphate, muscle glycogen), (2) reductions in energy stores, (3) accumulation of metabolites and (4) loss of water and changes in mineral balance. The above results show evidence that the volume of competitive activity is related to the location of the lactate line compared to the previous Mader Test. Those individuals involved in only a few races showed an expected movement of the lactate curve to the right consistent with the type of training undertaken. Conversely those individuals involved in more races showed no movement or a "left shift" in the lactate curve.

It does not appear that an increased volume of competition has any effect on muscle glycogen content since reduced muscle glycogen levels result in a "right shift" of the blood lactate curve due to decreased substrate availability (Costill *et al.*, 1971; Ivy *et al.*, 1981). However one point worth considering is the fact that swimmers training twice a day could became chronically glycogen depleted and that the blood lactate curve preceding the competition test could have been moved artificially to the right. Common sense dictates that athletes will probably eat, sleep and train sensibly before any competition thereby raising muscle glycogen levels to "normal" values. It therefore seems probable that the "left shift" results of the swimmers following competition could be attributed to lack of recovery following competitive events by factors at present undetermined.

Foster *et al.* (1988) has suggested "normalizing" blood lactate values based on peak blood lactate responses and it may remove the variability in determining lactate profiles in athletes during different stages of training. This may be one solution, although it depends on the athlete undertaking a maximal trial to determine peak blood lactate values and is also based on the assumption that reduced lactate levels are a consequence of reduced muscle glycogen. However submaximal lactate levels may also be reduced through induced acidosis (Kowalchuk *et al.*, 1984), acute consumption of fat (Ivy *et al.*, 1981) or dehydration (Saltin, 1964) and increased through induced alkalosis (Kowalchuk *et al.*, 1984), acute consumption of glucose (Ivy *et al.*, 1981) or abnormally high carbohydrate consumption for several days (Yoshida, 1984).

In conclusion results from this study indicate that competition volume does have some effect on lactate profiles of swimmers but that the mechanism involved is as yet undetermined. The results from lactate profiles *per se* should be treated with caution but standardization of volume and type of activity and of diet in the days preceding such tests could be an alternative to normalizing the blood lactate profile and removing the variability associated with such results.

References

Costill, D.L., Bowers, R., Branam, G. and Sparks, K. (1971). Muscle glycogen utilisation during prolonged exercise on successive days. *Journal of Applied Physiology*, **31**, 834-838.

Costill, D. L., King, D.S., Mamas, R. and Hargreaves, M. (1985). Effects of reduced training on muscular power in swimmers. *The Physician and Sports Medicine*, **13**, 94-101.

Foster, C., Snyder, A.C., Thompson, N.N. and Kuettel, K. (1988). Normalisation of the blood lactate profile in athletes. *International Journal of Sports Medicine,* **9,** 198-200.

Harre, D. (1986). "Recovery". Part 2. Science Periodical on Research and Technology in Sport, August.

Ivy, J.L., Costill, D.L., Van Handel, P.J., Essig, D.A. and Lawer, K.W. (1981). Alteration in the lactate threshold with changes in substrate availability. *International Journal of Sports Medicine,* **2,** 139-142.

Kipke, L. (1985). The importance of recovery after training and competitive efforts. *New Zealand Journal of Sports Medicine,* **13,** 120-128.

Kowalchuk, J.M., Heigenhauser, J.F. and Jones, N.L. (1984). Effect of pH on metabolic and cardiorespiratory responses during progressive exercise. *Journal of Applied Physiology,* **57,** 1558-1563.

Mader, A., Heck, H. and Hollmann, W. (1976). Evaluation of lactic acid anaerobic energy contribution by determination of postexercise lactic acid concentration of ear capillary blood in middle-distance runners and swimmers. *In* "The International Congress of Physical Activity Sciences". Vol 4, Exercise Physiology (Eds F. Landry and W.H.K. Orban), pp. 187-200. Symposium Specialists, Miami.

Madsen, O. (1983). "Aerobic Training: Not So Fast, There". Swimming Technique, November 1982/January 1983, 13-18.

Madsen, O. and Lohberg, M. (1987). "The Lowdown on Lactates". Swimming Technique, May/July, 21-26.

Maglischo, E.W. (1982). "Swimming Faster". A comprehensive guide to the science of swimming. Mayfield Publishing, Palo Alto, California.

Maglischo, E.W. (1985). Some observations on the anaerobic threshold concept of training. *New Zealand Journal of Sports Medicine,* **13,** 95-104.

Olbrecht, J., Madsen, O., Mader, A., Liesen, H. and Hollmann, W. (1985). Relationship between swimming velocity and lactic acid concentration during continuous and intermittent training exercises. *International Journal of Sports Medicine,* **6,** 74-77.

Prins, J., Merritt, D.M. and Lally, D.A. (1988). The results of administering a modified "Two-Point" lactate profile test on swimmers for two successive indoor swimming seasons. *Journal of Swimming Research,* **4,** 5-10.

Saltin, B. (1964). Circulatory response to submaximal and maximal exercise after thermal dehydration. *Journal of Applied Physiology,* **19,** 1125-1132.

Sharp, R.L., Vitelli, C., Costill, D.L. and Thomas, R. (1984). Comparison between blood lactate and heart rate profiles during a season of competitive swim training. *Journal of Swimming Research,* **1,** 17-20.

Van Handel, P.J., Katz, A., Troup, J.P., Daniels, J.T. and Bradley, P.W. (1988). Oxygen consumption and blood lactic acid response to training and taper. *In* "Swimming Science V". (Eds B. E. Ungerechts, K. Wilke and K. Reischle), pp. 269-275. Champaign, IL.

Yessis, M. (1986). "Recovery". Part 1. Science Periodical on Research and Technology in Sport, July.

Yoshida, T. (1984). Effect of dietary modification on lactate threshold and onset of blood lactate accumulation during incremental exercise. *European Journal of Applied Physiology*, **53**, 200-205.

13. A Comparison of Maximal Lactate Values in Selected Swimming Test Protocols

E. AVLONITOU, A.TSOPANAKIS, K. N. PAVLOU and E. SGOURAKI

Introduction

BLOOD LACTATE CONCENTRATION has become a popular training assessment technique among swimming coaches over the last few years (Maglischo *et al.*, 1982, 1984; Madsen, 1983; Sharp, 1984).

By determining the blood lactate concentration required to swim at a particular speed, the work physiologists and coaches are able to identify adaptations to training (Maglischo *et al.*, 1984; Sharp *et al.*,1984), determine optimal training intensities (Maglischo *et al.*., 1982, 1984) and predict optimal athletic performance (Eliot and Haber, 1983; Maglischo *et al.*, 1984).

Such information is very useful in indicating adaptations to both the aerobic and anaerobic component of training, motivating individual swimmers to achieve their best performance, while at the same time, help coaches make optimal use of training time and effort. However, in order to use lactate profiles to monitor training programs, the different tests used are determined by the parameters to be assessed.

Mader *et al.* (1978) proposed a practical model, describing the relationship between the dynamic work in swimming and the lactic acid energetic contribution. He used post-exercise peak lactate values obtained in two time trials, one at approximately 85% of best time at the particular distance and the other at maximal speed. By plotting lactate (mmol/l) and velocity values (m/sec) one can determine: first the optimal pace for training, by finding swimming speed at blood lactate content of 4.0 mmol/l, which is considered as the threshold of anaerobic energy supply, and second, predict maximal velocity of the individual swimmer by extrapolating the regression line to maximal values for blood lactate.

Another popular testing protocol, is the one which identifies the anaerobic threshold and determines the work load at a prefixed lactate concentration value of 4 mmol/l (Nader et al., 1980). However, because individual variation in muscle metabolism and lactate kinetics are not taken into account, erroneous results for the determination of performance capacity may result. For these reasons graded exercise tests have been developed for the determination of the individual's anaerobic threshold (Novak et al., 1988; Stegmann et al., 1981).

A popular test among coaches rests on the fact that maximum lactate accumulation can be produced during interval training (Fox et al., 1969), hence a broken 200 m test protocol (4 × 50 m) is used to ensure maximal lactate concentration.

Ideally, the ability to exhibit lower lactate values at a submaximal speed swimming velocity is indicative of adaptations to endurance-type training, while the ability to produce higher lactate values is indicative of anaerobic adaptation training.

Different tests have been used in swimming, to assess training intensities and/or adaptations to training programs. This practice is time consuming and unpopular among swimmers since lactic acid analysis requires frequent blood sampling.

The purpose of this study was, firstly, to compare maximal blood lactate values of selected swimming test protocols and secondly, to choose the appropriate test which, while giving maximal blood lactate values at the same time, provides the coaches with the most useful information to assess individual training programs.

Methods

The subjects who participated in this study were 10 male competitive swimmers, members of a swimming team in the Athens area of Greece.

Per cent body fat was determined by the Parizkova (1961) skinfold method (triceps, scapula). VO_2 max was assessed with the Sensor medics, MMC Horizon™ system 4400 to 1987 metabolic measurement chart using an increment test protocol with an initial speed set at 8 km/h and 2.5% inclination throughout the test. Speed was increased by 2 km/h every three and a half 3.5 min to exhaustion (R.Qmax > 1.05). At the time of the testing the subjects had undergone 10 weeks of training, 1 month before the winter competitive season. The tests took place in a 25 m indoor swimming pool during the early morning hours between 07.00-09.00 h a.m. All tests were administered after a 30 min warm up in the pool. Swimmers underwent four different experimental protocol tests within a 2 weeks period. The freestyle swim was employed and the tests were as follows:

1 A 2 × 200 m test with the first 200 m swim performed at submaximal speed, a pace corresponding to between 85 and 90 per cent effort of the best 200 m time, and the second 200 m swim was performed at maximal speed. A twenty minute rest was used between the successive swims.

2 A 2 × 400 m test administered in a similar fashion as the test 2 × 200 m swimming.

3 A 4 × 300 m consecutive swim test. The first 300 m length performed at a pace corresponding to 75 per cent of the velocity of the best time of this distance, the second at 83 per cent, the third at 90 per cent and the fourth one at a maximal speed effort. Each effort was interrupted by 2 min rest between the trials.

4 A 4 × 50 m test with 5 sec rest between the 50 m maximal efforts. The same protocol repeated with 85 per cent effort.

During the tests, heart rates were continuously monitored by the Sport Tester™ P 3000 Heart rate system (Polar Electro oy, Hakameamtie 18, df-90440 kempele, Finland).

Blood samples (0.04 ml) were taken from an arterialized fingertip before and after each trial as well as at the first and fifth minute after the termination of the test.

The samples were analyzed for lactate content by a PCA precipitation method modified by Tsopanakis et al. (1986), in a Kontron-Roche Automatic Lactate Analyzer. Velocity time for each effort was expressed in m/sec.

Analysis of Variance was used to compare the means between the treatment groups. Furthermore, wherever a significant P ratio was found the Newman-Keuls test was performed to identify the differences between the groups, with the alpha set at > 0.05 level of significance. Correlation was made by a linear regression between the maximal lactate values and the respective maximal valocity values.

Results

The means and standard deviations for age (15.3 ± 3.4 yr) and height

(172.2 ± 8.4 cm) are shown on Table 1. Body weight and % body fat mean values were 66.1 ± 10 kg and 15.6 ± 4.4% respectively. VO_2Max consumption value was 4102.7 ± 732.3 l/min or 62.1 ± 5.g ml/kg^{-1}.min^{-1}. No statistically significant differences were found (Table 2) in maximal mean lactate values among the four tests: 2 × 200 m (x = 7.4 ± 1.5 mmol/l), 2 × 400 m (x = 6.6 ± 2.3 mmol/l), 4 × 300 m (x = 7.6 ± 2.3 mmol/l) and 4 × 50 m (x = 8.0 ± 1.8 mmol/l). Similarly, maximal mean heart rate values were found not to differ significantly for the four tests (Table 2): 2 × 200 m (x = 192 ± 5.2 bpm), 2 × 400 m (x = 190 ± 7.4 bpm), 4 × 300 m (x = 198 ± 2.3 bpm), and 4 × 50 m (x = 192 ± 9.7 bpm). Mean maximal velocity values were found (Table 2) not to differ significantly between the 2 × 400 m (x = 1.33 ± 0.06 m/s) and 4 × 300 m (x = 1.34 + 0.07 m/s) tests. However, significant ($p < 0.001$) higher mean velocity values were recorded for the shorter distance tests of 2 × 200 m (x + 1.38 ± 0.05 m/s) and 4 × 50 m (x = 1.45 ± 0.07 m/s).

TABLE 1. *Anthropometric and physiological data of the subjects.*

n	Age yrs	Height cm	Body Weight kg	Fat %	VO_2 max ml/kg/min	VO_2 max ml/min
10	15.3 ± 3.4	172.2 ± 8.4	66.1 ± 10.0	15.6 ± 4.4	62.1 ± 5.9	4102.7 ± 732.3

TABLE 2. *Maximal and submaximal lactate, heart rate and velocity values of the various swimming tests.*

Distance m		Lactate mmol/l	Heart rate bpm	Velocity m/s
4 × 50	max	8.0 ± 1.8	192 ± 9.7	1.45 ± 0.07*
4 × 50	subm	4.0 ± 1.5	169 ± 9.8	1.38 ± 0.10*
200	max	7.4 ± 1.5	192 ± 5.2	1.38 ± 0.05
200	subm	3.6 ± 0.9	175 ± 4.8	1.29 ± 0.06
400	max	6.6 ± 2.3	190 ± 7.4	1.33 ± 0.06
400	subm	2.8 ± 0.9	175 ± 9.3	1.24 ± 0.04
2 × 300	max	7.6 ± 2.3	198 ± 2.3	1.34 ± 0.07
2 × 300	subm	3.5 ± 1.0	173 ± 11.5	1.24 ± 0.07

*$p < .001$

A graphical presentation of lactate versus velocity data, submaximal and maximal, is given in Fig. 1. As can be seen there is an order in the sequence of the distances of the various tests, while the slope remains unchanged.

Discussion

The ability to produce and sustain, during competition, high blood lactate levels has been associated with successful athletic performance (Elliot and Haber, 1983).

It is logical, therefore, that coaches develop training programs geared towards improving this ability, in an effort to maximize athletic performance. It has been the practice in coaching to assess long term adaptations to training, by following maximal and submaximal lactate profiles throughout the season, as well as comparing individual lactate values to the previous season's lactate data.

The highest ever measured maximal blood lactate values have been found following competitive 100 and 200 m swimming events, with a peak value of 25 mmol/l recorded in the 200 m individual medley (Sawka et al., 1979). However, values of this magnitude have been rare, since most studies report maximal blood lactates values, during competition of the magnitude of 15-17 mmol/l (Prins, 1987; Telford et al., 1988).

The mean blood lactate, ranging from (6.6-8.0 mmol/l found in the different distance tests in this study, is low when compared to values reported in the literature (Sharp et al., 1987; Chatard et al., 1988; Telford et al., 1988).

As it can be seen in Table 2, no statistically significant differences in maximal blood lactate levels were observed among the four tests in our study. However, there seems to be a tendency (r= 0.75) to increased blood lactate levels, from the longest 6.6 ± 2.3 mmol/l) to the shortest (8.0 ±1.8 mmol/l) distance test. Although our values seem to be lower when compared to post-competition values (Chatard et al., 1988; Telford et al., 1988), something which we have found also (unpublished data), they are in general agreement with other studies, reporting maximal blood lactates taken after routine assessment tests during the season (Caldwell and Pekkarinen, 1983; Van Handel et al., 1988).

Caldwell and Pekkarinen (1983) reported a maximal blood lactate values of 7.96 ± 2.42 mmol/l during a 2 × 200 m test, at 85% and maximal all out effort, a value very close to the 7.4 ± 1.5 mmol/l found in our study.

Similarly, Van Handel *et al.* (1988) reported maximal blood lactate values of 7.3 ± 1.5 mmol/l during a 2 × 400 m test conducted in a similar fashion as the 2 × 200 m test, a value very close to the 6.6 ± 2.3 mmol/l found in our study.

Higher maximal blood lactate values during testing have been found by Sharp *et al.* (1984) in competitive college swimmers during a 2 × 200 mtest. Blood lactic acid levels reached 11.76 ± 0.87 mmol/l. These higher values, when compared to ours, may be attributed to the age differences between the two groups (15.3 ± 3.4 yr).

Although the ability to produce greater maximal blood lactate concentration with increased age has been challenged by Cumming *et al.* (1980), the overwhelming evidence in the literature suggests the opposite (Bar-Or, 1983; Jacobs *et al.*, 1983; Eriksson *et al.*, 1974; Eriksson and Saltin, 1974). This has been thought to be based on the observed reduced maximal activity of glycolytic enzymes such as phosphofructokinase (PFK) during early ages (Eriksson and Saltin, 1974) as well as lower levels of testosterone (Krotkiewski *et al.*, 1980).

An additional explanation to the lower maximal blood lactate values observed in our study was the fact that the subjects were middle distance swimmers, and it is well known that the ability to produce high values of lactate is based on muscle fiber type composition. Costill (1978) for example, has shown that sprinters who are able to produce high blood lactate concentrations have 60-65% fast twich fibers. Furthermore, the low blood lactate concentration might be attributed to the fact that the tests were conducted at the end of the training phase, which emphasized the aerobic component of training. Our tests were performed on a 25 m indoor swimming pool, which has been shown to produce lower lactate values than tests conducted on a 50 m pool. In the study by Telford *et al.* (1988) maximal blood lactate values were 8.23 ± 0.4 mmol/l and 11.7 ± 0.65 mmol/l for the 25 and 50 m swimming pool respectively.

The trend to greater blood lactate levels observed in the 4 × 50 m test, when compared with the longer 400 m test, was not due to differences in achieved cardiovascular intensity during the tests, since no statistically significant differences in maximal heart rate were recorded among the four tests used in this study (Table 2). Analysis of the Sport tester telemetric heart rate values, revealed an initial sharp increase of heart rate to the magnitude of 180 bpm during the first 30 sec in all tests; thereafter, heart rates increased and maintained at the maximal possible individual value throughout the effort. The non-statistically significant trend to higher maximal blood lactate values observed with shorter distances, was associated with statistically significant (p <.001) swimming speed values observed in the shorter distance tests (200 m, 4 × 50 m).

From the presentation in Fig. 1, one can observe that there is a velocity displacement on the left, i.e. towards smaller velocities as the test distance is increased, while lactate values are dicreased also with respect to the distance, so that the slope = (LA max − LA submax)/Vmax − Vsubmax) remains statistically unchanged. That is in agreement with the results of other investigators (Mader *et al.*, 1980), who found a similar slope. This is an indication of a change in the lactate kinetics, so a different lactate curve and lactate threshold is to be expected.

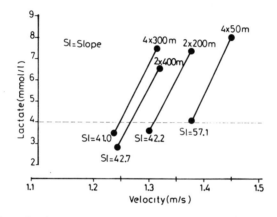

FIG 1. Submaximal and maximal swimming tests.

There is also a tendency of maximal and submaximal lactates to increase with respect to velocity (slope = 16.42), while the 2 × 300 m test is a special case, because it is the only one of the four tests in which there is no 20 min rest, but only a 2 min one, and obviously the lactate accumulates and appeared higher than the 400 m test.

These results indicate that for swimmers, if only the level of maximal lactate value is concerned, any of the tested protocols can be used to determine maximal lactate capacity. However, since there is a trend of differentiation in anaerobic contribution to energy needs during swimming, the selection of the test to be used should be determined by the additional information the coach needs to know in developing his training workouts.

References

Bar-Or, O. (1983). "Pediatric Sport Medicine for the Practitioner". pp. 165. Springer Verlag, New York.

Caldwell, E.J. and Pekkarinen, H. (1983). A comparison of the anaerobic threshold and blood lactate increases during cycle ergometry and free swimming. Biomechanics and Medicine in Swimming. *International Series on Sport Sciences*, **14**, 235-243. Human Kinetics, Champaign, Ill.

Chatard, J.C., Paulin, M. and Lacour, J.F. (1988). Postcompetition blood lactate measurements and swimming performance illustrated by data from a 400 m Olympic record holder. *International Series on Sport Sciences*, **18**, 311-316. Human Kinetics, Champaign, Ill.

Costill, D.L. (1978). Adaptations in skeletal muscle during training for spring and endurance swimming. *In* "Swimming Medicine IV". (Eds B.Eriksson and B. Furberg), pp. 233-248. University Park Press, Baltimore.

Cumming, G.R., Hastman, L., McCort, J. and McCullaugh, J. (1980). High serum lactates do occur in young children after maximal work. *International Journal of Sports Medicine*, **1**, 69.

Elliot, M., and Haber, P. (1983). Estimation of the peak performance in the 100 meter breast stroke on the basis of serum lactate measurement during two submaximal test heats at different velocities. *In* "Biomechanics and Medicine in Swimming". (Eds Hollander and Huijing, de Groot), *International Series on Sport Sciences*, **14**, 33-338. Human Kinetics, Champaign, Ill.

Eriksson, B.O. and Saltin, B. (1974). Muscle metabolism during exercise in boys aged 11 to 16 years compared to adults. *Acta Paediatrica Belgica* **28**, 257-265.

Eriksson, B.O., Golnick, P.D. and Saltin, B. (1974). The effect of physical training on muscle enzyme activities and fiber composition in 11 year old boys. *Acta Paediatrica Belgica*, **28**, 245-252.

Fox, E.L., Robinson, S. and Wiegman, D. (1969). Metabolic energy sources during continuous and internal training. *Journal of Applied Physiology*, **27**, 174-178.

Jacobs, I. Tesch, P.A., Bar-Or, O., Karlsson, J. and Dotan, R. (1983). Lactate in human skeletal muscle after 10s and 30s of supramaximal exercise. *Journal of Applied Physiology*, **55**, 365-368.

Krotkiewski, M., Kral, J.G. and Karlsson. (1980). Effects of castration and testosterone substitution on body composition and muscle metabolism in rats. *Acta Physiologica Scandinavica*, **109**, 233-237.

Mader, A. Heck, H. and Hollmann, W. (1978). Evaluation of lactic acid anaerobic energy contribution by determination of postexercise lactic acid concentration of ear capillary blood in middle distance runners and swimmers. *In* "Exercise Physiology". (Eds Landry and Orban), pp. 187-200. Symposium Specialists, Miami.

Mader, A., Madsen, O., and Hollmann, W. (1980). The evaluation of the anaerobic energy supply with regard to the performances in training and competition in swimming. *Leistungssport*, **10**, 263--279, 408-418

Madsen, O. (1983). Aerobic training: Not so fast there. *Swimming Technique*, **19**,

13-18.

Maglischo, E.W., Maglischo, C.W. and Bishop, R.A. (1982). Lactate testing for training pace. *Swimming Technique,* **19,** 31-37.

Maglischo, E.W., Maglischo, C.W. Smith, R.E., Bishop, R.A. and Hovland, P.N. (1984). Determining the proper training speeds for swimmers. *Journal of Swimming Reseach,* **1,** 32-38.

Novak, E., Mackova, K. and Bartos, O. (1988). Anaerobic threshold in training process of the swimmers. *Acta Universitatis Carolinae gymnica,* **24,** (2), 75-83.

Pariskova, J. (1961). Total body fat and skinfold thickness in children. *Metabolism,* **10,** 794-807.

Prins, J. (1987). "Lactate Analysis. World Clinic Yearbook". pp. 165-178. American Swimming Coaches Association, Las Vegas, Nevada, September 15-19.

Sawka, M.N., Knowlton, R.G., Miles, D.S. and Critz, J.B. (1979). Post competition blood lactate concentrations in collegiate swimmers. *European Journal of Applied Physiology,* **41,** 93-99.

Sharp, R.L., Vitelli, C.A., Costill, D.L. and Thomas, R. (1984). Comparison between blood lactate and heart rate profiles during a season of competitive swim training. *Journal on Swimming Research,* **1** (1), 17-20.

Stegmann, H., Kindermann, W. and Schnabel, A. (1981). Lactate kinetics and individual anaerobic threshold. *International Journal of Sports Medicine,* **2,** 160-165.

Telford, D.R., Hahn, G.A., Catchpole., A.E. Parker., R.A. and Sweetenharm, E.W. (1988). Postcompetition blood lactate concentration in highly ranked Australia swimmers. *International Series of Sport Sciences,* **18,** 277-283. Human Kinetics, Champaign, Ill.

Tsopanakis, A., Havale, I. and Tsopanakis, C. (1986). Enzymatic electrode blood lactate determination after muscular exercise. *Journal of Clinical Chemistry and Clinical Biochemistry,* **24,** (10), 814-15.

Van Handel, J.P., Katz, A., Troup, P.J., Daniels, T.J. and Bradley, W.P. (1988). Oxygen consumption and blood lactic acid response to training and taper. *International Series of Sport Sciences,* **18,** 269-274. Human Kinetics, Champaign, Ill.

14. Characteristic Blood Chemistry Results of Swimmers Following Various Training Periods

J.P. TROUP, A. BARZDUKAS, S.M. ARREDONDO, A.B. RICHARDSON and R. REESE

TRAINING IN THE SPORT of swimming involves a series of phases that vary in length, and in degree of volume and intensity of work. These phases are designed progressively to overload the athlete in an attempt to improve the level of performance capacity. However, should the training regimen be mis-designed resulting in a prolonged period of stress, the swimmer may mis-adapt and the resulting performances will decrease. In order to avoid the over-stressed condition some blood chemistries have been identified as useful in monitoring the response to training. Understanding fluctuations in these parameters will help avoid a high stress condition. The purpose of this study, therefore, was (i) to measure changes in blood chemistries of élite world class swimmers and (ii) to identify the response time for recovery and fluctuation periods following high volume and high intensity work.

Methods

Blood chemistry markers were followed weekly during a 6 week period of training in a group of highly trained, élite world class swimmers (n = 12). Markers included measurement of CPK, myoglobin, cortisol and SGOT. Additionally, a performance time trial was conducted weekly with measurement of energy cost at sub-maximal paces of 1.4 and 1.5 m/sec. Analysis of variance was used with appropriate *post-hoc* tests to determine significance at the $p < .05$ level.

The training program included 6 weeks of training divided into two, 3 week segments. The first segment included high volume, low intensity work, while the second segment involved high intensity, moderate volume of work.

Results

All blood markers increased ($p < 0.05$) at 3 weeks of training during the first phase of training. A similar increase ($p < 0.05$) was observed during the second phase of training but did not appear to differ from the initial increase observed during the first phase of training. During periods of peak fluctuations in each "overtraining" marker, performances decreased ($p < .05$) as well as the economy index of each swimmer. In order to establish the collective magnitude of the stress of each swimmer, a swimming stress index was developed. Following these weeks of training this index significantly increased and maintained that level until the first week of training.

Summary

In summary, changes in blood chemistries accurately reflect the level of stress that the athlete is undergoing. The use of these tests can therefore provide the sports practitioner a valuable marker to help in avoiding a misadaptation to training.

---

15. Hormonal Responses to Endurance Training in Swimming and their Dependence on Sex and Fitness

W. SKIPKA, U. KUNSTLINGER, E. ZIMMERMANN and T. ROHN

COMPARED TO EXERCISE on land, swimming has some essential, physiological differences:

    (a)   work in a horizontal position combined with a practical weightlessness,;

    (b)   water pressure;

    (c)   much less static and more dynamic ;

    (d)   altered conditions in temperature regulation of the body.

All this might suggest that the hormonal system is affected differently during swimming. Some investigators showed that the metabolic reactions to endurance training differ between males and females (Berg and Keul, 1981). The question rises in which degree sex specific hormonal reactions occur.

The aim of the present study was to investigate the influence of swimming exercise on the behaviour of catecholamines (adrenaline and noradrenaline), cortisol and aldosterone. Furthermore it had to be proved whether an influence of sex or performance capacity on the hormonal reactions exists.

Methods

With 15 male and 10 female swimmers of different performance capacity an extensive (high quantity) interval training in front crawl was conducted lasting about 90 min. The total training distance ranged from 3500 m to 4200 m. Distance, intensity and interval had been fixed individually. The subjects had been divided into well trained (WT) and less trained (LT) swimmers (Table 1). Before swimming, immediately as well as at 1.5 h and 3 h after cessation of the training both urinary and blood samples were taken to determine urinary excretion values of noradrenaline and adrenaline and the plasma concentrations of aldosterone and cortisol.

Urinary catecholamine concentrations were measured by gas-chromatography/mass spectrometry (GC/MS) (Zimmermann et al., 1982). Cortisol and aldosterone were analyzed by the RIA-method. Glomerular filtration rate (GFR) was analyzed by the measurement of creatinine clearance. Significance was tested by use of the Student t-test and analysis of variance.

TABLE 1. *Personal data and training distance of the groups. WT = well trained; LT = less trained. ($\times$ + S.D.).*

Groups	z	n	Symbols in figures	Age (yr)	Height (cm)	Weight (kg)	Training dist. (m)
males	WT	9	▲	24.1 ± 1.6	181.6 ± 6.9	75.6 ± 7.6	4050 ± 120
	LT	6	△	23.6 ± 1.1	180.0 ± 4.2	76.9 ± 8.2	3750 ± 150
females	WT	6	●	21.5 ± 2.7	172.4 ± 3.5	62.8 ± 6.1	4000 ± 130
	LT	4	○	22.7 ± 2.1	173.5 ± 6.1	68.5 ± 7.0	3600 ± 120

Results and discussion

During and after training a significant increase of GFR could be stated in some subjects thus influencing the excretion of catecholamines. Therefore catecholamine excretion was calculated per ml GFR; values are shown in Fig. 1.

As similar, or lesser increase in catecholamines is found with exercise in water as on land (Künstlinger *et al.*, 1987) thus giving no indications for an excessive increase of the secretion rate during swimming as reported by Weicker (1986). In males, basic values are slightly lower in WT and there is a smaller work-induced increase of the catecholamines in this group. This smaller increase of catecholamine excretion in WT males during swimming might reflect not only a reduced sympathetic reaction to work, but might also be combined with an abolished reaction in this group to the stress of water immersion, as shown in earlier experiments (Skipka *et al.*, 1976).

In females, the basic values of the WT are significantly smaller than in the LT; the exercise effect is just contrary to male results. The WT display a significantly higher increase while changes in the LT group are insignificant. A possible explanation might be that given by Freedmann *et al.* (1987) showing a lower sensitivity and/or density of peripheral vascular adrenergic receptors in women than in men.

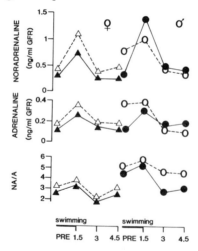

FIG. 1. Mean values of urinary catecholamine excretion before, during and 3 hours after extensive interval training in swimming. Closed symbols with solid lines represent values of well trained (WT), open symbols with dashed lines are values of lower trained swimmers (LT).

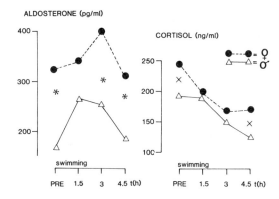

FIG. 2. Mean values of blood plasma aldosterone and cortisol concentrations before, at the end and after extensive interval training in swimming. For symbols see Fig. 1.

Blood plasma concentrations of aldosterone and cortisol are significantly higher in females than in males before and 3 h after swimming (Fig. 2). Especially in aldosterone pre-swimming mean values of females are nearly doubled compared with males, and after swimming they are about 60% higher. Only in the WT males, are the changes of aldosterone concentrations statistically significant. Three hours after swimming the values correspond to resting levels again. The swimming-induced rise by 75% is less pronounced compared to equivalent exercise on land, where augmentations by some 100% will be found. This can be explained by the immersion-induced inhibition of aldosterone secretion (Skipka et al., 1979). The insignificant increase of plasma aldosterone in LT males corresponds to results of Böening et al. (1988). In females the training-induced changes of aldosterone concentrations are most unhomogeneous and statistically not significant, even in WT, after training. As the increase of aldosterone during work depends strongly on the intensity of exercise, the observed influences of sex and performance capacity on the changes of aldosterone concentrations during and after exercise might be explained by differences concerning the swimming speed (Fig. 3).

In both sexes, aldosterone values before and 3 h after training are smaller in WT than in LT. There is a significant negative correlation between the basic levels of aldosterone and the performance capacity of the swimmers ($p < 0.05$). This effect has already been found in former investigations with untrained and endurance trained subjects and may be regarded as an adrenocortical adaption to the regular performance stress (Skipka *et al.*, 1979).

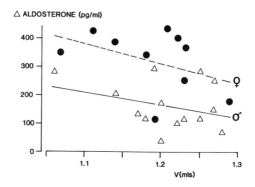

FIG. 3. Changes of plasma aldosterone concentrations during 90 min of training in swimming in relation to swimming velocity. Triangles represent values of males, dots values of females.

Plasma cortisol concentrations of the females display a significant decrease during training (Fig. 2). Values of the males seem to be unchanged during training and decrease more after it. The performance specific reactions during swimming in males show a small increase for WT and a small decrease for LT. In females the values of LT decrease more than those of WT during swimming. Evidently the basic values in cortisol concentrations are significantly higher compared to other findings (Künstlinger *et al.*, 1987). The influence of the circadian rhythm on cortisol concentrations has to be taken into account. While maximal values are observed at 08.00 h (i.e. at the time when we started our experiments), minimal values are measured at 12.30 h. This circadian decrement seems hardly to be influenced by exercise (Brandenberger *et al.*, 1982).

Besides this, exercise duration and intensity must also be considered. Raczynska and Opaszowski (1985) found a small decrease in cortisol excretion during a swimming training of 90 min, whereas swimming with higher intensity (5 × 400 m) resulted in an increase of excretion rate. In our study the above mentioned differences in swimming-induced changes of cortisol concentrations between the training groups in males as well as females might be the result of different absolute training intensities.

Conclusions

The last question refers to the meaning of the hormone aldosterone with respect to the performance capacity. Besides its well-known importance for the electrolyte balance, aldosterone has a positive effect on the aerobic metabolism leading to an improvement in performance capacity, as we have shown (Schramm *et al.*, 1983; Skipka, 1988). For this, an increased aldosterone secretion some hours before starting exercise might be beneficial, and a warming up by swimming slowly would have a contrary effect. As the aldosterone secretion depends on the exercise intensity you have to swim very quickly (Skipka and Künstlinger, 1988). Another possibility is exercise on land, in which you can achieve high aldosterone secretion rates without working as hard as in the water.

References

Berg, A. and Keul, J. (1981). Physiological and metabolic responses of female athletes during laboratory and field exercise. *In* "Medicine and Sport". Vol. 14. Women and Sport, (Eds J. Borms, M. Hebbelinck and A. Venerando). pp. 77-96. Karger, Basel.

Böening, D., Mrugalla, M., Maassen, N., Busse, M. and Wagner, T.O.F. (1988). Exercise versus immersion: antagonistic effects on water and electrolyte metabolism during swimming. *European Journal of Applied Physiology,* **57,** 248-253.

Brandenberger, G., Follenius, M. and Hietter, B. (1982). Feedback from meal-related peaks determines diurnal changes in cortisol response to exercise. *Journal of Clinical Endocrinology and Metabolism,* **54,** 592-596.

Freedmann, R., Sabharwal, S.C. and Desai, N. (1987). Sex differences in peripheral vascular adrenergic receptors. *Circulation Research,* **61,** 581-585.

Künstlinger, U., Ludwig, H.G. and Stegemann, J. (1987). Metabolic changes during volleyball matches. *International Journal of Sports Medicine,* **8,** 315-322.

Nielsen, B., Sjogaard, G. and Bonde-Petersen, F. (1984). Cardiovascular, hormonal and body fluid changes during prolonged exercise. *European Journal of Applied Physiology,* **53,** 63-70.

Raczynska, B. and Opaszowski, B. (1985). Lactate and cortisol response to swimming training in children aged 11-12 years. *Biology of Sport,* **2,** 207-216.

Schramm, U., Skipica, A. W. and Stegemann, J. (1983). Altered relationships between aerobic and anaerobic metabolic rate induced by aldosterone during short-term exercise. *In* "Sport: Leistung und Gesundheit". (Eds H. Heck, W. Hollmann, H. Liesen and R. Rost), pp. 57-62. Deutscher Arzte-Verlag, Köln.

Skipka, W. (1988). Relevance of the adrenocortical hormone aldosterone to long distance swimming. *In* "International Series on Sport Sciences". Vol. 18. Swimming Science V, (Eds B.E. Ungerechts, K. Wilke, and K. Reischle), pp. 237-241. Human Kinetics, Champaign, IL.

Skipka, W. and Küenstlinger, U. (1988). Hormonal reactions to swimming exercise, differing in intensity and duration. *Canadian Journal of Sport Science,* **13**, 31.

Skipka, W., Deck, K.A. and Böening, D. (1976). Effect of physical fitness on vanillylmandelic acid excretion during immersion. *European Journal of Applied Physiology,* **35**, 271-276.

Skipka, W., Böening, D., Deck, K.A., Kuelpelmann, W.R. and Meurer, K.A. (1979). Reduced aldosterone and sodium excretion in endurance trained athletes before and during immersion. *European Journal of Applied Physiology,* **42**, 255-261.

Weicker, H. (1986). Sympathoadrenergic regulation. *Sports Medicine,* **7**, Suppl. **1**, 16-26.

Zimmermann, E., Schänzer, W. and Donike, M. (1982). Stress hormones in the situation of competition and training. *In* "Sport: Leistung und Gesundheit". (Eds. H. Heck, W. Hollmann, H. Liesen, and R. Rost), pp. 277-282; Deutscher Arzte-Verlag, Köeln.

---

16. Changes in Peak Force and Work in Competitive Swimmers during Training and Taper as Tested on a Biokinetic Swimming Bench

J.H. PRINS, D.A. LALLY, K.E. MAES, J. UNO and G.H. HARTUNG

THE DEVELOPMENT OF MUSCULAR strength and power are recognized as important components in the training of competitive swimmers. Traditionally, dry-land training is stressed during the early months of a training season. The expectation is that once the emphasis shifts to swimming training, the improvements in strength and power may translate into improved competitive performances. The measurement of strength and power in swimmers has been facilitated by the introduction of the Biokinetic Swim Bench, a semi-accommodating resistance device which mimics the arm action of the freestyle and butterfly swimming strokes. This equipment has been used to measure muscular work and power during training as well as periods of reduced workloads (Sharp *et al.,* 1982; Neufer *et al.,* 1987; Costill *et al.,* 1988;).

In recent years, attention has been focussed on the factors related to sprint swimming. Counsilman (1981) noted the importance of hand speed and acceleration as it applies to increasing swimming velocities. Since these increases in velocity require the application of muscular forces at progressively higher limb speeds, the ability to measure these forces may provide information on the efficacy of the imposed strength-training regime.

Since maintaining muscular strength and power is important during all phases of training, especially during the taper, the purpose of the study was to monitor the changes in peak muscular force and work during the last 7 weeks of a swimming season, using a Biokinetic Swimming Bench. The variable-speed settings provided by the Biokinetic apparatus permit the measurement of peak muscular force and work at varied speeds. In addition, an attempt was made to determine if there were differences in these measurements when the subjects were categorized as sprinters in comparison to swimmers categorized as non-sprinters.

Methods

Eleven female and 9 male competitive swimmers volunteered for this investigation. Informed consent as outlined by the American College of Sports Medicine was obtained. Based on their primary competitive event, subjects were divided into two groups, sprinters (Sp) and non-sprinters (NSp). Subjects whose primary competitive distance was the 50 and 100 yd/m were classified as sprinters (Sp); non-sprinters (NSp) were those swimmers whose primary competitive distances were 200 yd/m and above. Mean subject characteristics for all participants and average weekly training distances are presented in Table 1.

All measurements were made using a Biokinetic Swim Bench (Sharp et al., 1982). Since the design of this machine permits both the speed of the pull and the resistance to vary over the course of a single pull, the following calibration technique was employed. An optical tachometer was installed in the machine to measure the velocities at which varying weights would drop through a known distance. To obtain the work done on the machine, the measured kinetic energy was subtracted from the total potential energy of each of the calibration weights. The same weights were used for calibration of the force output. The velocity was found to increase by 0.29 m/sec per speed setting for a given force. This figure was in close agreement with that reported by Sharp et al. (1982). The change in velocity of the machine as a function of applied force was approximately 0.005 m/sec. per newton of force.

TABLE 1. *Mean (±SE) characteristics of the subjects.*

	Age (yr)	Height (cm)	Weight (kg)	% Fat
Sprinters				
Male (n = 5)	17.2	180.9	73.1	12.8
	(± 0.2)	(± 1.2)	(± 3.0)	(± 10.44)
Female (n = 3)	16.0	172.2	59.2	19.7
	(± 1.0)	(± 2.9)	(± 0.4)	(± 1.8)
Non-Sprinters				
Male (n = 5)	16.8	172.2	63.2	10.8
	(± 0.5)	(± 7.0)	(± 3.3)	(± 11.5)
Female (n= 7)	15.9	161.5	52.1	19.9
	(± 0.4)	(± 2.6)	(± 1.7)	(± 1.3)

Maximal work (kpm/pull) was measured using the digital work integrator supplied with the Bench. Maximal peak force (Newtons) was recorded by connecting a Honeywell Oscillographic Recorder, Model 1858 (Honeywell Corp., Denver, CO.) to the apparatus.

Data were collected from each subject on 11 separate test dates. These 11 tests extended for 7 weeks, the last 4 weeks of which incorporated the period of the "taper" (Table 1). The test protocol consisted of three maximal double-arm pulls performed at four different speed settings (0, 3, 6, and 9). The movement used approximated the pull pattern of the butterfly stroke. Maximal work (kpm/pull) and maximal peak force (N) at each of the speed settings were recorded for each test. Data for peak force (PF) and average work (WK) per pull at each speed setting were analyzed. In addition, the percentage decrement (% Dec) in PF between the lowest and highest speed setting was recorded.

Differences between mean values for sprinters and non-sprinters were tested using a one-way analysis of variance, which was considered significant if P was less than 0.05. When a significant F was obtained, a *post hoc* comparison of means was made using a Sheffe test.

Results

Comparisons of peak muscular force (PF) and Work (WK) for the sprinters and non-sprinters are presented in Table 2. Significant differences (p <0.01) in absolute values for PF were observed between the Sp and the NSp group at all four speed settings. The average mean difference in PF between the sprinters and non-sprinters at the lowest speed setting (ss 0), was 18.2, and at the highest setting (ss 9) was 22.5%. When normalized for body weight, significant differences in PF were seen only at the highest speed setting. At speed setting "9", the average mean difference in normalized peak force between the two groups was 4.3 % and was statistically significant (p <0.01). To compare the relative decreases in peak force, the percentage decrement (% Dec) in PF between the lowest and highest speed settings were compared between the two groups (Table 3). For the Sp group the mean % Dec was 44.8% and for the NSp group, the mean % Dec was 48.2%. This difference of 7.1 per cent between the two groups was statistically significant (p < 0.01). The difference between groups for the normalized percentage decrements was 41% and was also statistically significant, (p < 0.01).

TABLE 2. *Mean PF (N), PF/bw (N/kg), Average Work/pull (kpm), Average Work/pull (kpm/kg) for speed setting 0, 3, 6 and 9.*

	Gr	Setting 0	Setting 3	Setting 6	Setting 9
PF	Sp	316.2(± 5.3)*	249.1(± 3.7)*	208.0(± 2.8)*	173.6(± 2.5)*
(N)N	Sp	258.8(± 3.1)	204.1(± 2.9)	166.3(± 2.8)	134.5(± 2.6)
PF/BW	Sp	4.66(± .05)	3.68(± .04)	3.07(± .03)	2.56(± .02)*
(N/kg)	NSp	4.74(± .05)	3.73(± .04)	3.03(± .04)	2.45(± .04)
WK	Sp	34.7(± 0.5)*	29.7(± 0.3)*	26.2(± 0.3)*	23.4(± 0.2)*
(Kpm)	NSp	29.8(± 0.3)	25.7(± 0.2)	22.9(± 0.2)	20.5(± 0.2)
WK/BW	Sp	0.52(± .00)	0.44(± .00)	0.39(± .00)	0.35(± .00)
(Kpm/Kg)	NSp	0.54(± .00)*	0.47(± .00)*	0.42(± .00)*	0.38(± .00)*

* Denotes that means are significantly different (p < 0.01)

The average work (WK) per pull for all subjects at each speed setting was analyzed. When the mean absolute values were examined, the Sp group demonstrated significantly higher (p < 0.01) average scores per pull than the NSp group at all speed settings. However when normalized for body weight, the mean values per pull for the NSp group, were observed to be significantly higher (p < 0.01), Table 2.

When analyzed for changes within each group over time, no significant changes in any of the variables were observed for either group during the 7 week period.

Discussion

Biokinetic resistance devices have been used for both laboratory testing (Campbell *et al.*, 1979; Costill *et al.*, 1988; Counsilman,1981; Coyle *et al.*, 1979), and as part of dry-land strength training programs in competitive swimmers (Heusner, 1980). The design of the apparatus permits the recording of muscular work, power and peak forces and provides a means of monitoring the changes in these parameters over time.

In this study, the mean absolute values for peak force between the Sprint (Sp) group and the Non-sprint (NSp) group were significantly different at all speed settings tested, ($p < 0.01$). These results are consistent if we take into account the physical characteristics of the subjects in the Sp group who may be assumed to be capable of exerting comparatively greater absolute muscular forces. When the data were normalized for body weight, no statistical dffferences in PF were observed between the two groups at speed settings "0", "3" and "6". However, at setting "9", the highest speed provided by the machine's design, the differences in PF between the two groups was significant ($p < 0.01$). This difference between the Sp and NSp group was 5.4% (Fig. 1) .

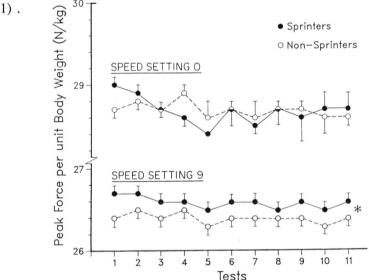

FIG. 1. Mean (±SE) values for peak force per unit body weight (N/kg) for test groups at highest and lowest speed settings during 11 tests. * = significantly different ($p < 0.01$) between groups at speed setting 9.

The above findings may lend further support to the belief that one of the factors which distinguishes sprinters from those athletes specializing in events of longer duration is their ability to exert comparatively higher forces at high limb velocities (Thorstensson, 1976; Campbell *et al.*, 1979; Coyle *et al.*, 1979; Dons *et al.*, 1979; Heusner, 1980; Komi, 1984). Studies by Thorstensson (1976) demonstrated that subjects with a higher proportion of FT fibers were capable of generating higher isokinetic forces as the velocities of contraction were increased. Coyle *et al.* (1979) concluded that "because Fast-Twitch muscle fibers are able to develop force more rapidly, the correlation between the percentage of these fibers and strength becomes progressively stronger as strength is measured at progressively higher velocities".

Differences between the two groups in the percentage decrement (%Dec) in PF IE. peak force between the lowest and highest speed settings, before and after normalization for body weight, were also noted. Before normalization, the %Dec in PF between speed setting "0" and "9" for the Sp group was 44.8% while that of the NSp group was 48.2% (Table 3). This difference of 7.1% was statistically significant ($p < 0.01$). A considerably larger statistical difference ($p < 0.01$) was noted in the percentage decrement when the data were normalized for body weight. This difference, 41 per cent, is also consistent with previous studies which indicate that subjects with a predisposition for short high-intensity work have demonstrated a larger proportion of maximum strength at higher limb velocities (Thorstensson, 1976; Heusner, 1980).

TABLE 3. *Per cent decrement of absolute peak force (%Dec) and peak force normalized for body weight (%Dec/bw), between settings 0 and 9 for each test group and percentage difference between groups.*

Group	PF at 0 (N)	PF at 9 (N)	% Dec
Sp	316.2 (± 5.3)	173.6 (± 2.5)	44.8 (± 0.4) *
NSp	258.8 (± 3.1)	134.5 (± 2.6)	48.2 (± 0.7)
Group	PF/bw at O (N/kg)	PF/bw at 9 (N/kg)	% Dec/bw
Sp	4.66 (± 0.05)	2.56 (± 0.02)	4.8 (± 0.4) *
NSp	4.74 (± 0.05)	2.45 (± 0.04)	8.2 (± 0.7)

* Denotes that means are significantly different ($p < 0.01$)

The physical work (kpm) recorded on the swim bench is approximately the product of the force and the length of the pull for each swimmer. Consequently, changes in the average work (WK) per pull over the 7 week period were dependent on changes in the ability of the subjects to exert muscular force while on the swim bench. In the present study, significant differences were noted in the absolute values for work output between test groups, Table 2. It is reasonable to assume that the Sp group, possessing a larger muscle mass, were exerting more force per pull and consequently were capable of performing more work on the swim bench. When normalized for body weight, the results were more difficult to explain. Statistical analysis of normalized values for WK indicated significantly higher values ($p < 0.01$) for the NSp group at each of the four speed settings. When the normalized data were used to cal-

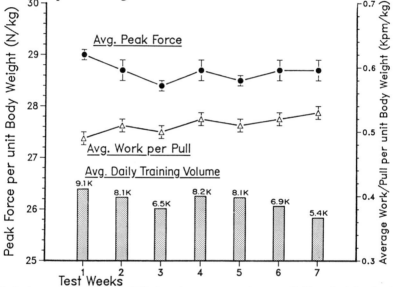

FIG. 2. Average peak force (N/kg) and average work per pull (Kpm/kg) for Sprint Group at speed setting 0, combined with average daily training volume for each week of study.

culate the percentage decrement in average work per pull, and compared to the average work at "0" speed setting, the NSp group showed significantly higher ($p < 0.01$) ratios between each of the higher speed settings. The explanation for these results may not be fully evident at this time. However, it appears that, as the machine speeds go up, the average work per pull is going down faster in the Sp group. This may be an indication of the ability of the NSp group to be capable of a more uniform application of force over the pull at all tested limb velocities and may be further evidence of the disassociation between the ability to exert peak force and perform muscular work.

Costill *et al.* (1988) and Neufer *et al.*(1981) used biokinetic devices to measure changes in muscular power in and out of the water in competitive swimmers during different phases of the season. These investigations reported no changes in work or swimming power when the swimming training was increased or during periods of reduced workloads. The findings of the current study concur with these reports. As shown in Fig. 2, even though there was a dramatic reduction in the volume of work over the 7 weeks, no significant changes in any of the variables were observed for either group.

Summary

It would appear from the present study that one of the distinguishing features between sprinters and non-sprinters in swimming is the ability to exert high muscular forces at high speeds of contraction as measured by peak muscular force. Sale (1988) observed that strength training may cause adaptive changes within the nervous system that allow a trainee to more fully activate prime movers thereby effecting a greater net force in the intended direction of movement. Sharp (1982), using a biokinetic swim bench, found a close relationship between sprint swimming speed and power output which suggested a causal relationship between these two parameters. Although swim bench measurements do not discriminate between swimming abilities or work output during the latter stages of a swimming season, the present study indicates that the pattern of force application may be different between groups and that force outputs characteristic of sprinters and non-sprinters may be distinguishable when measured at high limb velocities. The higher work outputs per body weight by the non-sprinters show evidence that at higher speeds, the ability to produce work outputs depends not only on the ability to exert peak force but on other variables, such as the pattern of force application within a pull.

References

Campbell, C.J., Bonen, A., Kirby, R.L. and Belcastro, A.N. (1979). Muscle fiber composition and performance capacities of women. *Medical Science on Sports*

Exercise, **11**, 260-265.

Costill, D.L., Flynn, M.G., Kirwan,J.P., Houmard, J.A., Mitchell, J.B., Thomas, R. and Park, S.H. (1988). Effects of repeated days of intensified training on muscle glycogen and swimming performance. *Medical Science on Sports Exercise*, **20**, 249-254.

Counsilman, J.E. (1981). Hand-speed and acceleration. *Swimming Technique*, **18**, 22-26.

Coyle, E.F., Costill, D.L. and Lesmes, G.R. (1979). Leg extension power and muscle fiber composition. *Medical Science on Sports Exercise*, **11**, 12-15.

Dons, B., Bollerup, K., Bonde-Petersen, F. and Hancke, S. (1979). The effect of weight-lifting exercise related to muscle fiber composition and muscle cross-sectional area in humans. *European Journal of Applied Physiology*, **40**, 95-106.

Heusner, W. (1980). "The Theory of Strength Development". pp. 285-311. American Swimming Coaches Association, World Clinic Yearbook.

Komi, P.V. (1984). Physiological and biomechanical correlates of muscle function: effect of muscle structure and stretch shortening cycle on force and speed. *In* "Exercise and Sport Science Reviews". Vol. 12, (Ed. R. Terjung), pp. 81-121. The Collamore Press, Lexington, Ma.

Neufer. P.D., Costill, D.L., Fielding, R.A., Flynn, M.G. and Kirwan, J.P. (1987). Effect of reduced training on muscular strength and endurance in competitive swimmers. *Medical Science on Sports Exercise*, **19**, 486-490.

Sale, D.G. (1988). Neural adaptation to resistance training. *Medical Science on Sports Exercise*, (Suppl). **20**, S135-sl45.

Sharp, R.L., Troup, J.P., and Costill, D.L. (1982). Relationship between power and sprint freestyle swimming. *Medical Science on Sports Exercise*, **14**, 53-56.

Thorstensson, A. (1976). Muscle strength, fiber types and enzyme activities in man. *Acta Physiologica Scandinavica*, Suppl. 443.

17. The Influence of Biological Factors and Training Load on Competitive Results in Junior Swimmers

H. KUŃSKI, A. JEGIER, E. RAKUS and A. MAŚLANKIEWICZ

APART FROM COGNITIVE aims, the analysis of factors which could determine performance, is applicable to the practice of partial selection for further sporting activity, as well as to make more reliable attempts to forecast further sports development (Nikitin, 1981). Anthropological and physiological parameters considerably affect the actual swimming performance in juniors (aged 12 to 14 years) during the period of intensive and unequal biological growth (Bulgakova *et al.*, 1985; Eriksson *et al.*, 1978). The essential relationship between these factors and swimming performance for a great many isolated parameters has been proved. The practical application of results of the investigations is difficult. There also exist some data that are indicative of an irrelevant consequence of sexual dimorphism in juniors, connected with the effort of swimming (Montpetit *et al.*, 1988).

It was assumed that the multiple analysis of the determinants of swimming performance would eliminate less relevant parameters and would leave only, highly essential mutually dependent ones.

We have sought a logical analysis of linear multiple regression equations, from which to estimate the determinants of swimming performance in junior males and females.

Procedures

SUBJECTS

Twenty-six boys, aged 13-14 yr, and 22 girls aged 12-13 yr, were examined, who were the elite of the Polish junior swimmers. The swimmers were divided into two male subgroups – a 100 and 400 m freestyle; and two female subgroups – a 200 and 400 m freestyle.

METHODS

A carefully standardized anthropological programme that included the following measurements was carried out: standing height, body weight, lean body mass, Rohrer index, upper and lower extremity length, shoulder and hip width and skinfold measurements. Physical work capacity (PWC/170) was measured using a mechanically braked bicycle ergometer (Monark) at a pedalling rate of 60 rpm. Heart rate was monitored from electrocardiographic tracings. Between the second and third minute after the submaximal effort, blood samples were collected from a non-pressed ulnar vein, and lactic acid concentration was determined with the Gutmann and Wahlefeld methods, using the Boehringer test. Let us consider the other variables in analysis of training load: the amount of training in water, duration of training in water, the amount of training on land, duration of training on land, mean swimming speed during training in the year (km/h).

Swimming performances were evaluated by means of the best time in the subgroups swimming distance in a 50 m pool during the summer. Multiple linear regression analysis was used as the best mathematical model to finding the simultaneous influence of anthropological, functional and training parameters on the best competitive result.

Results and discussion

Arithmetic means of those anthropological, functional and training parameters, defined as the essential ones in a regression function, have been listed in Table 1. The analysis of multidirectional determining has been presented in the form of linear multiple regression equations for both males and females in the shorter (100-200 m) and longer (400 m) distances in Table 2.

With regard to the equations, it has been found that only a few anthropological, functional and training factors had positive meaning for the actual determining of swimming abilities, despite accepting the previous greater class of 32 independent variables which were introduced into the regression process. Length of extremities, shoulder width, aerobic capacity (PWC/170), vital capacity, lactate concentration after submaximal effort and the number of trainings in water are these ones which are mainly related to the progress of swimming performance. The negative effect on sports performance is connected with body weight and hip width in girls.

TABLE 1. Mean and standard deviation of anthropological, functional and training parameters which are in linear multiple regression equations.

	S	Y s	H cm	W kg	E_1 cm	E_2 cm	S cm	P cm	M cm	F %	N l	C w	L mmol/l	T_w year^{-1}	T_1 year^{-1}	I km/h
Male 100m freestyle	15	100.4 ±3.4	175.1 ±5.9	64.3 ±5.4	78.0 ±3.2	92.5 ±4.3	–	–	–	–	–		195 ±38		312 ±42	2.36 ±0.4
400m freestyle	11	457.2 ±15.5	173.9 ±6.2	61.7 ±5.7	77.4 ±3.2	91.6 ±4.0	37.9 ±1.6	–	–	–	5.09 ±0.55	194 ±39	–	297 ±90	–	–
Female 200m freestyle	11	237.8 ±2.3	–	–	–	–	34.6 ±1.4	–	–	16.3 ±2.9	–	–	3.3 ±0.4	404 ±40	187 ±69	–
400m freestyle	11	492.7 ±10.2	–	47.3 ±4.4	72.3 ±2.8	85.4 ±3.4	–	25.7 ±1.3	46.1 ±3.1	–	3.65 ±0.27	–	3.2 ±0.5	414 ±95	–	–

Key: S= No of Swimmers; Y = Competitive results; H = body height; W = body weight; E_1 = upper-extremity length; E_2 = lower-extremity length; S = shoulder width; M= thigh girth; P = hip width; F = body fat; N = vital capacity; C = PWC$_{170}$; L = lactic acid conc. after submaximal effort; T_w = an amount of trainings in water; T_1 = an amount of trainings on land; I = intensity of training in water.

TABLE 2. *Linear multiple regression equations.*

Male
100 m freestyle
$$Y = 171.2 - 0.02\ H + 0.07\ W + 0.76\ E_1 - 1.25\ E_2 - 0.01\ C - 0.001 - 8.88\ I$$
    RR = 0.59   SE = 3.29
400 m freestyle
$$Y = 772.3 + 0.13\ H + 3.53\ W - 1.6\ E_1 - 2.42\ E_2 - 1.38\ S - 0.21\ C - 20.0\ N - 0.05$$
    RR = 0.99   SE = 3.90

Female
100 m freestyle
$$Y = 295.2 + 0.06\ F - 0.88\ S + 2.47\ L - 0.01\ T_w - 0.17\ T_1$$
    RR = 0.86   SE = 2.72
400 m freestyle
$$Y = 501.0 + 3.07\ W - 3.92\ E_1 + 2.21\ E_2 + 3,84\ P - 1.81\ M - 10.0 - 0.41\ L - 0.1\ T$$
    RR = 0.94   SE = 5.82

Key: Y = competitive result/s; H = body height/cm; W = body weight/kg; E_1 = upper extremity length/cm; E_2 = lower extremity length/cm; S = shoulder width/cm; P = hip width/cm; M = thigh girth/cm; F body fat/%; N = vital capacity/L; C = PWC_{170}/W; L = lactic-acid concentration in blood after submaximal effort/mmol/1; T_w = an amount of training in water/year^{-1}; T_1 = an amount of training on land/year^{-1}; I = mean of intensity of training in water/km/h

The logical analysis of obtained formulas leads to the following conclusions that might be practically useful:

1   the relationship between swimming performance and an aerobic capacity level was being shown in boys only, while the same correlation between a dependent variable (sports performance) and a lactate concentration level after submaximal effort was being observed, especially in girls;

2   the relationship between swimming abilities and vital capacity has existed in both males and females (more relevant in boys) under conditions of close analysis of sports performance in the longer distance (400 m);

3   the influence of the number of training sessions in water has been relevant in boys and girls; however, it is definitely greater when the analysis of the best competitive result was carried out in the longer distance (400 m).

The application of these investigations to the prognostic purposes of competitive results during the developmental period requires taking into consideration some growing trends of individual biological parameters that are typical of determined populations. The results proved a much stronger influence of the set of chosen biological parameters on swimming performance in comparison with the level of applied training load. It can also be seen that effects of the observation of biological factors do not vary from the previous ones which were published by Kuński et al.(1988). On studying the literature, we can realize that the competitive result in swimming depends not only on biological factors and training load, but also other factors such as the hydrodynamic properties of an organism, joint mobility, strength-testing preparations, physical immunity and the state of a swimmer's mental preparation (Bulgakova et al., 1985; Clarke and Vaccaro, 1979). The authors have also noticed that the influence of neuro-endocrine systems in children at this age, taking part in competitions, was so great that it became a screen for the representation of swimmer's technical-exercise preparation (Martirosov et al., 1984).

Conclusions

It has been emphasized in our work that biological factors were one of the main indicators of younger junior swimmer's high swimming performances, although their influence was different – it was dependent on sex and swimming specialization.

References

Bulgakova, N. Z., Woroncov A. P. and Radygina I. Ju. (1985). Sootnosheniie tiempov biologichieskogo pazvitija i prirosta osnovnyh morfofunkcionalnyh pokazatieliej junych plovcow. (The relationship between a rate of biologival development an on increment of basic morpho-functional parameters in young swimmers). *Theorja i Praktica Fizicheskoj Kultury*, **11**, 27-28.
Clarke, D. H. and Vaccaro, P. (1979). The effect of swimming training on muscular performance and body composition in children. *Research Quarterly*, **50**, 9-17.
Eriksson, B. O., Berg, H. and Taranger, J. (1978). Physiological analysis of young boys starting intensive training in swimming. *In* "Swimming Medicine IV". (Eds B. Eriksson and B. Furberg), pp. 147-160. University Park Press, Baltimore.
Kuński, H., Jegier, A., Maślankiewicz, A. and Rakus E. (1988). The relationship of biological factors to swimming performances in top Polish junior swimmers aged 12 to 14 years. *In* "Swimming Science V". (Eds B. E. Ungerechts, K. Wilke and K. Reischle), pp. 109-113. Human Kinetics, Champaign, IL.

Martirosov, E. G., Bulgakova, N. Z., Statkiavchienie, B. W., Filimonova, I. E. and Chebotarieva, I. W. (1984). Polovoj dimorfizm niekotoryh mofrofunkcjonalnyh pokazatielej i sportivnyh dostizenij w plavanii. (The sexual dimorphism of some morphofunctional parameters and competitive results in swimming). *Tieorija i Praktika Fizicheskoj Kultury*, **3**, 16-18.
Montpetit, R. M., Cazorla, G. and Lavoie, J. M. (1988). Energy expenditure during front crawl swimming: a comparison between male and females. *In* "Swimming Science V". (Eds B. E. Ungerechts, K. Wilke and K. Reischle), pp. 229-235. Human Kinetics, Champaign, IL.
Nikitin, J. P. (1981). Prognozirowanije pierspiektivnosti junych plocow s ychetom kliniko-fizjologicheskih dannyh. (The prognosing of a perspective in young swimmers on the basis of clinical and physiological data). *Tieorija i Praktika Fizicheskoj Kultury*, **9**, 22-24.

18. Longitudinal Morphofunctional Study in Young Cuban Swimmers

J. BLANCO HERRERA

Introduction

The foundation, in 1961, of the National Institute of Sport, Physical Culture and Recreation (INDER) began, in Cuba, a real development in the popular practice of sport as well as in the high performance sport. However swimming has lagged behind. This fact attracts attention because our country is an island, whose subtropical climate is ideal for the practice of this sport.

The situation is even more contradictory since in water-polo, an almost unknown sport in our country before 1959, Cuba ranks today among the first five in the world: and its technical basis is swimming.

Swimming is a really complex sport, one that demands a great expense of energy and which starts in early life, generally before puberty. This fact makes even more complicated the load training dosage during the different periods of training.

During puberty major metabolic changes take place and the athletes practising this sport are often subjected to intensive training loads; undoubtedly it is necessary to study whether at various grades this could overload the youngsters' organism.

A curious fact is shown statistically by the results obtained from our very young swimmers' categories in international events, where most of the swimmers in these ages do not get the same results compared with the same competitors 6 years later. On the other hand our record holders in different swimming events are younger than the world record holders at the same distances.

That is why the main aim of this work is to study morphofunctional variations produced in the swimmers' bodies at these ages.

Subjects and methods

Two groups of 20 swimmers were each studied for 3 years, starting from the age of 12. In group A, the sample consisted of children who had trained intensively since they were seven years old, while group B was made up of youngsters who knew only how to swim. During the research both groups had the same conditions, they lived in the same school, had the same food and the same recreational and resting conditions, the only difference between them being the training methods employed, because, while group A continued intensifying its training loads, group B worked on the basis of technique, volume, play and development of motor qualities.

The subjects were submitted to physical examination and clinical laboratory tests before the investigation started, when the results were considered normal.

In the same way, during the 3 years, both groups were studied and at the end of each year of training their aerobic capacity indicators, anthopometrical data, anaerobic threshold and oxygen debt were analyzed, making a total of 18 variables.

Results

1   At the beginning of the investigation, group A had better aerobic capacity indicators than group B; however when they were 14 years old, the children in group B were better than group A although the difference was not statistically significant.

2   During the 3 years a better development of the important parameter in the children, namely maximal oxygen uptake, was verified in group B.

3   The most significant result was the progressive decrease of fat per cent in group B in relation with group A.

4   With regard to the anaerobic threshold one can appreciate a tendency in children from group B to increase the percentage of maximal oxygen uptake, while in those of group A the tendency was to decrease.

5   A displacement to the right of the anaerobic threshold in the children of group B was shown.

6   The increase of the oxygen debt in group A is due mainly to an increase of the lactaside fraction. This is more easily appreciated analyzing the parameter lactaside fraction divided by maximal oxygen uptake, while the tendency in group B was to decrease this parameter and to increase the alactaside fraction which means a greater explosivity. The results shown allow one to conclude that intensive training at these ages does not help an adequate aerobic capacity development, it being necessary to make use of glycolysis as a main energetic source.

19. The Effects of Altitude Training on Sea-level Swimming Performance

J.T. DANIELS, J.P. TROUP, T. TELANDER, K. MILLER and A.B. RICHARDSON

Abstract

TWELVE SWIMMERS, PREVIOUSLY selected for participation in the Olympic Festival, volunteered as subjects and were randomly divided into a Sea-level (S), Control Group and an Altitude (A) Group; there were six swimmers in each group. Each subject signed an informed consent prior to participating in a series of tests that were administered to all subjects at sea-level at the beginning of the study. Following these initial tests (resting blood samples, body weight, blood lactate profiles, economy S swimmers performed the same training at sea-level for the same period of time. Many of the tests were repeated weekly during the training period and all tests were repeated again, at sea-level, during the final 2 to 5 days prior to competing in the Olympic Festival. Performances at the Olympic Festival were also compared with each swimmer's previous lifetime bests as a test of actual performance changes that may be attributable to altitude training. Finally, each subject recorded his or her subjective evaluation of the total study.

Following training at altitude, the A swimmers improved their 400 m freestyle time and fastest 200 m time (stroke specialty) during lactate profile tests, increased VO_2 max and showed a significant improvement in their test workout set of 10×100 m with 30-sec rests. However, none of these changes was greater for the A swimmers than was the case for the Control S swimmers. On the other hand, the A swimmers experienced a greater positive shift in their lactate profile curve compared to the S group, and the A group improved in swimming economy, whereas the S group did not. Further, in sea-level performances (races) the A swimmers recorded more personal bests and had a more positive reaction to the study than did the S swimmers.

It was concluded that training at altitude, (1) enhances sea-level performance; (2) elicits greater adjustments in the blood-lactate response curve; (3) improves swimming economy and (4) can be more positive subjectively, compared to equal sea-level training experience. With the availability of adequate eating, housing and training facilities, it is recommended that a period of altitude training, of 3 to 4 weeks' duration, be used prior to sea-level competition. It is important that the intensity and amount of training not be increased during this altitude training period.

20. Stroke Related Differences in Economy as a Result of Long Course and Flume Swimming

L.J. D'ACQUISTO, J. TROUP and S. HOLMBERG

Introduction

DETERMINATIONS OF MAXIMUM OXYGEN uptake (VO_2max) have been made during tethered swimming (Bonen *et al.*, 1980; Kohrt *et al.*, 1987), free swimming (Montpetit *et al.*, 1983, 1987; Van Handel *et al.*, 1988) and flume swimming (Holmér, 1972; Holmér and Astrand, 1972; Holmér, 1974; Holmér *et al.*, 1974; Holmér and Haglund, 1978; Kipke, 1978; Gullstrand and Holmér, 1983). However, few studies have included comparisons of the aerobic demands (i.e. economy profile) for each of the above mentioned modes of swimming (Holmér and Astrand, 1972; Holmér, 1974). If research conducted in swimming flumes is to have direct training applications, the energy costs associated with flume swimming must be determined. Hence, the purpose of this study was to determine the associated energy costs of stroke swimming in a long course pool and in a swimming flume.

Methods

Twenty-six (9 male, 17 female), highly trained, collegiate swimmers in the final month of their competitive season participated in the study. Two sets of swimming experiments were conducted. The first set took place in an indoor 50 m pool. Each subject performed 3 × 400 m efforts. An 800-1,000 m warm-up was followed by a 5 min rest period and each of the 400 m swims was followed by a 10 min rest period. Velocity was held constant by the use of pace lights placed along the bottom of the pool.

The swimmer wore a specially designed collection device which contained a Daniels valve (1971). Expired air was collected into meteorological balloons during the final 100 m of each swim. Fractions of expired oxygen and carbon dioxide were determined using an

AMETEK Oxygen analyzer (S-3A/I) and a Carbon Dioxide sensor (P-61B). Volume was determined by evacuating the balloon contents into a balanced Rayfield spirometer (RAM-9200).

Five cycle stroke rates were measured three times during the final 100 m of each effort. Post-swim heart rates were determined by taking the carotid pulse for 10 sec. Finger stick blood samples were collected immediately post-swim and analyzed for lactic acid.

The second series of swims took place in a swimming flume. Three work bouts at velocities identical to those performed in the 50 m pool were repeated. All flume swims lasted 5 min or until failure. The same equipment used to determine free swimming oxygen uptake values was employed to determine the flume values.

Five cycle stroke rates were measured three times once steadystate conditions existed. Heart rates and blood lactates were determined as previously described.

Statistical analysis

Repeated measures analyses of variance for each dependent variable were computed by the MANOVA procedure of SPSS-X (version 3.0). The independent variables for each analysis were stroke, a between subjects factor (four levels), velocity, a within subjects factor (three levels) and mode, a within subjects factor (three levels). The dependent variables were oxygen uptake, heart rate, blood lactate and stroke rate. Means ± S.D. were computed for each of the dependent variables. In all analyses, the 0.05 level of significance was used.

Results

Calculations of per cent differences between the oxygen uptake values for long course and flume swimming reveal flume swimming to require a greater amount of oxygen at the same velocity. A 23.7% difference was measured for backstroke swimming, a 12.3% difference for breast stroke, 24% for butterfly and 19.7% for freestyle swimming.

Analysis of variance for repeated measures demonstrated significant differences between long course swimming and flume swimming for heart rate ($F(df = 1,22) = 72.5$, $p = 0.00$), blood lactate ($F(df = 1,22) = 5.12$, $p = 0.034$) and oxygen uptake ($F(df = 1,22) = 69.06$, $p = 0.00$), but not for stroke rate. No significant differences were measured for the effect of stroke by mode or for the effect of stroke by mode by speed.

Discussion

Holmér (1972) reported that VO_2max values achieved during flume swimming were almost identical with values obtained during long course swimming. However, submaximal values were not determined. Hence, differences between free and flume swimming were not apparent. In this study, subjects required more energy to perform at the same velocity in the flume than in the pool.

The results of this study indicate that measurements of swimming economy depend on the mode of swimming, since each procedure yielded different oxygen consumption, heart rate, and blood lactate results at the same velocity.

References

Bonen, A., Wilson, B.A., Yarkony, M. and Belcastro, A.N. (1980). Maximal oxygen uptake during free, tethered, and flume swimming. *Journal of Applied Physiology*, **48**, 232-235.

Daniels, J. (1971). Portable respiratory gas collection equipment. *Journal of Applied Physiology*, **31**, 164-167.

Gullstrand, L. and Holmér, I. (1983). Physiological characteristics of champion swimmers during a five-year follow-up period. *In* "Biomechanics and Medicine in Swimming". (Eds A.P. Hollander, P.A. Huijing and G. de Groot), pp. 258-262. Human Kinetics Publishers, Inc., Champaign, IL.

Holmér, I. (1972). Oxygen uptake during swimming in man. *Journal of Applied Physiology*, **33**. 502-509.

Holmér, I. (1974). Physiology of swimming man. *Acta Physiologica Scandinavica* (Supple 407). 1-55.

Holmér, I. and P. -O. Astrand. (1972). Swimming training and maximal oxygen uptake. *Journal of Applied Physiology*, **33**, 510-513.

Holmér, I. and S. Haglund. (1978). The swimming flume: experiences and applications. *In* "Swimming Medicine IV". (Eds B.A. Eriksson and B. Furberg), pp. 379-385. University Park Press, Baltimore, MD.

Holmér, I., Lundin, A., and B.O. Eriksson. (1974). Maximal oxygen uptake during swimming and running by elite swimmers. *Journal of Applied Physiology*, **36**, 711-714.

Kipke, L. (1978). Dynamics of oxygen intake during step-by-step loading in a swimming flume. *In* "Swimming Science IV". (Eds B. Eriksson and B. Furberg), pp. 137-142. University Park Press, Baltimore, MD.

Kohrt, W.M., Morgan, D.W., Bates, B. and Skinner, J.S. (1987). Physiological responses of triathletes to maximal swimming, cycling, and running. *Medicine and Science in Sports and Exercise*, **19**, 51-55.

Montpetit, R.M., Lavoie, J.-M. and Cazorla, G.A. (1983). Aerobic energy cost of swimming the front crawl at high velocity in international class and adolescent swimmers. *In* "Biomechanics and Medicine in Swimming". (Eds A.P. Hollander, P.A. Huijing and G. de Groot), pp. 228-234. Human Kinetics Publishers, Champaign, IL.

Montpetit, R., Divallet, A., Cazorla, G. and Smith, H. (1987). The relative stability of maximal aerobic power in elite swimmers and its relation to training performance. *Journal of Swimming Research.* **3**, 15-18.

Van Handel, P.J., Katz, A., Morrow, J.R., Troup, J.P., Daniels, J.T. and Bradley, P.W. (1988). Aerobic economy and competitive performance of US elite swimmers. *In* "Swimming Science V". (Eds B.E. Ungerechts, K. Wilke and K. Reischle), pp. 219-227. Human Kinetics Publishers, Champaign, IL.

21. Specific Physiological Adaptations of Top Level Swimmers

F. SARDELLA, M. FAINA, C. GALLOZZI, P. DI CAVE, G. GUIDI and A. DALMONTE

IT IS REPORTED THAT THE maximum values of functional efficiency in swimmers are achieved in running rather than swimming (Astrand and Rodhal, 1970; Dixon and Faulkner, 1971; Holmér and Astrand, 1971; McArdle *et al.*, 1972). To accomplish such comparisons, a constant-speed treadmill with increase of gradient was used for running or walking; for swimming various ergometers were used: threaded swimming with increase of barbell weights, stroke-speed-increase swimming or constant-speed swimming in an ergometric pool. Owing to the different conditions under which loads are increased, we believe that the methods used, at least as far as swimming is concerned, are not exactly comparable to those of the treadmill and, therefore, we believed it appropriate to check these results by having 10 national level swimmers undergo a comparable work on two ergometers which were simlar in terms of design as well as functioning: treadmill and ergonometric pool.

The anthropometric and personal data of the subjects are reported in Table 1.

TABLE 1. *Personal data (± SD).*

Age (Yr, mm)	Weight (kg)	Height (cm)
17	70.9	179
± 2	± 5.6	± 7.5

Methods

The ergometric pool consists of open water conduit measuring 6.7 × 3 m in which the fluid is set in motion by four propellers. The swimmer swims against the water flow being motionless in relation to the walls of the pool. Before the beginning of the experiment, the subjects were invited several times to swim in the ergometric pool, so they could familiarize themselves with it. In the incremental test in the pool, the speed of the water, which had been calibrated in advance, using a flow-meter, was increased by 0.1m/s every 3 min (2 min 30 sec work, 30 sec rest) starting from 1.3 m/s. The test, which was preceded by a 5 min warm-up, finished at the point of volitional exhaustion. Every 15 sec during the test the HR was recorded and samples of expired air were collected and analyzed for ventilation and VO_2 using an automatic system (EDV 80 Jager). At the end of each bout of work, the value of the trend of the above parameters was calculated and considered as an expression of the steady-state performance for that bout.

A mouthpiece with two channels was used to gather the air from subjects' mouths; the expiratory channel was linked to analysis apparatus and the other, inspiratory channel, was connected to the external environment by a snorkel system. The "dead" space between the subject's mouth and the double-channel valve, which was kept as small as possible, was reproduced again later in the treadmill test. At the end of the test in the pool (stop, 2 min, 4 min, and 6 min) a sample of capillary blood (15 µl) was taken from the ear-lobe to determine the blood lactate level, using the enzymatic-amperometric method (Lactate Analyzer 640 Roche). On the second day following the test in the pool, and at the same time of day, the same subjects were studied in a treadmill test (Laufergotest, Jager) identical to the pool test as far as the organization of the exercise bouts and the parameters measured were concerned. In this case again, the subjects had performed some running tests on the treadmill during the previous days, as a trial run. The incremental treadmill test consisted of an increase in speed of 2 km/h every 3 min (2 min 30 sec work, 30 sec rest) starting from 8 km/h, after 5 min warm-up at 6 km/h. For the analysis of the results, only the following maximal parameters, taken during the test, were considered: VO_2 max, HR max, BF max, Ve max and La max. The Student t statistical analysis was carried out on the homogeneous groups of data to determine the significance of the differences.

Results

All the subjects performed the tests without suffering any feeling of discomfort; this applies to both the running, a non-specific exercise, and the swimming in the ergometric pool. In the latter in particular the subjects said they had felt the same proprioceptive sensations as they noticed when swimming in non-moving water. The mean values, plus the SD, of the parameters taken for the group of the subjects for the ergometric pool test (0) and the treadmill test (R) are reported in Table 2. The degree of statistical probability (p) that the differences between the two groups are not casual is also indicated.

TABLE 2.

	VO_2 max (l/min)	HR max (b/min)	BF max (f/mol)	Ve max (l/min)	La max (mmol/l)
Treadmill (R) = runners	4.410 ± 0.317	197 ± 7	60 ± 6	132 ± 8	8.10 ± 0.9
Swimming pool (S) = swimmers	4.110 ± 0.187	170 ± 10	47 ± 5	108 ± 7	6.00 ± 1.00
p	> 0.3	< 0.02	< 0.005	< 0.02	> 0.04
% R-S R	− 7%	− 14%	− 21%	− 18%	− 26%

The maximal values of VO_2, HR, Ve and La recorded for the subjects were higher in the treadmill running test than in the swimming test. The details are as follows: VO_2 max (R) proved to be 4.410 l + 0.317, while the value for (S) was 4.110 + 0.287; HR max (R) was 197 + 7 b/min and the (S) value was 170 + 10 b/min; BF max (R) was 60 + 6 F/min and BF max (S) was 47 + 5 f/min; Ve max (R) was 132 + 8 l/min and the (S) value 108 + 7 l/min; and, finally, La max (R) proved to be 8.10 + 0.97 mmol/l while La max (S) was 6.00+ 1.00 mmol/l. The differences found in VO_2 max and La did not prove to be statistically significant, while the HR max and Ve differences were significant $(0.02 > p > 0.01)$ and the differences in BF max were highly significant $(p < 0.005)$.

Discussion

The finding that the capacity of a subject, even a swimmer, reaches high values of functional efficiency, is greater in running than in swimming, is a datum that has already been reported in the international literature (Dixon and Faulkner, 1971; Holmér and Åstrand, 1973; Holmér et al., 1974). Our data confirm this by showing how the differences in the HR, Ve and BF are particularly marked. In fact, only the variations in these three parameters proved to be statistically significant, while this was not the case for VO_2 max and La max.

It could be said, therefore, that while the functional data evaluated from the individual's capacity to utilize all his or her aerobic power and to activate the anaerobic lactate metabolism to the highest possible levels, are only partly limited in swimming with respect to running, the conditions of activation of the cardio-circulatory and respiratory apparatus are on the other hand significantly different. In our opinion, this is due to the fact, and in this we agree with other authors, that in swimming, as we know, the legs, which are much more powerful than the arms, are used almost exclusively as stabilizing elements (Åstrand and Rodhal, 1970; Dixon and Faulkner, 1971; Holmér and Åstrand, 1971; and Holmér et al., 1974). In this case, they evidently do not require the same oxygen intake as we find in running and this, bearing in mind also their considerable muscle mass, is an explanation of the lower aerobic power recorded for the swimmers in the pool with respect to the treadmill test.

We can in addition assume that in swimming, because of poor stability of the point of contact (the water) in the pushing phases, the athlete cannot exert all the mechanical (and therefore metabolic) power he is capable of producing, which is a further factor in reaching lower maximal VO_2 and La values. Another point, which is of greater interest and which is not yet completely clear, is the different performance of the respiratory and cardio-circulatory parameters in the two tests. The lower

HR could in fact be indicative of a reduction in cardiac output (CO) and if this were the case, the oxygen consumption, an increase in the a-v O_2 difference would be on record; on the other hand, however, it might be the expression of an increase in stroke volume (SV), if the cardiac output has not changed. Water has a bradycardiac power and, according to some authors (McCardle et al., 1971) the horizontal position assumed by the subject in swimming encourages the venous return to the heart. These two factors would support the hypothesis of a redistribution, in the context of the same CO, of the relationship between HR and SV, with a decrease in the former and an increase in the latter. In our opinion, the rhythmic action of the muscle masses of the arms would act in the same way; with their pumping effect, they would further encourage the increase in venous return to the heart in swimming compared to running. Further light will be shed on these hypotheses by the research we have already begun into fin swimming in which, as we all know, only the legs are used to effect progression through the water.

As far as the lower breathing frequency is concerned, it should be noted that this is also accompanied by a reduction in ventilation and the relationship between the two (tidal volume) is practically the same in running as in swimming. We can assume that ln swimming the reflex mechanism, which comes into action following the regulation of the respiration according to the frequency of the arm-stroke, also acts in conditions like those of the test, in which respiration is free.

Since the variation in VO_2 max (–7%) is much less marked than the variation in Ve max (–18%), it is logical to suppose that in swimming the lungs have a greater oxygen extraction capacity. This could in our opinion, be caused by a higher ventilation/perfusion relationship value. In fact, the horizontal position of the subject could encourage a greater homogeneity of the circulation and ventilation through the pulmonary environment, so that a larger proportion of blood, would be oxygenated. It seems clear that all the considerations we have put forward, while they certainly require further examination, are in indication of the need for swimmers, in view of the particular functional adaptations they come up against in the practice of their sport, to be evaluated with specific methods as in our ergometric-pool.

References

Ästrand, P.O. and Rodhal, R. (1970). "Text Book of Work Physiology". McGraw-Hill, New York.

Cerettei, L.I.P. (1985). "Manuale di Fisiologia dello Sporte del Lavoro Muscolare". SEU, Rome

Dalmonte, A. (1977). "Fisiologia e Medicina dello Sport". Sansoni Edi Nuova, Firenze.

Dalmonte, A. *et al.* (1983). "La Valutazio one Funzionale Dell ' Atleta". Sansoni Editore, Firenze.

Dixon, R.W. and Faulkner, J.A. (1971). Cardiac outputs during maximum effort running and swimming. *Journal of Applied Physiology,* **36**, 6.

Holmér, I. and Åstrand P.O. (1972). Swimming training and maximal oxygen uptake during swimming and running by elite swimmers. *Journal of Applied Physiology,* **33**, 4.

Holmér, I., Lundin, A. and Eriksson, B.O. (1974). Maximum oxygen uptake during swimming and running by elite swimmers. *Journal of Applied Physiology,* **36**, 6.

McArdle, E. W. D., Glasser, R. R. M. and Magel, J. R. (1971). Metabolic and Cardiorespiratory Response during free Swimming and Treadmill Walking. *Journal of Applied Physiology,* **30**, 5.

Part 4
Pool Design and Safety in the Water

22. The Layout, Design, Operation and Maintenance of Diving Equipment in Regard to User Safety

J.E. SANDERS

IT IS EXTREMELY IMPORTANT that, in order to provide for the safest possible use, diving facilities be designed with care so that the operation of this equipment can be effectively supervised. This requires the input of proper knowledge by designers experienced in this area who understand the functions and use patterns of diving equipment. If the correct design is complemented by the facilities being correctly maintained in good functional order and supervised during use then there is no reason for injuries to be caused by unsafe facilities.

The provision of correct and safe facilities requires the following steps to be undertaken.

Analysis of functional use

The purpose and mode of operation of the facility must be clearly stated before design is commenced.

(a) Is it to be primarily a competition centre or an elite training centre, or do both have equal importance?

(b) What level of competition is to be catered for?

(c) What level of training is to be catered for?

(d) What is the estimated number of divers and coaches who will use the facility?

(e) What are the proposed hours of operation?

(f) Are platform facilities to be provided in addition to springboards?

(g) Will the facility be available for recreational use by either the general public and/or unskilled members of the controlling body. If so, what will be the times of operation and methods of control and supervision?

The last section (g) is by far the most relevant aspect regarding safety; data show that almost all accidents in diving facilities occur amongst untrained and unskilled people who are using the equipment for recreation. Patterns of use vary greatly from area to area and in particular from country to country, and these can and should be taken into account when establishing the layout of the facilities.

Layout of equipment

The correct layout of the boards and platforms relative to each other plus the water depths and distances to the side and end walls of the pool are very important components in making a facility as safe as possible.

(a) The FINA handbook specifies, for each apparatus, the following minimum dimensions which will allow for fundamental safety of use:

i. Water depth under, to the rear and to the front, and to both sides of the board or platform;

ii. Distance of the front end of the board or platform from the rear wall, side wall and front wall of the pool or to an adjacent board or platform;

iii. Ceiling height above, to the rear and to the front, and to both sides of the board or platform;

iv. Distance from the front end of a platform back to the front end of a platform-below;

v. Slope of the base of the pool upwards from the point of maximum depth.

These dimensions are covered in detail by FINA Rule D7.3, which is for pools designed and constructed after January, 1987. The minimum dimensions in metres for diving facilities are detailed on the table on page 115 of the hand book; and the diagram on page 114 shall prevail, using, as a basic measuring point of reference, the plummet line, which is a vertical line extending through the centre point of the front edge of the platform.

As pertinent is table on page 115 of the 1988-1992 FINA handbook.

(b) The minimum dimensions of springboards and platforms are:

i. "D7.1.1 The boards shall be at least 4.8 m long and 0.5 m wide, and shall be approved by the Technical Diving Committee before the contest.

ii. "D7.2.2 The minimum dimensions of the platform are:

0.6 m to 1.0 m platform	0.6 m width 5.0 m length
2.6 m to 3.0 m platform	1.5 m width 5.0 m length
5.0 m platform	1.5 m width 6.0 m length
7.5 m platform	1.5 m width 6.0 m length
10.0 m platform	2.0 m width 6.0 m length"

(c) The minimum projections of platforms and distances between centres of adjacent platforms are specified in FINA Rules D7.2.5, D7.2.6 and D7.2.9, which are: "D7.2.5 The front of 10 m and 7.5 m platforms shall project at least 1. 5 m beyond the edge of the pool. For 2.6 m - 3 m and 5 m platforms a projection of 1.25 m is acceptable, and for 0.6 m- 1 m platforms a projection of 0.75 m is acceptable.

"D7.2.6 Where a platform is directly underneath another platform the platform above shall project 1.5 m beyond the platform below."

"D7.2.9 The dimensions C from plummet to adjacent plummet in the table on page 115 apply to platforms with widths as detailed in rule D7.2.2. If platform widths are increased then the dimensions C shall be increased by half the additional widths."

(d) Other FINA Rules which refer to the layout are: "D7.1.8 The springboards shall be placed on either one or both sides of the platform".

"D7.2.10 It is preferable that a platform should not be constructed directly under any other platform.

"D7.6 In outdoor pools, springboards and platforms are recommended to face north in the northern hemisphere and south in the southern hemisphere."

(e) When placing a number of springboards and platforms of different heights together in the one facility, there is an almost infinite number of combinations in which they can be related. A large number of solutions may be possible in which each individual apparatus is safe and in accordance with the previous regulations but in which the combinations can prove to be very unsafe.

It is in this area where experienced knowledge and assessment of the use patterns must be made and a safe layout of all the components made.

The longitudinal section and cross section diagrams on page 114 of the FINA Handbook show indicative arrangements as to how these individual dimensions can be combined.

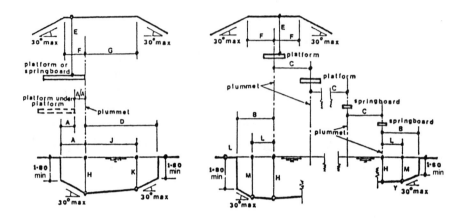

FIG. 1. Longitudinal section diagrammatic only; cross section diagrammatic only.

(f) The important fundamental rules to be kept in mind when laying out a diving facility are:

i. Locate the platforms in the centre of the pool with the springboards to the side (FINA Rule D7.1.8).

ii. Locate the highest apparatus in the centre and then the next highest, down to the lowest apparatus closest to the side walls. If a low board is placed between two high platforms, for example, the danger of collisions in the air or water is increased by several times.

iii. It is preferable that a platform not be constructed directly under another platform (FINA Rule D7.2.10). This ideal safety situation is difficult to obtain due to the additional cost involved in constructing the wider pool required to conform to this. It is generally recognized that the two training levels of (0.6 to 1.0 m) and (2.6 to 3.0 m) platforms can be placed under the 5 m and 7.5 m platforms respectively. Whether the 5 m platform is placed directly under the 10 m platform or not is related specifically to the method of operation and type of supervision, and this is where intelligent and knowledgeable assessment by the designer needs to be made.

Two examples illustrate this point. If the pool is being built in the USA for, say, a university where the only use is for training or competition, i.e. when it will always be supervised by a diving coach or official and used by experienced divers, it is quite safe to construct the 5 m platform under the 10 m. If the pool is being built in Australia for a local council where for long periods the facility will be used by the general public for recreation (often without any form of supervision) then it is very dangerous to construct the 5 m platform under the 10 m.

iv. The provision of continuous walk-out steps along the end wall behind the boards is a safety feature as it allows each diver to exit from his dive from under his own board without needing to cross the line of flight of someone coming off another board in order to reach a set of exit steps. Note that this situation applies to the coaching of competitive divers, where a diver enters the water vertically and generally emerges to the surface of the water close to the end of the board. The operating use of the general public in recreation is the opposite. These people normally enter the water at a short angle and scoop the entry to emerge at the surface a long distance out from the board. In this situation they must be encouraged to exit from the water by swimming forwards to steps at the far end or to steps at both sides close to the far end of the pool.

It is safer to place all the facilities along the one end of the pool. If facilities are placed along the side wall or along the far end wall then they must be only springboards and must be located so that there is no danger of an accident caused by a diver landing on a person emerging to the surface having dived off another board.

In the case of a 1m springboard at right angles, the centre of this should be located at a minimum distance of 13.0 m past the front end of a 3 m springboard or at a distance of 16.0 m past the front end of a 10 m platform.

In the case of a 3 m springboard at right angles, the centre of this should be located at a minimum distance of 14.0 m past the front end of a 3 m springboard or at a distance of 17.0 m past the front end of a 10 m platform.

In the case of diving equipment at opposite ends of a pool, the clear distance between the front ends of the highest piece of equipment at each end should be:

Between 1 m springboard and 1 m springboard	18.0 m
Between 1 m springboard and 3 m springboard	20.0 m
Between 1 m springboard and 10 m platform	24.0 m
Between 3 m springboard and 3 m springboard	22.0 m
Between 3 m springboard and 10 m platform	26.0 m

It should be noted that the supervision of safe operations is more difficult when facilities are located at right angles or at the opposite end of the pool.

Design of equipment

Once the various individual items have been incorporated into the general layout as previously described it is now the job of the designer to ensure that each piece of equipment is designed and installed in a correct and safe way and, where appropriate, in accordance with the manufacturer's instructions.

Listed below are details of the items which must be covered together with a reference to the relevant FINA rule (where there is one to cover the situation). This list is not comprehensive; there may be other factors not included due to a specific or different nature which can occur in a particular situation.

(a) The height of each item above the water level must be correct, with a tolerance of plus 0.05 m and minus zero (FINA rule D7.4)

(b) Depth of water over full water depth can vary by 2%. The minimum depth anywhere is to be 1.8 m (FINA rule D7.5).

(c) Lighting must be sufficient to allow the diver to safely view the water, which is a level of 500 lux at a level of 1m above the water (FINA rule D7.7.1).

(d) Sources of illumination are to be controlled to prevent glare, in order that a diver does not get blinded in the middle of a spin or a twist by a bright light (FINA rule D7.7.2).

(e) The surface of the water must be agitated continuously in order that a diver can visually locate the level of the surface of the water (FINA rule D7.8). This requirement should be given much higher importance than it normally is, as injuries can occur due to a diver not being able to judge the exact level of the water and consequently not be able correctly to prepare for entry. It is important that the surface agitation equipment be left on continuously while the centre is open, whether the diving pool is in use or not. Note that when injuries have occurred this equipment has been turned off.

(f) Springboards are to be provided with a satisfactory non-slip surface when wet (FINA rule D7.1.2)

(g) Springboards are to be installed dead level when the moveable fulcrum is centred (FINA rule D7.1.7).

(h) Springboards are to be erected with correct distances from anchor to fulcrum and the correct levels above the supporting structure (FINA rules D7.1.4 and D7.1.5).

i. 3 m high springboards should be provided with safety handrails as described in FINA rule 7.2.7. These handrails should extend at least to the edge of the pool.

j. Care must be taken to ensure that the anchor bolts of fulcrums and anchors to springboards are locked tight.

k. Platforms are to be rigid and constructed dead level. However, it is recommended that the top surface of platforms be provided with a slightly cambered surface in the longitudinal direction so that any surface water will run off from the centre of the platform to both sides. On no account must hollows occur in the top surface of platforms as this will allow water to lie.

l. The surface and the front edge of platforms are to be covered with a resilient surface which is non-slip when wet or dry (FINA rule D7.2.3).

m. The dimensions of the front edge of platforms are to be as described in FINA rule D7.2.3.

n. All platforms except 1 m levels are to be provided with safety handrails as detailed in FINA rule D7.2.7.

o. All diving facilities are to be accessible by suitable stairs (not ladders). See FINA rule D7.2.8. The stairs are to have non-slip treads and suitable handrails.

p. All pool decks are to be of a non-slip surface.

Maintenance of equipment

All the good work in providing a correct layout and design of facilities above can be undone over a period of time by poor maintenance which can lead to unsafe situations developing.

All aspects of all facilities should be given safety inspections and routine maintenance at appropriate intervals. The items which need to be checked include:

(a) That artificial lighting is maintaining its original brightness.

(b) That windows, etc., which allow in natural lighting do not get dirty and reduce the level of lighting.

(c) That the fixing and orientation of artificial lighting sources is not changed, especially during maintenance or changing of light bulbs.

(d) That surface agitation equipment is maintained in good order.

(e) That the internal pool surface does not deteriorate to a rough or dangerous situation.

(f) That the pool deck surface does not develop into a slippery situation or develop sharp-cornered areas which can cause injury.

(g) That the springboards maintain a non-slip surface.

(h) That the fulcrums and anchors of springboards are greased and maintained in accordance with the manufacturer's instructions, and that any replacement parts are installed when required.

(i) That the anchor bolts of springboard equipment are locked.

(j) That the surfaces of platforms maintain their non-slip finish and that they do not become worn, especially in the take-off area at the front of the platforms.

(k) That handrail supports do not become corroded at the base or anchors.

(l) That the treads on access stairs do not become slippery.

(m) If a springboard is reaching the end of its serviceable life and is becoming stiff or is developing surface cracks, it should be replaced.

(n) As previously described, the surface agitation equipment should be turned on continuously.

Supervision during use

It must be stressed that it is not possible to design a divin facility that is tolally safe from stupid or irresponsible use.

(a) A facility which has been correctly designed for safe use is unsafe resulting from the foolish action of just one individual who is dangerous to himself and/or others. Examples of this type of irresponsible action are:

i. Diving off the side of the springboard.

ii. Diving off the handrail of a platform to the side to see how close they can land to the side of the pool without actually hitting the concrete.

iii. Jumping off a platform to land on one of the springboards below in order to get a high spring.

iv. Bombing people who are in the water.

v. Diving off the back of the handrail on the 10 m platform into a swimming pool 5 m away which is 1 m deep.

vi. Swinging from the handrails of the access stairs.

(b) The incidents listed above are actual occurrences that have resulted in injuries and which have then been followed by the generalized claim that "diving facilities are dangerous".

(c) During diving training or warm-up prior to competition supervision will be by experienced diving coaches and officials, and problems would not be expected to occur.

(d) During use of the facility by the general public for recreation, supervision by the governing authority should be continuous and stringent. The supervisor must not only ensure that acts of stupidity like those previously described do not occur but that the swimming direction and movement as well as exit procedures are followed at all times.

23. Water Acceptability and its Problems

L. KIPKE

SWIMMING POOL WATER is the swimmer's daily environment – his/her equipment for training and competition. It is thus astonishing that this equipment had not been defined at all in international rules and regulations up till 1986. Even today little is known about swimming pool water, its quality, hygienic problems or processing – in order to avoid health risks when this equipment is used – by swimmers, trainers, coaches or by physicians taking care of the athletes.

There are, however, surprisingly scientific institutions in most countries dealing rather intensively with the problems of swimming water processing, and their findings are continuously being published in many scientific periodicals or specific journals. Unfortunately, the contact between these swimming pool experts and swimming sport is not as close in most countries as it should be. Despite Fabian's references to these problems during the 2nd Sport Medical Congress in Swimming in Dublin as early as in 1971, until 1986, no rules on water quality had been included in the FINA Rules and Regulations. Up to that date just the water temperature had been given and the requirement that it should be clear and without turbulence. Therefore, since 1982, the FINA MC has tackled the topic and in seminars staged in the GDR, the FRG, and specifically in Denmark in 1985. A proposal made by the FINA MC was accepted by the FINA Bureau and included into FINA's 1986-1988 and the 1988-1992 manuals.

We live in a smaller world. Modern means of transport applied no an increasing scale draw people from different parts of the world together by tourism and particularly by sport. They bring also germs which could not be classified as ubiquitous or pathogenic in any one place but could damage health in another. This fact is of particular importance in sport. A swimmer trains for many years to achieve a great athletic triumph and immediately prior to his goal, his health is reduced, possibly due to the transmission of a germ by water. It is, however, often difficult to prove that the water has been the source of the transmission.

Hygiene attempts to prevent diseases and to maintain and increase well-being and efficiency, and so, hygiene is also a kind of prophylaxis; and swimming pool hygiene should be regarded in the same way. It is frequently said "So far, nothing has happened." The answer can only be that unfortunately too much has happened and that there is no sense in putting a handrail to a bridge after somebody has fallen into the water.

During the last few years four seminars have been staged in the GDR. In the FRG, on the occasion of the INTERBAD International Exhibition, so-called status seminars in a bi-annual cycle, comprising the latest findings poor hygiene, have been held.

This short survey of the actual situation of swimming pool water processing – at first mainly from a European angle – results from additional literature analyses, consultations in leading institutes and with scientists like Brummel, Eichelsdorfer, Jessen, Theuss, Tiefenbrunner *et al.,* as from an almost 30 years experience as a physician who takes care of swimmers. The major part is related to problems arising in those swimming pools where competitions are staged. Hygienic aspects of swimming in natural water has not been taken into consideration.

Infective dangers in swimming pools

Infectious diseases transmitted by swimming pool water are occasioned by the presence of a virus or bacteria in it. Germs may either be present already in the water or get into it through an infective source, i.e. the swimmer or bather. There are numerous publications on this issue, and it seems to be generally accepted that the most important infectious source is with the bather and this has been experimentally corroborated.

Pool water is polluted or infected respectively, from the following parts of the bather's body:
(a)   the surface of his/her skin
(b)   the mucous membranes of mouth, nose, larynx, vagina

(c)   the anus

(d)   the urethra.

In most cases, the germs are apathogenic ones (Jentsch and Hafemeister, 1971). However, pathogenic germs are also emitted, and apathogenic germs may also become pathogenic in larger quantities.

Exner (1900) prepared a careful literature analysis surveying the germ transmission from man into bathing water and its significance to health.

Cerva's reports (1968 to 1972) are most informative on *naegleria fowleri* infections in the USSR between 1962 and 1969, when 17 people died from amoebic encephalitis. Up to 1974 some 100 cases had become known in Europe (Werner, 1975). It is, however, not certain, whether diseases of that kind have not been detected or not related to staying in water. The number of cases might therefore be higher. Diseases which have been considered to be STD diseases (sexually-transmitted diseases), like Trichomonas, have also been transmitted by swimming pool water.

In Exner's survey the sensibility of the best known germs against the most frequently used disinfectants in swimming pool water – chlorine vs bact. *escherichia coli* – has been shown. Gonococci, Treponema, Trichomonanes, and measle viruses have lower resistance. Equally resistant are Salmonella, Shigella, *Pseudomonas aeruginosa* and Adenoviruses, whilst Streptococci, Staphylococci, Enteroviruses (poly-coxsaeckie), ECHO-viruses, Para-influenza, Hepatitis viruses, water amoeba (Rhizopodes), and vermiculars show higher resistances. There is information from Jirovec and Kneiflowa-Jirocova (1970), Hermanne (1972), Kommel (1973), and Wanczuk (1971) that amoeba of the Limax group as well as Rhizopodes are vermiculars of the *Enterobius vermicularis* group and *Ascaris lumbricoides* do not react to chlorine in concentrations such as those used in swimming pools.

Microbic contamination of pool water by the bathing individual is affected by various factors like pre-purification of the individual, health status, age, season, number of people bathing or swimmers, participating in competitions or training activities, by his/her sex and other factors. In addition, to these there are pollutions from hair, skin furfur, saliva, rhinopharyngeal mucus, perspiration, excrement particles, urinary constituent, ointments, sun-oils, powder, soap rests, cosmetics, textile pieces, etc. According to Hasselbarth's findings (1965) about 500 to 1000 mg organic substances are delivered "by any one person" into the water during a stay of 20 min.

According to Hopf (1954) contaminations from organic substances are twice to three times higher by female than by male swimmers.

Organic and anorganic contaminations result from insufficient water turnover, inadequate processing and high load rates from visitors. These manifest in strong turbidity and also in problems of water disinfection and processing. A germ-rich superficial film will be formed which gives, by aggregation, some protection from the effects of disinfectants. Chlorine compounds will be produced irritating the mucous lining and reducing the efficiency of the water processing equipment.

The transmission of pathogenic agents by pool water

Pathogenic agents existing in pool water may infect a swimmer by various routes depending on his/her capacity to resist them:
(a)   the skin
(b)   mucous membranes, conjunctiva, rhinolaryngeal ways, vagina
(c)   oral or via the gastro-intestinal part.

The skin provides for a good protection; longer stays in water however abolish that protection because of softening, maceration and injuries – thus paving the way for infectious agents causing skin diseases, e.g. fungi, verrucae, viruses, Staphylococci, Streptococci, Tubercle bacilli, Pseudomonae and Leptospirae. According to our experience more than 50 per cent of the diseases fall to the mucous membranes, the rhinolaryngeal area, eyes or ears. One-fifth of the diseases concern only the gastro-intestinal part.

Hygienic measures to exclude health risks during swimming

Contamination from swimmers and bathing visitors into the pool water cause – with unprocessed water – strong concentrations of micro-organisms and organic and anorganic substances after quite short periods. As early as 1909 publications from a Berlin indoor pool said that the germ increase from 09.00 to 16.00 h – after having the water processed prior to opening the pool to the public – was from 1500 to 150000 germs/ml, i.e. a hundredfold. That is a great infectious risk. Interesting also are Jessen's figures (1986) that every bather deposits up to 3.0 million germs, 0.5 to 1.0 g dirt and 40 to 60 ml urine into the water. It was, therefore, a prospective aim to achieve a continuous quality of swimming pool water and to exclude infectious risks by applying technical means.

This way the history of swimming pool water processing in Germany can be traced back to the turn of the century, when in 1909 the cycling of water had been begun with filtration through rubble filters. First attempts at disinfection are known from the 1915, 1916 and 1929 (Wagenknecht) but in 1965 only Switzerland issued the first law on swimming pool water processing followed by other countries accepting guidelines, requirements, and laws. In basic studies Eichelsdorfer and Jandik (1985 to 1988) and Brummel (1988) at the last Status Seminar have recently referred to that issue. During the Interbad (1986) situation of swimming pool water processing in Europe was compared with that in other continents.

In accordance with actual findings the measures to prevent infectious dangers in swimming pool water can be divided as follows:

processing by flocculation and filtration;

suitable turn-over of the pool water;

and disinfection.

Processing by flocculation and filtration

To exclude even the smallest contaminations, which have been colloidally dissolved for their larger part or truly dissolved and which may also include bacteria or viruses, they are precipitated by additives like aluminium sulphate, Fe-Chlorine, or Fe-Sulphate, Na-alumnate, or activated silicic acid. Flocculation agents depend on the water's pH-value. The control of the flocculation process is here a great problem requiring wide experience from the technicians since so far no automatically controlled instruments are known. The flocculation will be followed by filtration, which has to be done through appropriate filters which have to be rinsed after pre-set periods.

Disinfection of swimming pool water

Practically all the oxydatory methods known for processing drinking water, can be used to disinfect swimming pool water, such as chlorine, chlor-dioxyd, bromine, iodine, ozone. Chlorine is, however, the most popular disinfectant for swimming pool water processing throughout the world even if there might be some exceptions.

Information on other disinfectants, like BIC, etc., may be important for private swimming pools; there is, however, neither the experience, nor the technology for applying them in large competitive pools, and it might also be too expensive.

A disinfectant is required to:
kill existing germs quickly;
have a high stability;
be easily verified;
cause no harmful side-effects for the bathing visitor.

Effective agents for the chlorification with various chlorine compounds HClO, the hypo-chloric acid and the ClO-ion. HClO has, however, the highest germ killing effect in non-dissociated conditions.

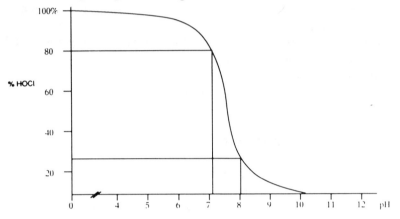

FIG. 1. Percentage of HClO in water against pH values.

Its reaction is pH-dependent having its highest effect at pH 5. Since pH 5 has a too high acid value for human beings, pH values of 7.0 are required for swimming pool waters, whereas 75 % HClO and 25 % of ClO-ions are available. At higher pH values the HClO contents are reduced, and the capacity to kill germs decreases. At a pH value of 9, HClO has been completely dissociated into H^+ and ClO^-. Disinfective capacities in water being dependant on chlorine concentrations, but not exclusively on them and affected by various water qualities, a chlorine concentration of 0.3 to 0.6 mg/l free chlorine is required at first. This chlorine concentration does not represent the disinfectant effect. The chlorine effect is reduced by other pollutants like organic and anorganic substances mainly ammonium compounds and resulting in a reduction of the chlorine effect, namely a chlorine consumption. We have to thank Carlson and Hesselbarth (1966 and 1968) for having made applicable the Theory of Redox-Potentials for the practical requirements in swimming pool water disinfection. They started from the fact that the survival of micro-organisims was only possible within a certain Redox-potential range which is limited by the relation between reducing and oxydizing substances. A slide of the Redox-potential into the oxydizible range results in dying micro-organisms. So the Redox-potential may be accepted as a criterion for the germ-killing effects of briefly present free or additionally of bound chlorine, considering the actual pollution. Redox-potentials should, therefore, be fixed at 6.5 to 7.5 at 700 mV within the pH range. (Fig. 2 shows the killing velocity against micro-organisms decreasing when the Redox-potential is reduced.)

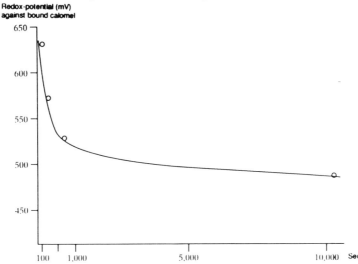

FIG. 2. Killing time for *E. coli* lengthens as the Redox-potential is reduced in the presence of pH7.

In some countries an ozone disinfection is inserted between flocculation and disinfection. Ozone causes a breakdown and, flocculation of organic and anorganic water contents and additionally a very effective sterilization because of its high oxydizing capacity.

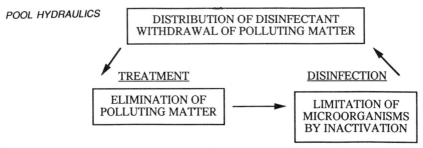

FIG. 3. Function diagram of pool hydraulics, treatment and disinfection within the circulation of swimming pool water.

Following ozonization, filtration by activated charcoal is necessary since the ozone content of swimming pool water should only be 0.01 mg/l. The water processing is then as follows:

(a) Flocculation – filtration (sand) – disinfection (Cl_2 NaOCl)

(b) with ozonisation: flocculation – filtration (sand) – oxydization (ozone) – filtration (activated charcoal – disinfection (Cl_2)

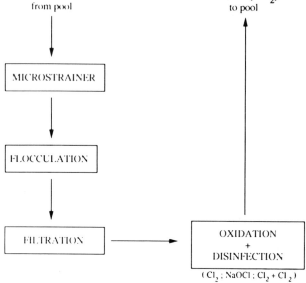

FIG. 4. Function diagram of pool water treatment according to the process combination: flocculation + filtration + chlorination.

In addition to the flocculation, filtration and disinfection measures, a reasonable flow of the pool water is of high relevance. To maintain acceptable water quality in all parts of the swimming pool, water must be sufficiently treated with disinfection agents and fresh water must be added, and all the swimming pool water must regularly be passed through the turn-over equipment to free it from micro-organisms and contaminations. Concerning these facts, a wealth of findings is available which should be taken into consideration when new facilities are to be constructed. Since hygienically correct swimming pool water depends to a far reaching extent on the pool flow, i.e. the pool hydraulics, the question has to be asked whether turn-over machinery should be switched-off during international competitions. Since Rule Sw 15,13 requires turbulence-free water this would otherwise not be the case. In accordance with leading experts the answer can be that the turn-over equipment should be working during the preparatory stages – warm-up swimming, but that it could be stopped during the contests which is normally no longer than two hours and contains about 100 swimmers without danger. In cases of longer duration contests the turn-over machines should be started from time to time.

From these findings the parameters have been defined as they are included in FINA Rule MC 1. The values for Free chlorine (0.3 to 0.6 mg/l) and Redox-potential (700 mV) are here the decisive ones.

Whenever they are maintained during continuous activities no health risks will occur. Recently it has been suggested that values for THM (Trihalomethane) should be considered; these should be nil, but up to 20 µg/l is acceptable.

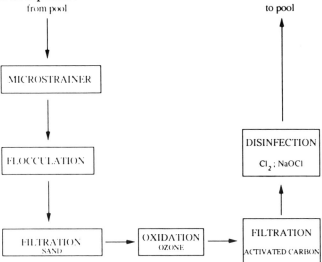

FIG. 5. Function diagram of pool water treatment according to the process combination: flocculation + filtration + ozonation + activated carbon filtration + chlorination ("ozone activated carbon process").

Bound chlorine values should be reduced from 0.4 mg/l to 0.2 mg/l. (Mr Kaas reports on this necessity in his paper, see p. 126).

In addition to these hygienic requirements for swimming pool water, which are equally valid for public pools in hotels, tourist facilities, and where institutions are following FINA rules and their stipulations, athletic requirements have to be considered that also are part of the definition for water.

One is the temperature, which has been empirically recommended to be 26 to 28°C, for water polo 24 to 26°C. Density is another important factor. Since density (which can be increased by higher salt contents) has an effect upon swimming velocities, this value is relevant when records have to be confirmed.

In some countries NaCl concentrations of 0.9 % are allowed for swimming pool water since that is an isotonic solution and better can be tolerated for health.

With the former rule "Records can only be recognize if achieved in freshwater" longer, a part FINA Rules and a definition where freshwater ends and salt water begins, the density value from Rule MC 1 is very important. It has been proposed to fix the density value at a 0.9% NaCl solution and a temperature of 26°C.

Maintaining the parameters in the FINA Rules during large international events (world championships, Olympic Games, European championships, etc.) is first and foremost a matter for the organizers. According to FINA Rules it is a responsiblity to present an expert or protocol on the pools' water conditions daily to the physician who is responsible for the event: a demand which has not been met so far.

Furthermore, representatives of the FINA MC should maintain continuous contacts with those scientists and technicians who work in the field of water processing. Time runs very quickly, and new findings should be expected continuously.

Auxiliary facilities, sauna pools, whirl pools, warm-up pools all are apart of swimming pool water processing; although they are not usually built into the water processing circuit. They require, however, special attention as specific problems which cannot be tackled more closely in this paper. Large amounts of money are often spent for the architectural outlay of a swimming pool.

A swimming pool with water in which one can swim without health risks, and a fully functioning water processing system and continuous control of the swimming pool water are nowadays a "must".

Swimming is generally considered as being one of those sports which is most suitable actively to prevent widespread common disorders, such as cardiovascular diseases, hypertonia, adipositas, postural weaknesses – to mention only a few, so the medium in which that prevention take places must also be free of health risks. Hygiene attempts to prevent diseases and to maintain and to improve wellbeing and fitness. So we are grateful to all the scientists, technicians, and personnel in swimming pools who contribute daily by their work so that swimming sports may be joined in all countries without dame to health from swimming pool water.

References

Brummel, F. (1987). Bewertungsgrundlagen für Verfahren der Schwimbeckerwasser auf. *BBR*, **38**, 105-106.

Brummel, F. (1988). Schwimmbeckenwasseraufbereitung Entwicklung – Status – Zukunft, *BBR*, **39**, 473-478.

Carlson, S., Hässelbarth, U. and Mecke, P. (1968). Die Erfassung der desinfizierenden Wirkung gechlorter Schwimmbadwasser durch Bestimmung des Redoxpotentials. *Arch. Hyg. u. Bakt*, **152**, 306-320.

Carlson, S., and Hässelbarth, U. (1968). Das Verhalten von Chlor und oxidierend wirkenden Chlorsubstitutionsverbindungen bei der Desinfektion von Wasser. *Vom Wasser*, **35**, 266-283.

Cerva, L. *et al.* (1968). An outbreak of acute, fatal amoebic meningoencephalities. *American Journal of Epidemiology.* **88**, 436-444.

Cerva, L. *et al.* (1969). Meningoencephalitis durch Amoebidae Naegleridae *Münchener Medizinischer Wochenschrift*, **41**, 2090-2094.

Cerva, L. (1972). Quantitative follow up study of the frequency of Limax group amoebas in the Podoli swimming pool. *Parazit. Odd. Hyg.Stan. Cs. Epid.* **21**, 203-210.

Eichelsdörfer, D. and Jandik, J. (1984). Erforschung und Entwicklung der Schwimmbad wasseraufbereitung III. Mitt.: Badewasseraufbereitung mit Ozon im Langzeitkontakt. *Zeitschrift fur Wasser und AbwasserForschrift.* **17**, 148-153.

Eichelsdörfer, D. and Jandik, J. (1988*a*). Der Einsatzz von Ozon bei der Schwimm-Badewasser-Aufbereitung in der BRD. *Offentliche Gesuncheitwesen Monatsschrift*, **50**, 363-366.

Eichelsdörfer, D. and Jandik, J (1988*b*). Application of ozone for treatment of swimming pool water in the Federal Republic of Germany - Review Paper - Ozone: *Sci.Eng.* **10**, 393-404.

Exner, M. Beiträge zum Stand der Kenntnisse der Risiken in öffentlichen Badeanstalten aus hygienischer. Sicht. Aus dem Hygiene-Institut der Universität Bonn.

Fossa, A. (1970). Benutzung des Schwimmbeckens. *Med. Trib*, **44**, 13.

Hässelbarth, U. (1965). Wasserhygiene in Schwimmbecken. Aufbereitung, Desinfektion und Uberwachung. *Bundesgesundheitsblatt*, **8**, 353-357.

Hässelbarth, U. (1984). Aufbereitung und Desinfektion von Schwimm-und Badebeckenwasser. *Archiv des Badewesens*, **37**, 253-256.

Hässelbarth, U. (1988). Die Desinfektion von Schwimmbeckenwasser und ihre Auswirkung. *Offentliche Gesuncheitwesen Monatsschrift*, **50**, 360-362.

Hermanne, J. *et al.* (1972). Meningo-encephalite amibienne primitive en Belgique. *Annales de Pediatrie.* **19**, 425-436.

Herschman, W. (1987). 75 Jahre Verfahrenstechnik der Schwimmbadwasseraufbereitung. *Gesundheits Ingenieur*, **108**, 17-22.

Hopf, W. (1954). Ideales Schwimmbeckenwasser, Theorie und Praxis. *Archiv des Badewesens*,, **7**, 21-41.

Höppner, A. (1986). Nachweis von *Pseudomonas aeruginosa* im Schwimmbeckenwasser. Offentliche *Gesuncheitwesen Monatsschrift,* **48,** 39-41.

Jentsch, F. and Hafemeister, G. (1971). Betrieb and Uberwachung Kunstlicher Schwimmbader. *Ges. Wes. Desinf,* **63,** 19-23.

Jessen, H.-J (1986). -J Erfahrungen bei der Badewasseraufbereitung nach TGL 37780 *Zeitschrift für gesamte Hygien,* 171-174.

Jessen, H.-J (1987). Gewahrleistung der Saunatauchbecken - Wasserbeschaffenheit in der DDR. *Archiv des Badewesen,* **40,** 549-551.

Jirovec, O., und Kneiflowa-Jirocova, J. (1970). La resistance des amibes du type limax quelques facteurs externe. *Journal of Parasitology,* **56,** 172-173.

Kommel, H.G. (1973). Uber das Vorkommen tierischer Organismen in Hallenbadern. *Archiv des Badewesen.* **26,** 226-229.

Metzner, P. (1982). Chlorisocyanurate zur Desinfektion von Schwimmbadwasser - Wirkungsweise, Kontrolle und technische Vorteile, *Archiv des Badewesen.* 373-376, 379-380.

Pieekarski, Saathoff, G.M. and Stier, D. (1973). *Trichomonas vaginatis* Infektionen durch Benutzung offentlicher Badeanstalten und Schwimmbader. *Immunität und Infektion,* **1,** 22-25.

Symmers. W. (1969). Primary amoebic meningoencephalities in Britain. *British Medical Journal,* **4,** 449-454.

Wagenknecht (1922). *Veroffentliehungen der Deutschen Gesellschaft für Volksbäder,* **7,** 16-27.

Wanczuk, I. (1971). The influence of chlorine and iodine on the viability in swimming pools of eggs of the human intestinal helminths. *Roczniki Panstnowego Zakladu Higieny,* **22,** 179-187.

Werner, H. (1975). Amöben-Meningo-Encephalitis. Schwimmbadhygiene. Stuttgart, S. 177 ff.

24. The Pool of the Future and Water Problems

P. KAAS

Development trends

THE USE OF AQUATIC FACILITIES

THE POOL OF THE FUTURE is quite an ambitious title for a paper within the space available. I will therefore concentrate on the main conclusions and venture into some detail only on the subject of certain pool water pollutants and on how to deal with them.

The present trend in Europe and in North America is to establish leisure pools which are not fit for swimming or other aquatic sports. Even existing facilities are reconstructed with added equipment which hamper the aquatic sports. In certain European countries existing swimming pools have even been closed in order for the municipalities not to spend more money on what is pejoratively referred to as "muscle-temples".

This is a matter of concern to the different national swimming associations. An effort must be made to influence this development so as to obtain multi-purpose facilities which can be used for play and leisure as well as for the various aquatic sports.

This can actually be achieved by relatively simple means. If only the main pool has the minimum dimensions required for competition sports, then the addition of movable partitions and the like in the pools can transform these to be fit for play and leisure as well.

It could even become a point of attraction for the visitors to the different subtropical and architecturally quite fancy water worlds of today if certain times were reserved for sport competitions or training like diving and synchro-swimming. Ideas and suggestions should be issued by FINA as the single national swimming associations often do not have the necessary specialist knowledge.

FINA-RULES

FINA has issued rules for pools to be used for different types of competitions. These rules are changed from time to time as the world changes or when new knowledge is acquired. It is however frustrating for owners of new swimming facilities to see that important parameters like pool depths or widths are changed a few years after the facility has been established.

Especially on the subject of pool dimensions, it is felt that a study should be made of the change of the size of individuals over the last 50 years. This serves to provide a forecast for pool dimensions which will be valid for at least a couple of decades. Then the resulting amendments should be made to the FINA rules at one time.

Water quality

The quality of the pool water is the most important concern of any user of a swimming pool.

The primary objective is that the water does not cause problems for the user. It must therefore be practically free from pathogenic micro-organisms and it must also be as free from harmful chemicals as possible.

A secondary, but still important concern is to assure standardized conditions for competitions so that the results obtained are comparable from one pool to another.

DISINFECTION OF POOL WATER

Kipke (see p.115) has mentioned some of the pathogenic micro-organisms which can be spread among users of swimming pools. It is therefore obvious that a proper disinfection of the water is required. This disinfection is achieved by the use of either gaseous chlorine or of sodium hypochlorite. In both cases hypochlorous acid which is the true germ-killing agent, is formed.

No chemical other than these two should be used. Firstly, hypochlorous acid has been proven to be the best disinfectant, and secondly the side-effects in terms of toxicity towards man of hypochlorous acid as well as of its reaction products are well known; and so are the means to deal with these problems.

The level of hypochlorous acid in the pool water should be as low as possible in order to reduce to the minimum the toxic effects while assuring a sufficient germ kill. The present FINA rules of min 0.3 and max 0.6 mg/l of free chlorine are quite appropriate for this purpose.

Calcium hypochlorite is frequently used as a pool disinfectant as well. And from the simple point of view of disinfecting properties it is as good as sodium hypochlorite or gaseous chlorine. Because of certain technical, corrosional and health hazard (for the pool attendants) problems it is however recommended not to use calcium hypochlorite.

With regular intervals other pool disinfectants are being proposed. Usually their germicidal effects are poorly documented and other side-effects to man are completely unknown.

It is therefore important to maintain the principle of a positive list of permitted disinfectants for swimming pools. At present this list contains:

sodium hypochlorite;
gaseous chlorine; and *perhaps*
calcium hypochlorite.

Other chemicals cannot be accepted on the list till their germicidal effects, their toxicity as well as the toxicity of their reaction products have been well documented for a period of time, say 10 years. It took some 70 years since chlorine was first used as disinfectant before the health problems with trihalomethanes were realized.

Since the germicidal effect of hypochlorous acid is strongly dependent on the pH value of the water, this parameter must be fixed as well. This is why the FINA rules stipulate a maximum of pH = 7.3.

NOXIOUS PROPERTIES OF POOL WATER

Too low pH-values on the other hand, cause skin irritation, and a lower limit of pH = 7.0 is therefore also set by the FINA rules.

When swimming pools are used, organic components are transferred from the bathers to the pool water. And even the fresh water used to refill the pool at some locations contains organic constituents.

When aqueous chlorine is used as a disinfectant it reacts with organic matter in the water. It is this reactivity which is responsible for the desired germicidal effect of aqueous chlorine. But it is at the same time also the reason why aqueous chlorine reacts with the organic impurities of the water to form a number of chlorinated constituents of which some are quite toxic or even carcinogenic to man. Additionally some are quite obnoxious as well causing foul odour and, for instance, eye irritation.

The most well known type of these constituents is the chloramines which are formed when aqueous chlorine reacts with nitrogen-containing constituents such as:

proteins;

urea;

ammonia.

It is the chloramines which are responsible for the well known pool odour as well as for the irritation of mucous membranes resulting for instance in red and irritated "rabbit" eyes of the swimmers.

For these reasons it is important to reduce the content of the chloramines and of other chlorinated organic components like haloforms to as low levels as technically and economically feasible.

In the existing FINA rules a limit of max 0.4 mg/l is set to the content of combined chlorine (chloramines). There is a proposal to reduce this figure to 0.2 mg/l and at the same time it is being proposed to set a limit of 20 g/l of trihalomethanes. These limits will truly assure a satisfactory water quality as to low concentrations of chlorinated constituents in the water. To comply with these limits may require a number of modern methods. First of all it is necessary to minimize the amount of organic constituents in the water by proper construction and operation of the swimming facilities. Secondly it is necessary to purify the water by one of two modern technologies.

This paper will give some more details on these methods. But before that there is one more parameter of importance for the well-being of the swimmers: the salt content.

Tests have shown that in a swimming pool with:

24 to 36°C, and

0.9 % sodium chloride (salt),

less than 0.1 to 0.05 mg/l of combined chlorine (chloramines),

it is possible for swimmers to train for competition swimming, diving and other activities without swimming goggles and without having reddened eyes or other irritations. The salt content of the water contributes to this result, and these parameters should therefore be complied with in the pool of the future.

Another positive effect of the 0.9 % salt in the water is a significantly reduced irritation of the mucous membranes in the nose and mouth. As a consequence less saliva and slime is excreted by the swimmers and a cleaner water is the result.

EQUAL COMPETITION CONDITIONS

The sodium chloride does however also have another effect on the water: the density is increased by 0.64%. This is enough to change the performance of the competition swimmer. Examples are known in which Danes – being used to this chloride level – could not swim as fast abroad as in their own country. Inversely, swimmers of other nationalities have come to Scandinavian saline pools in order to make new world records.

Also the temperature has an effect on the water density. It is therefore necessary to set a narrow temperature range as well an upper limit to the concentration of salt in the pool used for competitions. Otherwise it will not be possible to compare results obtained in two different pools.

The salt also has one negative effect. If the pool is not prepared for salt in the water, it may cause serious corrosion in the purification installations as well as in the concrete of the pool. It is therefore usually not possible to start using saline water in existing pool which has been designed for such service.

On the other hand neither is it possible to set a very low limit to the salt content in order to avoid corrosion problems. The use of chlorine as a disinfectant as well as of hydrochloric acid for pH-control leads to the accumulation of sodium chloride in the pool water, and actual levels are typically varying around 0.04 to 0.1%. So, clearly, some limit needs to be set to the water density and thereby to the content of sodium chloride (or other salts). It is proposed, that this limit be 0.1% in old installations and 0.9% in new installations.

Architectural impact on water quality

As already mentioned, the best water quality is obtained by a number of measures aiming at minimizing the contamination of the pool water with organic matter. Only after this effort has been made is it economically feasible to remove the rest of the contaminants down to the desired levels by water purification methods.

Since the measures to minimize the pollution of the water with organic matter involve construction requirements to the swimming facilities, it is very important that these requirements be spread among architects and engineers working with the design of new facilities. Some important aspects therefore follow here:

1 There must be a clear distinction between the shoe walking areas and the barefoot walking areas. For the same reason areas for visitors and bathers at the pool must be kept separate and visitors forbidden access to the barefoot areas.

2 Barefoot areas must be regularly disinfected by appropriate chemicals. These are however of such a nature that they must not be spilled into the pool water. For this reason the floor around the pool must be made to slope away from the pool with gullets along the walls so that the floor can be flushed with disinfectant and water in the direction away from the pool. Vacuum cleaning of the whole pool bottom must be carried out every morning and must be accomplished at least half an hour prior to allowing people into the pool. The pool sides must be brushed once a week.

3 There must be one shower with soap for each 10 bathers. It must be obligatory for all bathers to wash under the shower without clothes prior to using the pool.

4 There should be one toilet for each 20 bathers established in such a way that the bathers use a shower after the toilet and prior to re-entering the pool. Taking a shower without clothes may in certain cases constitute a cultural or religious problem. At international competitions there should therefore be established a few lockable shower cabins.

Numerous investigations have shown that proper washing by the bathers under showers prior to using the pool has a marked influence on the pollution of the pool water.

Unfortunately it has also been established that frequent users of pools such as like competition swimmers contribute the most to polluting the pool water. They do not wash prior to entering the pool nor after visits to the toilets, and they even often urinate in the pool water. "Instead" they take showers after the swim in order to remove the smell of chloramines to the formation of which – by their own malpractices – they have significantly contributed.

Both physicians, pool attendants and trainers therefore face a significant educational task as a contribution to achieving the water quality goals for the pool of the future.

Water purification methods

I will concentrate on how to remove the chloramines, which among other things give rise to irritations like "rabbit" eyes. Different methods do exist. But from a technical and economical point of view two methods only are really feasible, and they will be explained in some detail.

OZONE

Ozone followed by an activated carbon filter is in itself a technically good way to remove chloramines as well as organic matter from the water. Generated in an ozone generator, the resulting ozone is mixed with the water and allowed sufficient time to react with the pollutants in the water.

Ozone treatment is especially used at new swimming pools. Capital costs are quite high, as are the space requirements. This is why ozone treatment is seldom used for upgrading of water treatment equipment at existing swimming pools. Ozone is toxic to man, and the remaining ozone in the water after the ozone treatment step must therefore be removed in a carbon filter before the water can be recirculated to the pool.

One reason for the high capital costs is that it takes at least 15 min of retention time before the reactions between ozone and the organic matter have come sufficiently to an end. Some persons with technical insight even state that 20 to 30 min should be the minimum – anything below this figure they claim as being of symbolic efficiency only. A 50 m olympic pool would typically require an extra basin of some 150 m^3 in order to give a retention time of 20 min.

CHLOROMINATOR

The second and more recent method consists of treating the water with light at different wavelengths in a special sequence. Some of the wavelengths used are in the UV-range. This takes place in a so-called Chlorominator. The treatment destroys the different chlorinated pollutants in the water in the same time as it significantly reduces the quantity of organic matter.

In this way the effect of the Chlorominator is very much the same as that of the ozone treatment. At a saline concentration of 0.9 g/l, it provides a water quality such that one can swim in for hours without the use of swimming goggles.

Figures 1 and 2 show bacterial counts and chlorine/chloramine levels in a pool equipped with a Chlorominator. Figure 3 shows the water quality in a pool before the Chlorominator was installed, during its operation and after it was removed again. It can be seen that the level of chloramines responsible for the "rabbit" eyes was reduced from about 0.70 mg/l to about 0.10 mg/l.

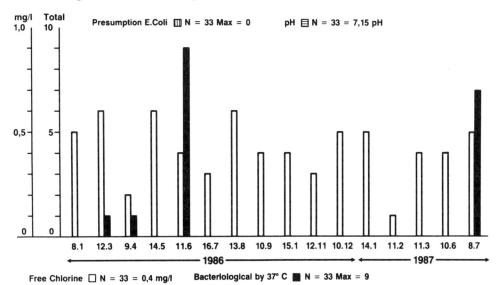

FIG 1. Bacterial counts in a pool with a chlorominator.

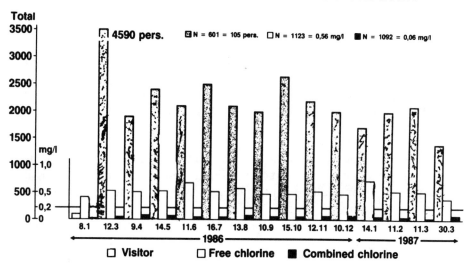

FIG 2. Chlorine/chloramine levels in a pool with chlorominator.

Combined Chlorine

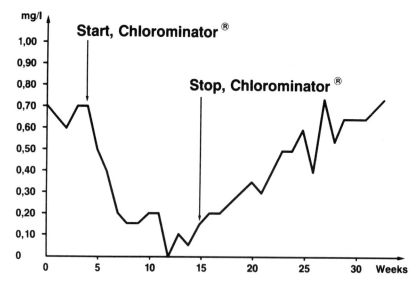

FIG. 3. Water quality before, with and after using a chlorominator.

An important difference however is that the chemical reactions are extremely fast. Therefore no extra basins are required for retention time for the recirculating water. Another difference is, that the Chlorominator comes in a modular form, so that it is possible to obtain exactly the water quality one wants to pay for. The Chlorominator requires very little space so that it is usually possible to add this equipment to existing facilities without building modifications.

The modular form of the Chlorominator also makes decentralized installations possible at individual pools, such as for instance in a larger sport complex. Both the Chlorominator and the ozone methods save important quantities and thereby costs of fresh make-up water to the pool which would otherwise be used to keep down the level of noxious constituents in the water. The cost of the chlorominator is so relatively low, that the savings in water consumption gives a typical pay-back time of a few years.

Some people confuse the water treatment in the Chlorominator with simple UV-radiation. Simple UV-radiation can only disinfect the water but does not remove the chlorinated pollutants like the chloramines. One Dutch company has started selling simple UV-radiation equipment claiming that it removes the chloramines. Some six installations so far have proven that this equipment cannot remove the chloramines.

The pool of the future

It is technically as well as economically feasible to achieve a satisfactory water quality in swimming pools. The parameters to be monitored daily are shown in Table 1 together with their limits.

All parameters but one can be achieved in existing pools – if necessary by retrofitting better purification equipment. Only the chloride level may constitute a problem to existing facilities not designed for saline service. But, as new facilities become designed for saline service, the goggles, the red eyes and the foul smell of chloramines will become a thing of the past.

The pool must be designed so that it takes a maximum of 5 min for the recirculated water to mix completely with the water in the pool. A colour test should be carried out once for all new facilities to verify compliance with this requirement.

The visual observation through an underwater window obviously requires that at least one such window is installed in each pool allowing observation in the longitudinal direction through the water. Apart from the above parameters, the levels of nitrate and aluminum should be monitored from time to time.

If the above limits to the physical and chemical parameters of Table

1 are monitored and fulfilled, then an occasional (say once per 3 months) verification of the bacteriological parameters below will suffice. This verification of the actual disinfection of the pool water should show:

TABLE 1. *Parameters for day-to-day monitoring.*

Free chlorine:	≥	0.3mg/l
Free chlorine:	≤	0.5mg/l
Combined chlorine:	≤	0.1mg/l
Trihalomethanes:	≤	20μg/l
pH:	≥	7.0
pH:	≤	7.3
Redox potential (Silver elect.):	≥	770mV
KMnO$_4$ (above value of fresh water):	≤	3mg/l*
KMnO$_4$ (absolute value):	≤	6mg/l*
Turbidity (after filter):	≤	0.1 FTU
Visibility of pool water:		Visible
Visibility through underwater windows:	≥	50 m
Temperature:		26 ± 1°C
Relative density from salts (mostly as NaCl):		1.0064
Air temperature minus pool temperature:	≥	3°C

* If there is > 0.9% salt in the water, then another analysis method must be used.

TABLE 2. *Bacteriological parameters for occasional checks.*

Bacterial counts at 21°C:	≤	10/ml
Bacterial counts at 37°C:	≤	10/ml
Presumptive *E.coli* at 37°C:		Untraceable in 100 ml
Pseudomonas aeruginosa at 37°C		Untraceable in 100 ml

The bacteriological counts should be made in accordance with the ISO standard, using the resuscitation method with tryptone agar at 37°C.

The bacteriological parameters should also be monitored prior to larger international competitions as well as in case of significant deviations from the above limits to physical and chemical parameters of the water.

Hot whirl pools are used more and more and are for instance often at the disposal of divers. Such hot whirl pools are specially problematic in terms of maintaining an appropriate water quality (Kipke, p.124 supra).

It is necessary to develop special rules for the water quality of such installations. As an example it can be mentioned that the bacteriological tests should encompass *legionella pulmonaris* in the water as well as in the air above such a pool.

Lighting

Another detail for the pool of the future is, that the lighting system should be designed so as to fulfill the four different lighting requirements for:
    swimming,
    diving,
    synchro-swimming, and
    water polo.

Technical committee under FINA

From the above discussion of the interrelations between water quality and the design and operation of the swimming pool facilities it is apparent that, although it is a relatively simple matter to verify whether a given installation complies with a given set of water quality parameters, it is much less simple to tell:

(a) what to do in case a given installation does not live up to the requirements;

(b) how to construct a new facility so that the FINA rules for water quality will be complied with.

(c) It is therefore proposed, that a hygienical/technical committee (or subcommittee under the Medical Committee) should be established under FINA with the purpose of:

(i) verifying that the water quality criteria of FINA are complied with at swimming pools where international competitions are to take place;

(ii) offering advice to such installation, where the rules are not complied with, of the cheapest way to comply with the requirements during the international competition;

(iii) offering advice on the plans for new international swimming facilities prior to the construction thereof in order to assure that hygienic and water quality requirements will be lived up to.

Many parameters relevant to water quality interfere with each other and the technical problems are diverse and numerous. This is why there is ample scope for a technical committee, which should deal with problems such as:

Filtration velocities,
Back washing procedures,
Flocculation methods and aids,
Materials of construction,
Proper dimensioning of water treatment equipment,
Safety precautions in chemicals storage and handling,
Water quality monitoring (hereunder check list and hand-held monitoring equipment),
Water toxicology,
Filtration systems,
Bacteriological proliferation,
Disinfection of surfaces (especially noxious fungi such as mycosis).

It is the multitude and the complexity of these problems which call for the insight of technical experts with a long technical experience to become members of the proposed technical committee. An important tool for such a technical committee could be some kind of transportable laboratory, possibly in a container for monitoring of water qualities prior to large international competitions. Another task could be to set pool dimensions such that they will be valid in the foreseeable future.

25. The Canadian Lifeguard Emergency Care Programme

S.B. BEERMAN

THE ROYAL LIFE SAVING SOCIETY Canada provides training courses for lifeguards. The RLSS is the sole provider of these courses and they are nationally standardized. The National Lifeguard Service (NLS) Award Course has now been offered for 25 years. The Aquatic Emergency Care (AEC) Course has been available for 12 years. A dual certification in NLS and AEC awards provides skilled lifesavers with an excellent preparation to undertake the professional role of lifeguard.

A National Lifeguard service course is available in all provinces in Canada. The current pre-requisites are, 16 years of age, and the holding of a Bronze Cross and Senior Resuscitation Award. There is a core control and optional component available, depending on the environment that the employment training may best suit. There are four course options available to candidates, swimming pool, waterfront beach, surf bench and waterpark.

In the waterfront option, candidates would learn principles of water rescue and advanced resuscitation including the principles of emergency management of near-drowning and spinal iniury. They would also learn the principles of group supervision and crowd control. Environmental conditions, as they influence the beach and patrons are all part of the content. Employers usually require this certification prior to employment.

The Aquatic Emergency Care Award is a "learn by doing" course to provide knowledge and techniques of emergency care which are useful in the aquatic environment. The emphasis in this course; is on assessment of vital signs, prioritizing patient problems and basic aquatic emergency care principles. There is no pre-requisite for this course; however, a successful completion of a Bronze Medallion is recommended. At the present time certification in Cardiopulmonary Resuscitation (CPR) is not available within any RLSSC award. Certification is provided only by an external agency. All lifeguards are encouraged, and usually required to have certification in basic CPR. In the near future the RLSSC will include CPR certification within the award program. Until that change takes place CPR is introduced at all levels of the RLSSC award program and emergency cardiac care is practised at the AEL and NLS award levels.

Much has been learned from many years of providing, teaching, examining and revising our professional training award program. These include:

1   A simple approach is always best. The introduction of a few simple principles for a few important problems is always superior to imparting large quantities of information that confuse the students and do not improve performance comfort.

2   In the management of near-drowning, airway concerns cannot be overstated. In review of resuscitation attempts a common source of frustration was airway management after submersion injury. The degree to which this challenges rescuers has been an unexpected frustration.

We must improve our teaching in this area to raise performance comfort.

3   Cold water is a frequent factor in many drownings. Understanding the principles of hypothermic protection in cold water near-drowning is important. Initiation of resuscitation efforts and prolonged resuscitation efforts are justifiable when hypothermia might otherwise prevail.

4   Spinal cord injury has an important economic and social morbidity that may result from diving into shallow water. In Canada approximately 60 aquatic spinal injuries per year cause a massive rearrangement of life goals and function for the individual involved. The initial medical management cost is approximately $10 million, and the subsequent annual support costs are approximately $2 million per year. Therefore the prevention of a small number of these injuries has a huge pay-off. Twenty-five per cent of all aquatic spinal iniuries have no spinal cord injury and 50 per cent of aquatic spinal injuries have only partial cord damage. Therefore correct management has a good outcome potential.

5   Most drownings and near-drownings do not occur in supervised areas. There is little point in teaching lifeguards to protect the bather in a designated swimming area if there is no carry-over to the "real" risk areas. It makes little sense to have such constraining rules on activity that high risk individuals and behaviours go elsewhere without supervision and assistance. All communications between lifeguard and bather should be friendly, encouraging and educational. We must try to be available for the "teachable moment".

References

The Canadian Life Saving Manual (1985). Royal Lifesaving Society Canada, Toronto, Ontaria, Canada.
The Near-Drowning. Drowning Symposium (1989). June 12 York University, Toronto, Canada Unpublished.

26. Safety in Aquatic Sports: What Are the Risks?

B.V. SIMS

BY WAY OF AN INTRODUCTION I shall identify three main areas that will be considered in this short paper.

It is important (1) to examine the current situation as it affects drowning statistics in recent years; (2) to identify the possible risks involved by those persons who take part in aquatic sport; (3) to establish some framework that might be considered to tackle the problem of drownings.

The current situation with regard to drowning figures for the British Isles, and although much of the material being shown will be for some few years ago it is qualified by current trends shown through media reporting over the past 6 or 7 years the patterns and situations remain constant.

If we take Drownings by Age and Sex we can see that of the 485 cases in 1983 the vast majority was male – some 382 in fact. To follow this we can see also that the age range for the most drownings was in the 15-24 group; closely followed by those of 30-40 years. (Fig.1.)

When we now look at the statistics for their swimming ability we find that of these previously identified Male Age ranges the majority of those who drowned could swim. What we do not know is how well they could swim and whether this skill could have prevented their death. This is one of the major issues to be undertaken (Fig.2).

It is also important to identify the type of water in which these drownings occur. It will be seen that this is within rivers and closely followed, as is traditionally thought, by drownings in the sea. It will be noted also that drownings in swimming pools reflect only a small percentage of the total.

We should also note the ratio of drownings by activity and, as has already been identified, a large proportion of drownings has occurred within the swimming activity, although it is important to note the other areas which are affected by possible sporting activity, such as those of boating and fishing (Fig.3).

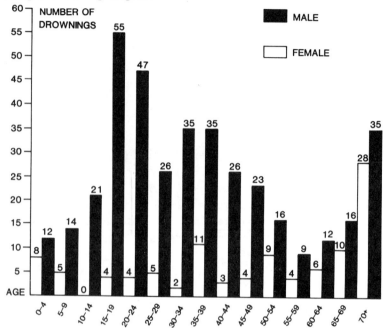

FIG. 1. Drownings by age and sex in the British Isles, 1983.

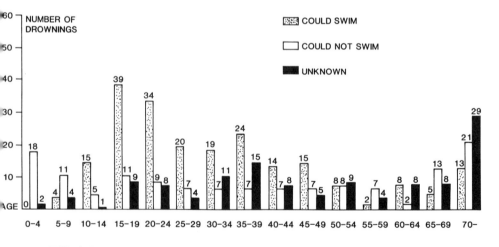

FIG. 2. Drownings by age and swimming ability in the British Isles, 1983.

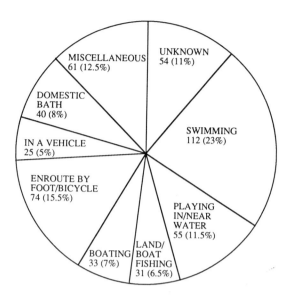

FIG. 3. Drowning by activity.

Finally, in considering the statistics, we should take note of the very sad fact that a large proportion of drownings has occurred within a very short distance from a point of security, and in some cases even within a hand reach distance. The need therefore for wider education in emergency rescue must be considered.

In addition we find some other factors that need to be mentioned, namely that more people drown in the afternoon. Although the summer can be seen as the most likely period for persons to drown, we are also drawn to the conclusion that of flooding, ice, snow and other similar occurrences will increase the winter toll of death by drowning.

When we start to examine the attempts by rescuers we find some important issues. The effect of cold water, the currents, and degrees of pollution all make a significant contribution to the difficulties. In addition to this we find the majority of rescuers is male and falls within the 20 to 30 age range. The water is over 3 m deep in most cases where drowning has occurred. For obvious reasons the majority of rescues is carried out by swimmers, of varying ability: only 8% of rescuers were qualified in lifesaving techniques. It is also interesting to note that in more than half the rescues no equipment was used and therefore physical contact was made between rescuer and casualty, thereby increasing the likelihood of a successful conclusion.

We find very few cases reported where resuscitation was applied in the water. Once casualties had been brought to land the majority of techniques used was Expired Air Resuscitation, and within this mouth to mouth was more widely accepted.

It is galling to imagine the consequences of failure in either the teaching of water safety or rescue. One needs only to look at the number of water hazards in this country, the number of people unable to help themselves, the number of people thrown inadvertently into danger and the number of rescues each year, to realize the importants of prevention and cure.

These statistics and reports in as far that the fact of being in, or near the water must have a recreational purpose.

What then are the responsibilities of those who govern sport? In the first instance it is important to identify the area of control. Traditionally those activities which occur under the direct control of governing bodies, for example programmed training, or competition, pose a limited risk – always provided qualified support is available. It is in the area of general participation, where an individual or group has taken up an aquatic activity, not directly controlled by the governing body, that more risk occurs. For example the leadership of a local youth group which wishes to take part in a boating activity is possibly qualified in general terms but may not be specifically competent in an aquatic emergency. This is not to say that there is any disregard for safety as set out by a particular governing body, but in practice, unless leadership is trained regularly in an understanding of water safety and emergency skills, the risk within the activity is increased.

When we look at the great number of participants engaging in aquatic sport singularly or in small groups – all under the "banner" of sport of recreation – unless those persons have received some safety training during the acquisition of skill and knowledge for their particular sport, the risk factor will remain an important factor.

Obviously it is up to the individual governing body of a sport to identify the potential risk involved in taking part in its activity, whether this be for a well ordered group at the highest level of training and competition, or for the individual, possibly occasional, participant. The hazards are the same, the risks can be reduced.

In attempting to manage the risk and thereby reduce the incidence of an aquatic emergency we need to be clear as to what that risk is. Knowing the hazards, the risks, and the preventative methods will go a long way toward a safe sporting environment. If we look at the swimming pool environment as it affects the casual swimmer, here we are usually assured of an organized, safe, and guarded situation. If that same swimmer seeks to undertake the same activity in open water the risks can increase significantly. This is also true for other swimming pool users with boats, and underwater activity. The key factor is to build in to the training required for the sport a total awareness of safety and emergency procedures. Of course all responsible sporting bodies already take this matter seriously, but do they review and control it successfully?

Change does occur in the aquatic environment. There is always the search for more danger within an activity, for more fun, for a greater involvement. This requires the governing bodies regularly to identify the aquatic environment, the equipment being used, the number of persons undertaking a sport in one given situation, and the ongoing need for awareness of hazards. So far as this control of risk affects the controlled swimming and related activity in the swimming pool environment the full weight of the law entrusts all managers and users alike to take note of the Health and Safety at Work Act 1974 and the subsequent Regulations and Codes of Practice for the Safe Supervision of Swimming Pools. It is important that governing bodies be very sure of their responsibilities and for the required actions to be taken.

The whole area of regulation and control does give rise to adverse comment on the reduction of the enjoyment factor in sport and recreation where it is recognized that participants usually require a challenge in some shape or form and indeed do not always identify a potential risk to themselves. Any control must measure the risk factor against frequency of occurrences, the consequences and the measures to be taken. The important factor is to reduce the minor incidents which unless controlled seem to graduate into major situations. In this respect the common sense approach to what is reasonably acceptable and safe will be a useful guide.

There is no doubt that regulation and enforcement will continue, based on reported incidents and dangerous occurrences, and may extend to a wider range of activity and environment. With this in mind governing bodies of sport and recreation will be advised to consult with specialists to arrive at the best result for their need.

This specialist advice may contain a range of suggestions to fulfill the requirements under legislation.

First the sporting body must identify this need to allow for safe participation in its sport, not only for groups but also for the individual and occasional user.

This may take the form of the production of a safety policy or statement, the provision for training toward awareness and emergency procedure, the safer way of enjoying the sport, the need to report even the most minor occurrence, and the establishment of a control system by the governing body.

The governing body will need to be sure of its organization, to identify and measure the risk for participants within a sensible and plausible constraint.

This organization can take place in two parts: organizational culture; aims and objectives.

In this respect the organization will need to adopt the most appropriate measures to fit the culture of their participants. Although swimming pool establishments are controlled under the Health and Safety at Work Act since 1974, nevertheless they were set on a panic course especially with regard to qualification of pool lifeguards and the numbers of participants using their facility. The lesson is to know just what is required under legislation, what is required for safe participation (even if no legislation exists) and to implement any recommendation conducive to the culture of the organization. Within the concept of aims and objectives, as has already been mentioned, the need for a written policy for safe participation and emergency procedure should be included in the broader terms for the organization. It may be that the pursuit of excellence, at whatever participant levels may produce an unacceptable level of risk. The organization should identify to its members its aims and objectives for participation and the incorporation of safe practices. It is also to accommodate, so far as is practicable any local, requirements and to estimate the likely cost involved in the application of safer practices. This is especially relevant as it affects the hiring and use of premises for aquatic sport, whether this be an indoor or outdoor environment.

Regrettably the introduction of legislation always seems to create an initial outlay of expenditure, and governing bodies of sport are under constant threat of higher operating costs to accommodate safer practices. In this respect it is even more important that a full understanding of legislation is applied not only by the national and regional controllers, but also by the local groups, and possibly the individual participant. This also applies to firm recommendation for safer activity required by the governing body, but not forming part of legislation by act of parliament.

By a reasonable understanding of the requirements, for the identification of local needs and the application of an "in-service" type of continual training in safer practices and emergency procedures, the organization can achieve a higher degree of competence.

Participants at all levels should be encouraged to have an understanding of what the governing body reflects. This means that the avenues of communication must be examined and any problems dealt with. This requires regular assessment with positive action undertaken to ensure that all members, and interested persons, are given the opportunity to understand what is considered safe practice.

The individual therefore has a responsibility to acquire a full knowledge of the sport, for its safe practices, and for an acquisition of skills based on that understanding.

It might be considered that some communication to the participant shall include the requirement to understand safe practice and the ongoing need for those involved at teaching/coaching levels to be equipped with the knowledge and skill to prevent emergency situations developing.

In conclusion the purpose of managing is to achieve results. In the field of risk, the results are probably intended to be a safer environment for those taking part in in aquatic sport. However, such broad objectives cannot be grasped as a basis for action and the question is always "What do we do next?". The end product is an action plan. Action plans present progress to a desired goal in a sequence of steps. The objectives must be clear and able to be understood by all participants so that progress toward a safer activity can be measured. Objectives must also be stimulating and avoid imposition. They must be realistic and attainable. Failure will benefit no one, but success in a safer sporting and recreational environment is essential.

27. The Development of a Pool Lifeguard Training Programme

A. J. HANDLEY

Two YEARS OR SO AGO, there were huge headlines in one of the national newspapers announcing: "Swimming - the most dangerous sport". As is so often the case, the quoted statistics were misleading. If everybody who takes any form of recreation in the water is considered a swimmer then this statement is correct but sports swimming has a very good record.

Swimming pools are safe places: only about 4.5% (22 cases) of UK annual drownings occur in pools. Even this is an overestimate as far as competitive swimming is concerned, since private pools are included in the figures.

The public assumes, correctly, that when it is invited to pay and participate in the facilities of a swimming pool, the proprietor has taken care to make it a safe environment. It is a reasonable assumption, since it is, in fact, the proprietor's duty, under the Health and Safety at Work Act of 1974 to ensure public safety. Many proprietors take this duty seriously and provide well-trained lifeguards. Unfortunately, the job of the lifeguard has, until recently, been very ill-defined and throughout the UK there have been a wide range of standards.

The Health and Safety at Work Act is typically British in that the general duty to ensure safety extends only "... so far as is reasonably practicable". This "reasonableness" lacks definition and cases have had to pass through the Courts for decisions to be made as to what constitutes negligence. In 1983 a working party, with wide representation including the ASA and RLSS, met to draw up guidelines to help those who were responsible for implementing and enforcing the Act. This led to the publication, jointly by the Health and Safety Executive and the Sports Council, in 1988 of: "Safety in Swimming Pools". This book contains five chapters covering, amongst other matters, safe pool design, maintenance, water treatment and pool equipment. The chapter with which we are most concerned is: "Supervision Arrangements to Safeguard Pool Users". Within this is specifically defined the role, training and work of pool lifeguards.

Until the publication of "Safety in Swimming Pools" there was no nationally recognized scheme for the training and certification of lifeguards, although there was in existence the RLSS Pool Bronze Medallion award. Following publication, the RLSS has embarked upon a National Pool Lifeguard Training Programme and I would now like to discuss the concepts which underlie this programme and which we believe will lead to a higher standard of training and professionalism for pool lifeguards.

It is important to understand what lifeguards are not. They are not administrators or collectors of tickets but are there to ensure the safety of pool users. Equally, however, they should not be regarded or behave as police, taking on a purely prohibitive or negative role. Instead, their function should be that of facilitators of safe recreation. The public goes to swimming pools for fun and enjoyment. The lifeguard should be there to help it realize this in a safe environment. Emphasis should be placed on guiding and educating pool users rather than inhibiting their enjoyment.

It is important not to forget that the prime duty of a lifeguard is to prevent accidents, but if one should occur he must have the skills necessary to effect a rescue and carry out resuscitation or first aid procedures. Before discussing the training requirements of lifeguards, it is important to understand the conceptual differences between lifesaving and lifeguarding. A lifesaver is a member of the public who is trained to deal with an aquatic emergency that chances to happen when he is in the vicinity. He puts his own safety first, before that even of the casualty. A lifeguard, however, owes his prime duty to the public whom he has volunteered or been employed to guard. He puts the safety of the casualty before his own.

With this in mind, a lifesaver is taught to consider methods of rescue in ascending order of personal danger. He considers first the possibility of reaching the casualty, then throwing a rope or floating object, then wading or rowing in a boat. Only if none of these methods of rescue is feasible does he resort to swimming, even then preferring to take with him some form of rescue aid. The lifeguard, on the other hand, is much more ready to enter the water quickly to ensure that the casualty's head is lifted above the surface. He is able to do this with confidence because he is part of a team that will quickly back him up with the necessary skills and equipment. The pool lifeguard is also taught the importance of pool safety procedures and awareness of the early signs that indicate that a swimmer is getting into difficulty.

An aspect of pool lifeguarding that is being developed by the RLSS is the management of spinal injuries. We are all aware of the vulnerability of the human spinal cord when there is any damage to the protective spine. The commonest mechanism of injury is severe flexion of the head following a dive into shallow water. The incidence of spinal cord injuries in swimming pools decreased in the 1960s when many diving boards were removed from inappropriately shallow pools. This was achieved largely because of the FINA regulations which specified maximum diving board heights related to pool depth and lateral clearances.

Unfortunately a new cause of spinal cord injury has appeared with the explosive increase in the number of leisure pools and their attendant flumes. These water slides are quite safe when entry at the top is controlled and where there is a deep splashdown pool. The danger comes when a second user follows too closely after the first. The resulting injury is often to the lower thoracic or lumbar region rather than the neck.

Careful handling of casualties with definite or suspected spinal cord injury is of immense importance. It is a team procedure and a series of manoeuvres to right the injured swimmer in the water, without disturbing the lateral and antero-posterior relationship of the head to the neck, have been developed. This is followed by "trawling" the casualty to shallow water where specialist teams are able to land him safely.

The objective of the new Royal Life Saving Society National Pool Lifeguard Training Programme is to provide a safe environment for the enjoyment of aquatic recreation. Life is inherently dangerous and some sense of danger is exhilarating. However, the risks must be controlled and reduced to low and acceptable levels.

28. The Possibility of Transmission of Infection (including AIDs) to the Rescuer during Resuscitation Procedures

M. F. CUTHBERT

ALTHOUGH IT IS THEORETICALLY possible for a number of infections to be transmitted to the rescuer during expired air resuscitation (EAR), for practical purposes we need consider only infectious hepatitis and the Acquired Immune Deficiency Syndrome (AIDS).

Hepatitis B is an inflammation of the liver which may have several causes, one of which is the Hepatitis B Virus (HBV). The virus is spread by direct contact with infected body fluids through broken skin or mucous membranes. The incidence of Hepatitis B in England and Wales is low (about 1000 cases a year in the population as a whole). There is, however, a relatively high incidence of the disease in drug addicts, male and female prostitutes and homosexuals. The risks of contracting Hepatitis B are greatest amongst those who are likely to come into contact with the body fluids of persons in those groups. HBV is much more infectious than the virus of AIDS (HIV) and unlike HIV, has been found in virtually all body secretions and excretions in infective quantities.

The risk of HBV transmission during mouth-to-mouth and mouth-to-nose resuscitation is regarded as negligible and EAR should not be withheld. Where blood is present (e.g. after an accident) the risk of infection is higher. The procedure to be followed when spillages of blood occur is considered later.

AIDs is a serious and newly recognized disease which is not yet fully understood.

In the USA and the UK, the occurrence of AIDS has been predominantly confined to male homosexuals, intravenous drug abusers and haemophiliacs. In this respect, the disease is transmitted through intimate sexual contact or through contaminated blood or blood products. There is no evidence that the disease has been acquired through casual contact with an AIDS carrier or victim.

While the AIDS virus has been isolated from saliva, there is no evidence that the disease can be transmitted by this route. No case of AIDS has been shown in the UK or abroad to have been transmitted by mouth-to-mouth or mouth-to-nose resuscitation. EAR does not therefore appear to carry any risk of transmitting the disease.

Since both AIDS and HBV are transmitted by blood-to-blood contact, lifeguards and lifesavers should avoid such contact during rescue and resuscitation procedures, particularly if they have any breaks in the skin (e.g. cuts and grazes). For this reason the Health and Safety Executive have issued advice as follows: "Any exposed cuts and abrasions should be covered with a waterproof dressing before treating a casualty whether or not any infection is suspected. Whenever blood or other body fluids have to be mopped up, it is strongly recommended that disposable plastic gloves and an apron be worn and paper towels used; these items should then be placed in plastic bags and safely disposed of preferably by burning."

The AIDS and HBV viruses are killed by household bleach and the area where any spills have occurred should be disinfected by using one part of bleach diluted with ten parts of water; caution should be exercised since bleach is corrosive and can be harmful to the skin. If direct contact with another person's blood or body fluids occurs, the area should be washed as soon as possible with ordinary soap and water. Clean cold tap water should be used if the lips, mouth, tongue, eyes or broken skin are affected and medical advice sought.

When blood is present the risks are marginally higher. In order to avoid direct contact between the rescuer and the casualty, some authorities have advocated the use of resuscitation airways or masks. It must be remembered that special skills are needed to use these devices safely and effectively; in any case, they do not guarantee protection from the interchange of secretions.

In conclusion, the risk of the transmission of HBV and AIDS during EAR is negligible. There is no doubt EAR is the most effective and easy-to-learn form of artificial ventilation. The technique has been responsible for saving countless lives in the past and it is essential that it remains the fundamental part of the standard first aid treatment given to non-breathing casualties.

Part 5
Diving Injuries and Physiological Constraints

29. Diving Injuries: the Diver's Input

F. DUFFICY, A. CHILDS and C. SNODE

Introduction

THIS PAPER DISCUSSES DIVING injuries in a descriptive and non-medical sense, as would a diver describing the activities he/she performs in everyday training, and the injuries sustained. This description is not intended to provide an exhaustive list, nor to suggest any medical or any other technical analysis of what is taking place during the various diving activities, or as and when injuries are sustained.

Training takes place in the pool and the gymnasium, mostly in the pool and consists of a variety of dives, including those which make up a competitor's list.

Diving competitions are divided, broadly speaking, as follows:
Highboard – a firm platform: 5 m or 7.5 m or 10 m above the water;
Springboard – a metal alloy construction 1 m or 3 m above the water.

In competitions, typical dives and boards are:
Women:
   Platform: 5 m, 7.5 m or 10 m – eight dives (including armstand group);
   Springboard: 1 m or 3 m – ten dives;
Men:
   Platform: 5 m, 7.5 m or 10 m – ten dives (including armstand group);
   Springboard: 1 m or 3 m – eleven dives

Divers often compete in both highboard and springboard at the same competition.

Divers will usually dive from the board in any of these four directions: Forward; Backward; Reverseward; Inward.

In each of the above directions, divers perform a range of somersaults, twists or a combination of both. In highboard diving, divers also perform a range of somersaulting movements from handstand or armstand takeoffs. Very broadly speaking, the aim of the diver is to perform the dive with the correct technical execution and as gracefully as possible, to enter the water as near vertical as possible, and with as little splash as possible. For the purposes of this discussion, the physical activity for performing dives can be divided into the following categories: Takeoff; Flight; Entry into water.

The general requirements of the diver are: Flexibility, Strength, Orientation, Confidence (in coach and self), Competitive instinct.

In the gymnasium

Gymnastics: This is often used by divers and coaches in the development of strength, flexibility, agility and orientation.

Weight training: This is used by many coaches. Some use an "off season" period of intense weight training followed by a less intense programme during the competitive season.

Dance/ballet: This is being used more commonly to increase strength of the lower body, aid flexibility and stretch, improve posture and general deportment and develop co-ordination.

Trampoline: The diver performs complete diving movements in a safety harness suspended over a trampoline. This aids work intensity because trampoline training is dry and therefore it permits greater repetition of movements. The trampoline also helps orientation and general fitness.

Portapit: The trainee dives onto a large sponge bed or into a pit filled with foam rubber slices. It may be equipped with a safety harness suspended over the pit or bed.

Cardiovascular Training: This consists of running and skipping and aids general fitness.

Mental Rehearsal: Used more frequently to assist concentration on the movement to be performed and concentration on the competition.

In the pool

Practice in the pool is usually preceded by a general physical warm-up. The diving practice consists of repeated dives from one or more diving boards and allows practice of the takeoff.

The entry path into the water can be one of the three following types: Straight to the bottom, Somersault roll, or Scoop.

Common injuries

HEAD AND NECK

Head striking the board
This happens when a diver has not moved his centre of gravity far enough away from the board. This is likely to occur when a diver is performing a dive of a complexity that may be at the threshold of or just beyond his ability. Another reason may be an imbalanced takeoff or buckling of the legs which can occur in springboard takeoffs.

Head hitting pool bottom
This is more common with accidents happening to lay persons enjoying recreational diving. It is usually attributable to the depth of water being too shallow at the point of entry.

The more the body is lined up from hands to toes in a straight line and the greater the stretch in the body at the point of and through the entry, the faster the body will move through the water. Normally, a competitive diver will be aware of the depth of water but occasionally the water may be shallower than recommended and a difference of 18 inches can be dangerous if the diver has not noticed it.

Black eyes
A diver hitting the water face-first is quite likely to emerge with a pair of black eyes. This can also occur if a diver enters the water in the tucked position because the knees may be pushed into the face and eyes.

Ears
A burst eardrum can occur if a diver lands awkwardly on one ear on the water.

Sinus problems

These afflict some divers. They may be exacerbated by continual diving into deep water and seem to be associated with pressure: the deeper the diver's entry the more sinus difficulties seem to occur. Divers who suffer from these have used nose clips in the past, but such use seems to be less common today.

Neck

A very common problem is neck strain ("ricked neck"). This usually occurs on entry into the water especially from the 10 m platform. It may result from the diver "landing" awkwardly or not being strong enough to maintain the correct position on entry.

UPPER LIMBS

Shoulder dislocation

Usually anterior dislocation occurs on entry into the water where the diver is not strong enough to maintain the arms in the entry position.

Divers tend to be very mobile around the shoulder region and unless strong enough, the force of hitting the water on entry can cause problems in this area.

Elbow: hyperextension/dislocation

Hyperextension injuries to the elbow can arise on entry especially in younger divers who are diving from the 10 m platform, who may not have the strength to withstand the force entry into the water.

It has also been known for triceps to rupture. This can arise if the diver does not achieve full extension at the elbow before entry and has to rely on strength in the triceps to help withstand the impact of entry.

Wrist/hand injuries

An illustration of the handgrip of the diver on entry shows that the hands are fully extended with one hand gripping over the back of the other. The force of impact is taken on or about the palms of the hand.

Joint Capsule Injuries can be sustained from entries and also seem to arise from constantly climbing out onto the poolside.

Scaphoid problems arise from constant impact on entries.

Severe bruising can occur to the back of the hand when the diver's arms are not locked or strong enough to withstand the impact on entry: the arms give and the hand strikes the diver's forehead.

Tenosynovitis of the wrist/finger extension

This injury is fairly common due to the grip and overuse. It also arises if there is continual striking of the hand against the head at the point of entry. Thumbs are prone to injury due to the handgrip: hyperextension of the thumb seems to be a problem and capsule strains seem to arise at the first CMC joint. Fractures of fingers are also common. They can arise easily if the diver is too close to the board and his hand strikes the board during the dive.

SPINE

Overextension

This occurs in the air during a dive or on entry into the water – what is known as a scoop entry. If there is frequent repetition of the scoop entry the back may be overextended and become strained, usually in the region of the lower back. In extreme cases, it seems to aggravate spondylolysis and spondylolysthesis. Extension injuries may also occur to the back when the diver is working on the trampoline. Such injuries may occur when the diver is practising in a spotting rig. Lower back injuries can also occur if the diver is not supple enough to achieve efficient compact positions, particularly in the pike position.

Thoracic injuries

These may be more of a problem when there is a slight muscle imbalance. They may lead to problems with the upper thoracic area and pain from nerve root involvement.

Sacro iliac

Problems here tend to be common.

THORACIC/ABDOMINAL

Viscera

Injury to this area can arise when the diver misjudges the point of entry and lands horizontally on the water, such that he/she strikes the water on flat outstretched legs and back, stomach and chest. It is commonly known as landing "flat". Risk is greater when the diver is performing from the 10 m platforms and it can lead to haemoptysis. Usually it does not lead to any further problems that the diver becomes aware of but it can cause extreme distress at the time.

Abdominal
These strains may occur in the gymnasium when performing, e.g. sit-ups or in the pool. Tears may occur in overextension accidents.

LOWER LIMBS

Knee
Osgood Schlatters seems to be a risk in young divers. Shin splints tend to be common to divers of all ages.

Achilles tendon
The diver is constantly standing up on his toes and jumping off his toes. Overuse may lead to tendonitis.

Feet
Fractures may occur where the feet hit the end of the diving board during the flight of the dive.

_____

30. Taping for the Prevention and Treatment of Diving Injuries

R. MACDONALD

_____

IN THE SPORTS INJURY CENTRE at Crystal Palace National Sports Centre we have treated a variety of injuries arising from 108 different sports. The Diving Institute is situated on the floor above our clinic and over the years we have developed expertise in the treatment of diving injuries and a close liaison with the coaches.

The diver suffers many injuries to various parts of the body during his career and not all injuries occur during the performance of the sport itself. As in all other sports injuries may occur at any time during everyday activities and these injuries affect the diver's performance.

Cause of diving injuries

BACK AND NECK

Improper execution or improper entry, accompanied by shoulder sprains and strains.

HEAD INJURIES

Hitting the board or platform.

LIMBS

(a)   Sprained ankles: foot-first entry from 10m platform. Loss of balance on either forward or backward take-off from the springboard.

(b)   Shin splints: constant use of poorly mounted non-flexible springboards or gymnastic training on a poorly sprung floor.

(c)   Quadriceps tendon strains: from effort to gain height on "take off" and often accompanied by: cysts in tendons; Osgood Schlatters disease; thickening of the tendon, Patella Femoral Syndrome.

Contributing factors to the condition: Genu recurvatum; weak vastus medialis muscle; mal tracking; CMP in its true sense (occasionally).

(d)   Tendonitis and tenosynovitis of the forearm: the forearm flexors are prone to hyperextension injuries from failure to adopt the correct entry position into the water (the clasped hands and extended arms protect the diver by making a well in the water for the remainder of the body to pass through). The flexor tendons may also be stressed during handstands, push off, and the diver levering himself out of the water.

Prevention of injury

The diver must develop strength, power and flexibility in order to execute the gymnastic type moves in space under perfect control. The high board event demands jumping power and agility to achieve height off the board. Flexibility is essential in the shoulders, hips and back for the aerial acrobatic movements. Training and perfecting the stunts on a trampoline with a safety harness avoids the stress of repeated impact on water. The bubble machine also lowers the entry impact.

Taping and strapping techniques are widely used in the prevention and rehabilitation of sports injuries by physiotherapists, doctors and podiatrists. Tape provides support and protection for soft tissues and joints with minimal limitation of function. Therefore, it is important to understand the anatomy and kinesiology of the parts involved, and have an accurate assessment of the injury.

Treatment

Some of these injuries may be taped during the treatment and rehabilitation programme and for return for activity – some more successful than others.

WHY AND WHEN TO TAPE

For protection, support and treatment during rehabilitation and for injury prevention on return to activity. Stretch tape is used to compress and support soft tissues:
    1   to apply anchors for muscle;
    2   to hold protective pads in place;
    3   *but* it will not give mechanical support.

Non-stretch tape is used:
    1   to support inert structures e.g. ligaments and joint capsules;
    2   to limit joint movement;
    3   to protect against re-injury.

Sprains

The ankle is the joint most often taped *because of the degree and extent of disability after injury*. Ankle taping varies for different sports. It is important to be aware of the type of activity for which one is taping and know which structures must be protected, restricted and supported. Most sports have dorsiflexion action as in team sports, such as football and basketball. However, many are *plantarflexion* sports such as diving, gymnastics and some forms of dance.

Metacarpals or *phalanges* and *wrists* may be *supported* by adhesive tape procedures, which can act as *effective splints* which is important where unyielding substances applied to the part are illegal.

Strains

The *stresses associated with training* cause marked tissue overuse which results in soft tissue damage, for instance tendonitis.

Tape around the *shin* can reduce stresses on the tendons of tibialis anterior and posterior, e.g. shin splints.

A firm wrap will reduce the pull at the attachment of a muscle or tendon to bone thereby reducing pain.

WHEN NOT TO TAPE

(a) As a *first aid measure,* before assessment. Tape must be applied with a specific purpose in mind. Therefore one must know what structures are damaged so that they may be supported and protected from further abuse.

(b) If not familiar with the *taping techniques* for the specific injury, when in doubt – *don't* – as further damage may be caused, thus delaying the recovery.

(c) Known pathologies with vascular and neural impairment.

Tape application

When applying tape consider all the various tissues which will be affected by the taping technique, e.g. skin, tendons, muscles, ligaments, blood vessels and nerves – all are intimately related.

Avoid

1 Excessive traction on skin = breakdown.
2 Gaps and wrinkles = blisters.
3 Bony areas = will ache after a short time.
4 Continuous circumferential strips – will impede circulation
5 Too many layers of tape = alteration in neural transmission – pins and needles.
6 Too tight an application = alteration in neural transmission – pins and needles.
7 Non-stretch tape around muscles = alteration in neural transmission – pins and needles.

Tape removal

Avoid leaving tape on for too long a period = skin breakdown.
Never rip tape off. Remove tape carefully.
Check the injured area on removal, e.g. skin. Then question the athlete:

Was there adequate stability and control?

Are any changes necessary next time?

Remember that taping techniques are not "cure-alls". The techniques are only "skin deep" – the deeper structures are not affected to the same extent as the skin and superficial structures. Consequently, these techniques do not create total soft tissue control. Taping techniques function only as part of a total injury care programme.

31. Age:Height Ratio for Diving at Extremes of Age

J.M. CAMERON

FOR SOME TIME CONCERN has been shown regarding the heights from which competitors should enter the water in diving, particularly at the extremes of age. The medical committee of the Federation Internationale de Natation Amateur (FINA) had rather strict views on the matter but all members had difficulty in expressing them in a simple way.

It was for that reason that Fig. 1 was prepared to illustrate the recommendation.

It will be seen that the recommendation is, for competitive diving:

(a)   under 10 and above 60 years not above 5 m, and

(b)   over 10 but under 14, and over 45 but under 60, not above 7.5 m.

It is felt that little control can be held over the age:height ratio in out-of-competition or recreational diving. The reason for choosing the age: height figures was that over 45 years in females the possibility of post-menopausal osteoporosis (bone softening) must be considered and over 60 years in men the possibility of silent prostatic secondary deposits in the spine must also be considered, in addition to hypertension on climbing.

In the developing child it was felt that 7.5 m should be the limit up to 14 years of age and 5 m up to 10 years of age in order that they not only protect their skeleton but develop a proper respect for the boards and the discipline of diving.

These figures were subsequently given by the Medical Committee to the FINA Bureau as recommendations and referred to the Diving Technical Committee; these would not be rigid, but open for discussion.

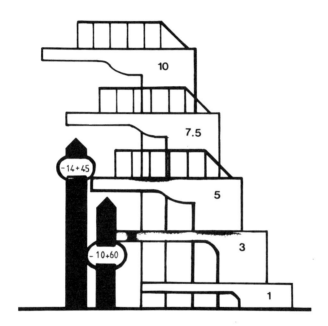

FIG.1. Recommended diving heights by age.

Part 6
The Law and Drugs

32. Tort in Sport

R. HENDERSON QC

ACCIDENTS, BOTH GRAVE AND TRIVIAL, will happen in all forms of sport. It is easy to envisage how competitors in swimming, in driving and in water polo can be injured. Swimmers may cut themselves in or en route to or from the changing rooms. There may be a risk of injury on or near the starting blocks and injury in the pool itself perhaps caused by improper chlorination or by the lane dividers or by the edge of the pool. A remote possibility might even involve the risk of electrocution if timing or lighting or broadcasting equipment were dangerous. Divers can be hurt by the dangerous state of the board or of the pool, or more probably from an error of judgment on their part. In water polo, collisions can easily cause injury.

Not all accidents result from tort or delict (the Scottish term). Tort means a civil wrong, as opposed to a criminal wrong, but of course some criminal acts are also torts.

Officials and spectators and coaches can likewise be injured, but ordinarily one would expect such injury to arise from some condition of the premises themselves. However, crowd control is a topical subject and we must recognize that in unexpected circumstances engendering panic or fear, people can be crushed or endangered by the spontaneous and ill-considered reactions of others. How will the law treat such accidents and disasters?

First, it will consider any contractual provisions which exist, because it is open to people to agree that liability for such accidents will be allocated in particular ways. If a contract based upon the purchase of a ticket were to provide that the occupiers of premises will be liable for all accidents to spectators caused by crushing, and a spectator was crushed, his claim could and probably would be a claim for damage pursuant to the liability in contract but he or she would supplement it by a claim in tort, probably for negligence.

What a person cannot validly do in the business of providing for the use of premises or of sporting services or facilities, is, by reference to a contract term or notice given generally or specifically, to "exclude or restrict his liability for death or personal injury resulting from negligence": Section 2 of the Unfair Contract Terms Act 1977. That Act severely curtails the right of anyone to exclude or restrict his business liability for negligence, and that entailment applies as much to occupiers as it does to others in the sporting business.

Of course, in the ordinary way, contracts will seek to minimize rather than to confer rights. But as between an owner of a sports hall, and an occupier of that sports hall, and a company supplying equipment or services to it, there may be vitally important and relevant conditions which allocate liability between them and thus their insurers.

How will the common law approach the determination of liability for such accidents? Subject to certain glosses imposed by statute, such as the Occupiers Liability Act 1957 and the Defective Premises Act 1972, it will apply the tests derived from a vast mass of case law by which negligence is judged. The existence of a separate Act, namely the Occupiers Liability Act 1957, has preserved and created the appearance of occupiers' liability as something distinct, but in its substance it is very much the same as the common law.

I will mention two other Acts, only to dismiss them from consideration of tort in sport: the Safety of Sports Grounds Act 1975, and the Fire Safety and Safety of Places in Sport Act 1957. By Section 13 of the 1975 Act and Section 12 of the 1957 Act, the provisions of those Acts confer no right of action in any civil proceedings, other than proceedings for recovery of a fine, in respect of contravention of those statutes.

Roscoe Pound said many years ago in the Harvard Law Review: "There is a strong and growing tendency where there is no blame on either side, to ask, in view of the exigencies of social justice, who can best bear the loss and hence to shift the loss of creating liability where there has been no fault". That approach remains very much alive today, if perhaps not so well resisted in truth, because there is a strong inclination to find fault when in fact there may be little or no fault. That is especially so when the Plaintiff's injuries are grave or fatal.

And so to the nub of the case law, and the tests which the Courts will apply in cases of alleged negligence. The clearest and most dominant exposition of the law is that of Lord Atkin in *M'Allister (or Donoghue) a pauper v. Stevenson (1932) AC 562 at 579 et seq:* a Scottish case considered by the House of Lords. On 26th August, 1928, at a cafe in Paisley a shop assistant called M'Allister or Donoghue consumed part of the contents of a bottle of ginger beer. She had no reason to suppose, because of the opaque glass, that the bottle contained anything but ginger beer. Her friend was proceeding to pour the remainder of the contents into a tumbler when lo and behold a decomposed snail emanated from the bottle. The nauseating apparition and impurities in the liquid were said to have caused injury to the pursuer, i.e. the claimant, perhaps not unreasonably, and the claim was ultimately settled for a few hundred pounds. From such apparently inapt and trivial beginnings, we find the formulation of the law which will still be applied in sport and all other areas of possible negligence today.

Lord Atkin said this: "The law of both countries [i.e. England and Scotland, but Wales is no different] appears to be that in order to support an action for damages for negligence the complainant has to show that he has been injured by the breach of a duty owed to him in the circumstances by the Defendant to take reasonable care to avoid such injury". He went on to say how the Courts had engaged upon an elaborate clarification of myriad different types of circumstances and then distilled the infinite variety of circumstances in these words: "The liability for negligence, whether you style it such or treat it as in other systems as a species of 'culpa', is no doubt based upon a general public sentiment of moral wrongdoing for which the offender must pay. But acts or omissions which any moral code would censure cannot in a practical world be treated so as to give a right to every person injured by them to demand relief. In this way rules of law arise which limit the range of complainants and the extent of their remedy. The rule that you are to love your neighbour becomes in law, you must not injure your neighbour; and the lawyer's question, Who is my neighbour? receives a restricted reply. You must take reasonable care to avoid acts or omissions which you can reasonably foresee would be likely to injure your neighbour. Who, then, in law is my neighbour? The answer seems to be – persons who are so closely and directly affected by my act that I ought reasonably to have them in contemplation as being so affected when I am directing my mind to the acts or omissions which are called in question".

If I had taken a few of the innumerable examples of claims arising in sporting accidents, the collapsing stands, the slipping cases, the electrocution cases, the flying object cases, I would have obscured the vital general tests:

1 all the circumstances must be considered;
2 did those circumstances give rise to a duty to take care;
3 was reasonable care taken to prevent injury or damage;
4 did the injury or damage result from not taking such a degree of care. The foreseeability of risk is plainly vital.

If you look up "Sport" in the Index to Charlesworth on Negligence (7th Edition) you will find it between skylarking, spacecraft, spectacles, spikes (not the sporting variety) spring guns, squibs, squatters and stairs. It is actually headed "Sport: see also cricket ball". I hope that in the 8th edition we will not find "Sport: see also swimming pool".

---

33. Inaugural Bleasdale Memorial FINA Lecture: some legal aspects in regard to doping controls

H. BEYER

Introduction

AFTER THE OLYMPIC GAMES of Seoul, the public discussion about doping in sport, proclamations against doping in sport and the demands to fight any doping in sport have greatly increased. Hardly a day passes when you *cannot* read or hear about the problems of doping.

Everyone who is engaged in sport – athletes, doctors, officials, coaches all – assure us that they reject any doping in sport. In major events such as the Olympic Games or World Championships, athletes and officials swear that they are willing to compete without any violation of the rules and laws of sport. However, again and again we have doping cases, sometimes extremely spectacular, as for example in Seoul, and in increasing numbers.

This proves that it is not enough to proclaim opposition to doping in sport. Medical care is needed as well as a judicial basis on which to fight it.

The legal position

I would like to give you some impressions of how difficult all these questions are and how numerous. It is very easy to demand random tests, unannounced and during training times in any place in the world, but it is extremely difficult to establish a judicial basis for it.

First of all, we have to take into account the fact that individual athletes nowadays have become increasingly aware of their rights and are ready to claim them; they are no longer willing to obey the authorities or organizers unquestioningly. When individual athletes are to be disciplined or sanctioned, they are ready to fight defend themselves. In their efforts to get their "rights", athletes nowadays even appeal to public Courts against decisions made by the authorities in sporting organizations. The "mature" athlete, responsible for himself, has been an aim in sport for many years. This aim has been reached but the time of ideals has gone. Commercialization – money – is now governing sport and therefore successful athletes are more prepared than ever before to fight for their rights and against any personal restrictions and sanctions. This attitude, of course, is also applied to doping controls, and therefore we need rigid rules and regulations for doping controls and we need a legal basis.

There may be some countries where the public laws state that everybody who is taking part in a sporting competition has to accept doping control. In most countries, however, there are no public laws and so the only legal way to establish doping controls is by the voluntary agreement of the athletes, or on a contractual basis. This leads to the difficult question of whether an international sports federation such as FINA has the power to force an athlete to accept doping controls.

The structure and constitution of FINA – like those of other international sports federations – do not establish contractual relations between FINA and individual athletes. Individual athletes are not members of FINA, but only of the club, university, college, etc. which they have joined. Membership of a club carries with it various rights and duties between the club and the individual athlete, but not between the international swimming federation and the individual athlete. The club to which the individual athlete belongs is a member of a national swimming federation (or in some cases of a regional swimming federation) and only this national federation is member of the international federation. The question is: can Rules and Laws, established by an international federation such as FINA, have any standing at all in relation to the individual athlete?

There is a body of opinion which says that membership of a national federation in an international federation does establish a contractual relationship between the international federation and the individual athlete, with the consequence that the international federation has the power to demand obedience to its laws and rules. I think it is correct to maintain the view that the individual athlete who joins a club does not automatically become a member of the international federation. From this it follows that an athlete who joins a club, will generally come under the jurisdiction only of that club and not the jurisdiction of either the national or the international federation. The club has no automatic power, or even the right, to bring its members under the jurisdiction of the national or even international federation.

The jurisdiction of a federation can apply to the individual only by subjugation: subjugation of the athlete to the jurisdiction of the club, subjugation of the club to the national federation and subjugation of the national federation to the international federation. But the subjugation of the individual athlete to the jurisdiction of the club does not imply subjugation to the jurisdiction of the international federation.

For the international federation to have any jurisdiction over the individual athlete, a clear ruling would have to be made to that effect. The constitution of the club, of which the athlete is a member, would have to state that all club members come under the jurisdiction not only of the club, but also of the national federation, where the club is a member of that federation; and the constitution of the national federation would have to state that any individual who has come under their jurisdiction will automatically also come under the jurisdiction of the international federation.

A clear statement in the constitution that the potential member of the club knows that he/she will come under the jurisdiction of the national and international federations will provide a legal basis for carrying out doping controls against individual athletes.

Everybody who is aware of this legal situation and who knows the organization, structure and constitution of FINA, the national member federations and their member clubs, will agree that this demand for judicial doping controls under the jurisdiction of the international federations in relation to the individual athletes cannot be achieved easily within FINA. There are too many countries whose federations are members of FINA, and all these national federations have many regional federations, clubs, etc. and these regional clubs have millions of individual members. To organize all of them into a system, like the one outlined above would seem impossible. However, a legally viable possibility, which could be achieved within an international sport federation such as FINA, would be to establish regulations for participation in events. This would mean that whenever a sporting event was going to be held by FINA, the international federation could state in the competition rules that the laws of FINA with regard to doping controls, and sanctions in case of a positive test, must be observed.

In this case, the individual athlete who is going to take part in the competition will be obliged to accept the doping controls of the international federations on a contractual basis, as he/she has accepted the conditions under which the competition is held.

There would be some doubts as to the validity of this view if FINA had a monopoly to hold competitive events in aquatic sports, and in fact FINA is claiming for such a monopoly, especially in regard to World Championships.

However, even if there is such a monopoly, it will not invalidate all the contractual relationships between the individual and FINA as organizer of the event, but only those regulations which abuse the monopoly, and this could not be said about the regulations regarding doping controls and sanctions in case of a positive test. Of course, the monopoly, if there is any, does not force the individual to take part in the competition; he/she is still free to decide whether or not to take part.

More serious doubts arise when you consider that in most cases the entries for FINA events are made not by the individual athlete, but by the national federation. When FINA state in their regulations for an event, that doping controls will be in place and that there will be sanctions in the case of a positive test, these regulations will usually come to the notice of the federations rather than the individual athletes.

Therefore it seems to be doubtful to assume that an athlete taking part in a FINA event has agreed to the regulations regarding doping controls, even if this is part of the laid down regulations for that event.

On the other hand, no athlete entered by his/her federation in a FINA event is unwilling to take part in that event. The athlete has agreed to take part in that competition before being entered by the federation. This might be interpreted as meaning that the athlete has authorized the federation to agree to all regulations laid down for that competition.

There is another way to create an unassailable legal basis for doping controls of individual athletes, either in FINA competitions or during training times at home, and this is the easiest to organize and administer: the voluntary agreement of the individual athletes to any doping control. If the athlete signs a document stating that he/she agrees to any doping control carried out according to FINA rules by an authority of his/her club and/or Federation and/or the International Federation FINA, he/she cannot possibly refuse or object to any doping control.

A RECOMMENDATION

I can recommend very strongly that the international federations as well as the national federations establish a legal basis along these lines: it is simple, clear and without any doubts. This recommendation is obviously finding open doors: the athletes themselves are very interested in having a guarantee that among themselves there is no doping. At the European Championships this year, the athlete Stephan Caron (France) started an initiative in this regard. He presented a proclamation saying that he is ready to accept doping controls at any major event as well as during training times at home or anywhere. He invited other athletes to follow his example and to sign this proclamation also. He was followed by famous athletes, such as Michael Gross (FRG) and Kristin Otto (GDR), and in just the few days of the European Championships more than 200 athletes signed this proclamation. Had this been a FINA-document, FINA would have now an unassailable legal basis for doping controls with regard to these athletes. This method would solve a lot of legal problems.

TESTING IN TRAINING

When you consider what I have said so far, and of course I have not gone into detail, you will also understand how difficult it is to find a legal basis for random doping tests, unannounced and during training times. If this is done in a country where there is a public law that you have to accept doping tests at any time and any place, this is, of course, a legal basis.

But in countries where there are no laws like these, the creation of contractual relations between the individual athlete and the international federation holding sporting events, is not possible. Generally the international federation, FINA, has no power to demand any doping control during training at home at a club. If an athlete is suddenly requested by a FINA-authorized doctor to give a urine specimen for a doping control, and refuses to do so, FINA has no power to force the athlete to do it. In my opinion, a random test during training ordered by the international federation can be taken only with the voluntary agreement of the athlete.

However, FINA has the power to decide who is allowed to take part in FINA-events. The regulations for FINA-events may state that only athletes who have agreed to accept unannounced random tests during training periods are allowed to take part in FINA competitions. This leads us back to the question, whether there is a monopoly held by FINA in regard to that event and whether it is to be considered as an abuse of this monopoly to demand agreement to doping tests during training times.

But this I have already denied. FINA, which is in general interested to carry out random tests during training times, must in fact include in their regulations for participation in FINA events for the future, a stipulation that athletes are allowed to compete only if they have agreed to accept doping controls during training times.

TESTING PROCEDURE

There are not only problems in regard to the legal basis of doping controls, but also in regard to the procedure used to take test.

First of all, it cannot be denied that the procedure impinges on the privacy of the athlete; the question is whether a sport federation like FINA is allowed to violate this privacy. According to FINA rules, the athlete chosen for a doping control "must produce a specimen of urine under the direct supervision of a Member of the MC" (who is not necessarily a doctor!). On the other side, the examination of the urine specimen is accepted as sufficient test. As yet it is not required so to take blood from the athlete. This may be considered more a violation of the privacy of an athlete, than the request to give an urine specimen. In my opinion, there cannot be legal objections to that. Many mistakes are made when carrying out the controls. In common with all other international sport federations, FINA has a clear ruling on how to conduct doping controls. However, there is almost no major event where you cannot find mistakes. FINA rules are very detailed and very clear and they must be followed. Everyone who is in charge of carrying out doping controls, must take care that these rules are observed.

Whenever mistakes are found and the case is brought to Court, you can be sure it will lead to a verdict of "not guilty".

This very short account shows how difficult the whole matter is, and that it will need some more time before we find a reliable and sound legal basis for doping controls. All of us engaged in the promotion of swimming and the aquatic sports are really anxious to fight doping. But we must be aware that in the future there will be some violations. If we are to exclude those who do not behave according to our rules, we must have secure grounds for doing so.

Some proposals

The judicial discussions in relation to doping controls will continue until a reliable judicial ground has been found, so I now make some proposals, which FINA should adopt.

1   At all FINA events the regulations for participating competitors shall include the ruling that any competitor may be chosen for a doping control and that he/she agrees to that. When there is such a ruling every federation entering athletes for that event knows beforehand that they may be chosen for a doping control, and if they are chosen they cannot refuse.

2   All participants in any FINA event shall sign a declaration that he/she agrees to doping controls also during training at home. Only those athletes who have given such an agreement shall be allowed to compete in a FINA event.

Given the doubtful legal basis for doping controls carried out by FINA authorities on athletes during their training times at home, FINA should use its power to decide who is allowed to take part in its events. To require the declaration above is not an abuse of any monopoly FINA might have in regard to some aquatic events. Athletes having signed such a declaration can have no legal objections to doping control during training. This will guarantee FINA an unassailable judicial basis for doping controls during training of all the athletes competing in FINA events.

3   FINA shall amend its constitution so that only those federations can be or become members of FINA whose constitution states that the individual swimmers of that federation shall come under the ruling and jurisdiction of FINA in regard to doping controls.

I have explained that doping controls need a legal basis, that it is doubtful whether there is such a basis as long as there is no public law, and when the athlete concerned has not accepted doping controls by signing a document to that effect, and as long as there are no contractual obligations for the athlete concerned. To establish such contractual obligations it would be helpful to have rules in the constitution of FINA as well as in the constitutions of the member federations, that the individual athletes in every member federation of FINA are under the jurisdiction of FINA, at least in regard to doping controls.

4   No World Record shall be recognized without a doping control which has turned out to be negative. This was recommended by FINA's Medical Committee some time ago, which I first opposed. Since then I have changed my mind. It might happen that a World Record is set at a competition, but that it cannot be recognized because it was set at a competition without doping controls. However, the importance of high-level sport free of cheating makes it necessary to adopt such a rule. Of course, this assumes that only doping controls carried out according to FINA rules can be considered sufficient for the recognition of a World Record. This might cause objections by some member federations, since not all of them are able to carry out doping control as required by FINA rules.

5   On invitation, FINA shall inspect federations with regard to their measures to prevent doping. FINA, if satisfied, will issue a certificate stating that doping controls are in accordance with FINA's requirements. This Certification shall be publicized to all member federations.

Wherever you look at the Rules and Laws of FINA to be observed by their members, you will find sanctions, disqualifications and other consequences in the case of a violation of the rules. It may be better to follow a system of "awards" in cases where rules are observed rather than a system of "sanctions" in cases where rules are violated.

Any member federation of FINA, which is certain that in regard to doping controls everything is organized and practised in accordance with FINA standards and requirements, should be able to apply for an "award" from FINA. My proposal is that, at the request of the federation, a delegation from FINA (preferably members of the Medical Committee) go to that country and inspect its doping controls – how everything is organized, who is responsible, by what system athletes are chosen for doping controls, how often this is done, whether there are doping controls during training, what laboratory is used to test the samples, whether FINA rules are observed etc.

Such an inspection should lead to the Certification above which shall be advertised and published in FINA's official files as well as in the minutes of the FINA Bureau and in the FINA News and other publications. This will encourage other Member federations to organize their own doping control procedures according to FINA requirements and to apply for such a certificate.

As long as a Federation does not have this FINA certificate it could be suspected by others that in this country doping controls might not be in accordance with FINA requirements.

Other legal aspects

There are many other legal and judicial aspects in regard to doping in sport. There is not enough to deal with all of them. However, it is necessary, to mention the criminal aspects of doping:

1   taking drugs may lead to illness and even death; whoever is giving drugs to an athlete must be aware, therefore, that he/she may be liable to criminal proceedings and may be responsibly for the death of a human being;

2   this raises the question, of course, of whether it is a criminal offence to give drugs to an athlete who is aware of the danger and takes them voluntarily – probably not; but what is the situation if the athlete, voluntarily taking the drugs and knowing everything, is not an adult but only a child? Will the agreement of this athlete to taking drugs protect the person who supplies them? And what is the situation if the parents have agreed?

3   It must be considered also that in many countries the possession of drugs and, of course, the giving and taking of drugs are criminal acts. According to the public laws in these countries, anyone – athletes, coaches, doctors, team managers, etc. may be sentenced, if they take, give or even just possess drugs forbidden under this law, regardless of whether the athlete has agreed to accept drugs, whether he/she is doing it voluntarily and whether he/she is aware what he/she is doing.

The taking and giving of drugs to athletes may also lead to judicial questions under civil laws. If someone is giving drugs to an athlete – coach, manager, doctor, physiotherapist, functioneer, whoever – and if this leads to an illness or injury, or even to death, he/she may be liable to pay all the financial damages which might be caused by this.

Conclusion

It was my intention to give just some impressions about the many, various and difficult problems and judicial questions which are to be considered in connection with doping controls in sport.

It is not possible to deal with all these questions in the space which is available here. However, I do hope that I have succeeded in demonstrating that the legal and judicial aspects of doping in sport are as many, as important and as difficult as the medical aspects. All of us will continue to fight against drugs and doping in sport, doctors as well as lawyers. I do hope that we will be successful.

---

34. Anabolic Steroids and Diuretics

ARNOLD H. BECKETT

Introduction

THE TOPIC ASSIGNED TO ME is defined, but it is necessary to realize the problem in the context of drug misuse in society. The latter is beginning to undermine the fabric of society, e.g. drug misusers in the USA commit at least 40% of all property crimes and more than 250 000 of them are infected with AIDS; the cocaine traffic in Columbia has destroyed their criminal justice system and led to a virtual civil war between state and drug barons; WHO has stated that drug misuse could become the endemic disease of the Third World (Table 1). The question must be posed: Although sport is heavily infiltrated with drug misuse, can we prevent it being destroyed by a suitable blend of controls and education, so that those entering sport and their advisers will regard drug misuse and misusers as being "anti-sport", and therefore totally unacceptable in this portion of society? Can those involved in sport become role models to lead future sportspersons and even society, away from its destructive drug misuse culture? Anabolic steroids and diuretics were included in the IOC list of Doping Classes in operation for the Seoul

TABLE 1. *Drug misuse - 1985*

Approx
30 million cannabis users
1.7 million opium dependent
1.6 million cocaine users
0.7 million heroin dependent -

A W.H.O. Study has estimated
that there are some 48 million
illicit drug users in the world

Olympic Games (see Appendix 1). More recently a new class has been introduced, of which some examples, e.g. HGH and HCG have relevance to the anabolic steroid class. It should be noted this list represents examples of the different dope classes to illustrate the doping definition. Unless indicated, all substances belonging to the banned classes may not be used for medical treatment even if they are not listed as examples (see Appendix I).

Anabolic steroids

These are synthetic drugs modelled upon the male sex hormone testosterone. They were designed to constitute drugs with reduced androgenic, i.e. masculinising, effects relative to that of the hormone, but to retain the anabolic, i.e. weight gaining, properties. For dope control purposes testosterone is considered under the anabolic steroid heading. Testosterone is secreted predominantly by the testes but the adrenal glands also secrete the chemical; its production is under the control of hormones produced by the pituitary gland.

During the 1950s, some doctors began to adopt the anabolic steroids used in medicine as chemical aids in sport. In the 1960s their use in sport increased greatly because suitable analytical methods for their detection were not available.

The first testing for these drugs using methods, providing results upon which action could be taken, took place in the Olympic Games in 1976 in Montreal. However, some of the investigational work involving testing occurred earlier at the Commonwealth Games in 1974. At the 1976 Olympic Games some competitors, mainly from weight-lifting, were disqualified for the misuse of anabolic steroids. In the 1970s anabolic steroid misuse became widespread in some sports, e.g. weight-lifting, track and field ("Steroids: The Growing Menance", 1979).

Public awareness of the problem was high-lighted because of the disqualification of Ben Johnson in Seoul and the subsequent Dubin inquiry (1990). The statement of Ben Johnson's doctor (Astaphan) and coach (Francis) was very revealing as are the allegations of widespread misuse at top levels in sport. Most Americans were shocked at the disqualifications at the Pan Am Games in Venezuela in 1983, and the attempt to smuggle anabolic steroids from the USSR to Canada by Canadian and USSR sportsmen, and the revelations at the trial of David Jenkins of the high amount of anabolic steroids provided and distributed illegally (those approved for human use as well as veterinary ones sold for use in humans). The attempted smuggling of 200 kilos of anabolic steroids for use in sports into Sweden in 1988 indicated the high amount of the drug circulating illegally in Europe while the increasingly wide distribution of "The Underground Steroid Handbook" showed just how widespread had become the interest in and potential misuse of these drugs in sportspeople and those on the fringes of sport. Drug misuse in sport is not only at top level. Young teenagers thinking about their possible involvement in sport, or boys trying to look better for the girls, are going to gyms to get their supplier and advice, sometimes the quality of the oral products they receive is doubtful and the injections sometimes are not sterile and contain adulterated material. Middle aged people have joined this drug subculture just to attempt to better their own performance even when not involved in highly competitive sport. Frequently so-called experts who are remote from the drug misuse problem, have denied that these drugs improve performance or that they have serious side-effects; Ron Pickering summed up the situation admirably in his presentation to the second IAF World Symposium on Doping in Sport held in Monaco in 1989.

Side-effects

IN MEN

1   Large doses suppress spermatogenesis and cause degenerative changes in the seminiferous tubules.

2   Can accelerate the growth of malignant neoplasms of the prostate.

IN WOMEN

3   Suppression of ovarian activity and menstruation because of the inhibitory activity of the anabolic steroids on the activity of the anterior pituitary.

4   Large and continued doses produce:
   (a) Symptoms of virilism, such as male-pattern hirsutism.
   (b) Deepening of the voice.
   (c) Atrophy of the breasts and endometrical tissue.
   (e) Hypertrophy of the clitoris.

IN BOTH MEN AND WOMEN

5   May cause liver carcinomas and jaundice (Griffiths *et al.*, 1989; Vesselinovitch, 1989).

6   Increase sodium and fluid retention.

7   Can increase trygylcerides and cholesterol levels in blood.

8   The influences in 7 and 8 increases susceptibility to arteriosclerosis and the risk of cardiac disease.

9   Muscle volume increases more rapidly than tendon strength; greater frequency of injuries to joints and tendons thus results.

10 May produce psychological and personality changes (Pope and Katz, 1989).

If they are misused on young people whose growth is not complete, the epiphyses, i.e. the growing plates at the end of the long bones, can become fused so that no further longtitudinal growth takes place and shortened stature results.

It takes much time to establish unequivocally that serious problems result from the use of a drug when controlled investigations are not possible for ethical reasons, e.g. the ethics of giving massive doses well above the recommended therapeutic dose. Only epidemiological studies therefore are possible in this situation. The recent IAAF meeting in Monte Carlo addressed the problem. As far as the serious psychiatric side-effects are concerned there has been no doubt for some years.

REVERSIBILITY OF SIDE-EFFECTS OF ANABOLIC STEROIDS

Many of the effects are reversible when drug administration is discontinued.

However, this is not certain and the risk of permanent alterations is greater when large doses of anabolic steroids are taken for long periods.

The call for action

If effective action is to be contemplated, then not only is there the need to realize that a problem exists, but there is a need for a consensus of informed opinion amongst athletes, coaches, parents, sports doctors, sports administrators, politicians, etc. Leading athletes have stated their position, and politicians have reacted (see Ottawa, 1988; Moscow, 1988 and Reykjavik, 1989), the IOC has acted for many years and now has an agreement with the organization of summer sports, and GAISF has already stated its position (see Appendices II-III).

NUMBER OF POSITIVE TESTS

The results of testing, 1986-88, from IOC Accredited laboratories is shown in Table 2; the results only indicate the tip of the iceberg, since the majority of tests is carried out on those who know they might be tested. Anabolic steroids represent the highest percentage in 1988 (Table 3) of the banned classes of drugs (the result for diuretics is shown in Table 3).

TABLE 2. *Summary of samples analyzed by IOC Accredited Laboratories - 1986 to 1988.*

Number of samples	Number of negative samples	Number of analytically positive A-samples	Percentage	Year	N (labs.)
32982	32359	623	1.89	1986	18
37882	37028	854	2.25	1987	21
47069	45916	1153	2.45	1988	20

TABLE 3. *Summary of the samples analyzed by the IOC accredited laboratories 1988. Total 1353.*

Substances identified in A-samples - IOC List (*Anabolic Steroids* - 791)			
Nandrolone	304	Oxymetholone	12
Testosterone	155	Meaterolone	11
Stanozolol	89	Clostebol	6
Metenolone	60	Drostanolone	4
Methandienone	54	Formebolone	2
Methyltestoterone	33	Fluoxymesterone	
Oxandrolone	22	HCG	
Boldenone	19	Methandriol	
Dehydrochlormethyl-testosterone	16	Trenbolone	

TABLE 4. *Summary of the samples analyzed by the IOC accredited laboratories 1988. Total - 1353.*

Substances identified in A-samples - IOC List

Diuretics		*Beta-Blockers*	
Furosemide	35	Propranolol	7
Hydrochlorothiazide	17	Metoprolol	
Triamterene	2		
Bendroflumethiazide	1	*Masking Agents*	
Bumetanide			
Canrenone	1	Probenecid	19

Philosophy of dope control

It is important in considering dope control in sport that plans be based on a coherent philosophy and moral basis. Some have stressed simply the moral argument. However it is difficult to write rules and regulations on such a basis. In fact, how can we plan to match the natural capabilities of athletes when athletes from richer countries are able to train at high altitudes and then compete at lower altitudes, which athletes from poorer countries cannot do? Richer countries have many facilities for their athletes, poorer countries have not.

The IOC stressed the pragmatic approach, though of course realizing that there were moral aspects to what it was doing, the main points of which are:

1 Moral Argument: their use contravenes the basic characteristics of sport – the matching of the natural capabilities of the participants.

2 Pragmatic Arguments
   (a) Competitions should involve competitors, not pharmacologists and physicians.
   (b) Competitors should not be used as guinea-pigs.
   (c) The use of some drugs can cause aggression and loss of judgment – hazards to other competitors, spectators and officials.
   (d) Danger of bad examples to young people.
   (e) Danger of drug dependence.

The IOC policy on dope control is as shown:

To prevent the use of those drugs in sport which constitute dangers when used as doping agents.

To prevent drug abuse with the minimum interference with the therapeutic use of drugs.

To ban only those drugs for which suitable analytical methods could be devised to detect the compounds unequivocally in urine (or blood) samples.

To ban classes of drugs based upon the pharmacological actions of members of the classes but not to attempt to produce a complete list of banned drugs.

The emphasis is upon obtaining objective scientific evidence of drug misuse, rather than having to rely upon denunciations and doubts. Also very detailed considerations were given as to whether to try to draw a line between allowable and correct use of drugs for therapeutic treatment in sport and the area where a variety of drugs could not be used. Sometimes, doubts are expressed as to whether the line should be drawn at all, but in general the approach of the IOC Medical Commission has commanded international support.

It cannot be emphasized too frequently that in the dope control system it must be the deterrent and educative aspects which are emphasized rather than the punitive aspect. In dope testing at present, urine is the biological fluid analyzed for presence of drugs and metabolites to indicate misuse of a drug of the banned classes. These aspects of control of sampling, transfer of samples, reporting of results, etc. are equally as important as the analytical aspects. In fact, most of the challenges to the system have arisen around these general aspects, rather than around the final analytical results. The Medical Commission must consider each case on its merit. It is the Medical Commission which must decide whether the rules are infringed and not the laboratory.

Anabolic steroids and related compounds – developing problems

Testing for anabolic steroids at big events does not solve the problem of anabolic steroid misuse in sport. These compounds are used for two main purposes; namely, with a high protein diet to increase weight and muscle mass, but the other aspect of the misuse is because of the effect of the drugs on the central nervous system, to produce more drive, competitiveness and aggression.

A nabolic steroids are used during training and then the use is stopped within a certain period before a major competition where testing is expected. However, after misuse of anabolic steroids has stopped the performance tends to be reduced because the competitor becomes depressed and loses his drive and competitive edge. To cover this gap between ceasing the use of the drugs and the competition, other drugs have been misused. First of all, the endogenous material testosterone was used on the assumption that no one could act, since the drug was already present in the body. After much detailed research, the appropriate test was implemented. It centred around the fact that the body produces equal amounts of testosterone and epitestosterone; thus when extra testosterone was administered the ratio between the testosterone and epitestosterone increased. A rate of 6 was set at the level which must not be exceeded. However, in declaring a positive in misuse of testosterone, use is also made of the fact that the testosterone/luteinizing hormone ratio is also increased. Laboratories dealing with dope testing are asked to produce more evidence before declaring a positive testosterone analytical result than simply using the testosterone/epitestosterone ratio.

It has been reported that people are attempting to circumvent the testosterone/epitestosterone ratio test by administering epitestosterone along with testosterone, so that the ratio is then not exceeded. Professor Brooks has shown, however, that this misuse can be detected by using a testostesterone/luteinizing hormone ratio, but much more work is necessary before this can become definitive as far as decision making about drug misuse cases is concerned.

There are also many reports that the gap between misuse of anabolic steroids and testing at big events is being covered by the use of HGH. This material has a very short half-life in man, so the problem of analysis is very great, and no definitive test to indicated misuse is currently available. Now HGH releasing factor is available, this also will constitute a major challenge to those involved in testing for drug misuse. HCG increases the production of testosterone in males and misuse of this material is also now constituting a problem.

These developing problems have resulted in the IOC Medical Commission banning these materials. In these moves, however, the Commission has been forced to depart from its normal rules of not banning any material unless there were an appropriate analytical test available at the time of the ban. The challenge of these new materials, and others which will become available arising from recombinant DNA techniques, will constitute increasingly searching challenges to the system. These challenges must be met and if this not possible by analytical techniques, then government approaches such as mandating the introduction of inert marker materials into certain products will have to take place, otherwise the whole system of control will be in danger of collapse. There is no point in having a sensitive analytical approach for compounds which can be tested accurately, if many other compounds giving the same effects for which there are not appropriate tests are being misused. Any control based upon such a system would be morally and philosophically indefensible.

We must consider the challenge posed by Thomas Sewell: "Policies are judged by their consequences, but crusades are judged by how good they make the crusaders feel."

What are the motives of the sports leaders and politicians who have recently suddenly trumpeted their calls to the war which they have allowed to be almost lost before they even realized there was one? Their desire to be seen to be involved often overwhelms their limited understanding of the motive of the war and leads to their proposing or supporting battle tactics divorced from reality.

Diuretics

Diuretics are misused in sport with two main purposes in mind. Firstly, they are to remove liquid from the body quickly and reduce weight in those sports where weight classes are involved. Thus the individual who is over the weight limit for a certain class strips away much body water, makes the weight, then reinfuses salts and dextrose before the competition, so he competes at his more natural weight which is above the weight class in which he is competing. The second purpose is to produce very dilute urine to make the task of those who are analyzing drugs in urine much more difficult.

However, it is important to consider if there are no better alternatives than testing for these drugs, and certainly in my opinion there should not be testing for these drugs in out-of competition testing. Those sports involved in weight classes could easily deal with the problem of diuretics without testing, by arranging final weigh-ins just before the competition is due to commence. This would stop the nonsense that is going on.

Also, why should drugs be banned just because they might produce problems for laboratories? It would be more logical for laboratories to test the density of the urine and if the density were low then to take a bigger volume of urine for the analytical steps.

There is a strong body of medical opinion which is opposed to the ban on diuretics; and, their criticisms have not been dealt with appropriately, because adequate justification for the ban on diuretics has not been forthcoming from those who support it. Deliberately, therefore, I have concentrated my main emphasis in this paper on anabolic steriods because their misuse is so great and this misuse is producing so many problems for sport and for the individuals involved.

Chorionic gonadotrophin (HCG – human chorionic gonadotrophin): it is well known that the administration to males of Human Chorionic Gonadotrophin (HGC) and other compounds with related activity leads to an increased rate of production of endogenous androgenic steroids and is considered equivalent to the exogenous administration of testosterone.

Corticotrophin (ACTH): Corticotrophin has been misused to increase the blood levels of endogenous corticosteroids notably to obtain the euphoric effect of corticosteroids. The application of corticotrophin is considered to be equivalent to the oral, intra-muscular or intravenous application of corticosteroids. (See section III. D).

Growth hormone (HGH, somatotrophin): the misuse of Growth Hormone in sport is deemed to be unethical and dangerous because of various adverse effects, for example, allergic reactions, and acromegaly when applied in high doses.

All the respective releasing factors of the above-mentioned substances are also banned.

References

Dubin, C.L. (1990). Commission of therapy into the use of drugs banned practices intended to increase athlete performance. Toronto, Canada.

Griffiths K. *et al.* (1989). Misuse of anabolic steroids: potential ill-effects on the prostate. IInd IAF World Symposium on Doping in Sport, Monaco.

Pickering, R. (1989). A moral dileimona for Sport and for Science. IInd IAF World Symposium on Doping in Sport, Monaco.

Pope, H.G. and Ratz, D.L. (1989). Psychiatric Effects of Doping with Anabolic Androgenic Steriods. IInd IAF World Symposium on Doping in Sport, Monaco.

Resolution No. 1 on Doping in Sport and the Draft Anti-doping Convention Council of Europe, 1989

Steroids: The Growing Menace. (1979). From *Sports Illustrated,* November 12th.

The European Ministers responsible for Sport, meeting at Reykjavik for their 6th Conference from 30 May to 1 June 1989. Welcome the adoption by the 1st Permanent World Anti-Doping in Sport Conference in Ottawa (26-29 June 1988) of the text, based on the European Anti-Doping Charter, and supported by the 2nd International Conference of Ministers and Senior Officials responsible for Sport and Physical Education organised by UNESCO at Moscow (22-25 November 1988.)

Vesselinovitch, S. D. (1989). IInd IAF World Symposium on Doping in Sport, Monaco.

Appendices

APPENDIX I. *IOC 1990 List of doping classes and methods.*

I. Doping Classes
A. Stimulants

amfrepramine	amfetaminil	amiphenazole	amphetamine
benzphetamine	caffeine*	cathine	chlorphentermine
clobensorex	chlorprenaline	cocaine	cropropamide**
crothetamide**	dimetamfetamine	ephedrine	ethamivan
etilamfetamine	fencamfamin	fenetylline	feproporex
furtenored	meclofenoxate	mefenorex	methamphetamine
methoxyphenamine	methylephedrine	methylephenidate	morazone
nikethamide	pemoline	pentetrazol	phendimetrazine
phenmetrazine	phentermine	phenylopro-	pipradol
prolintane	propylhexedrine	panolamine	pyrovalerone
strychnine and			
related com-	pounds		

*For caffeine the definition of a positive depends upon the following – if the concentration in urine exceeds 12 µg/ml.
** component of "micoren".

Sympathomimetic amines of which ephedrine, pseudoephedrine, phenylpropanolamine, and norpseudoephedrine are examples. They are often present in cold and hay fever preparations which can be purchased in pharmacies and sometimes from other retail outlets without the need of a medical prescription.

Thus no product for use in cold, flu or hay fever purchased by a competitor or given to him/her should be used without first checking with a doctor or pharmacist that the product does not contain a drug of the banned stimulants class.

The choice of medication in the treatment of asthma and respiratory ailments has posed many problems.

The use of *only* the following beta2 agonists is permitted in the aerosol form: bitolterol; orciprenaline; rimeterol; salbutamol; terbutaline.

B. Narcotics

alphaprodin	anileridin	buprenorphin	codeine
dextropropoxyphen	diamorphine (heroin)	dihydrocodeine	dipipanone
ethoheptazine	ethylmorphine	levorphanol	methadone
morphine	nalbuphine	pentazocine	pethidine
phenazocine	trimeperidine and		
	related compounds		

Appendix I (cont'd)

C. Anabolic Steroids

bolasterone	boldenone	clostebol	dehydrocholormet-
fluoxymesterone	mesterolone	metandienone	hyltestosterone
metenolone	nandrolone	norethandrolone	oxandrolone
oxymesterone	stanozolol	testosterone* and	
		related compounds	

* For testosterone the definition of a positive depends upon the following – the administration of testosterone or the use of any other manipulation having the result of increasing the ratio in urine of testosterone/epitestosterone to above 6.

D. Beta-blockers*

acetbutolol	alprenolol	atenolol	labetalol
metoprolol	nadolol	oxprenolol	propranolol
sotalol and related			
compounds			

* Beta-blockers could be tested for in Diving with the proviso that if an athlete has a certified medical need, Beta-blockers could be allowed.

E. Diuretics

acetazolamide	amiloride	bendroflu-	benzthiazide
bumetanide	canrenon	methiazide	chlormerodrin
chlortalidone	diclofenamide	ethacrynic acid	furosemide
hydrochloro-	mersalyl	spironolactone	triamterene and
thiazide			related compounds

F. Peptide hormone and analogues

chorionic gonado-	corticotrophin	growth hormone	Erythropietin
trophin (HCG)	(ACTH)	(HGH)	(EPO)

All the respective releasing factors of the above mentioned substances are also banned.

II.*Methods*

A. Blood doping

Blood transfusion is the intravenous administration of blood cells or related blood products that contain red blood cells. Such products can be obtained from blood drawn from the same (autologous) or from a different (non-autologous) individual.

Blood doping is the administration of blood or related blood products to an athlete other than for legitimate medical treatment. This procedure may be preceded by withdrawal of blood from the athlete who continues to train in this blood depleted state.

Appendix I (cont'd)

These procedures contravene the ethics of medicine and sport. There are also risks involved in the transfusion of blood and related blood products.

The practice of blood doping in sport is banned by the IOC Medical Commission.

B. Pharmacological, chemical and physical manipulation

The IOC Medical Commission bans the use of substances and of methods which alter the integrity and validity of urine samples used in doping controls. Examples of banned methods are catheterization, urine substitution and/or tampering, inhibition of renal excretion, e.g. by probenecid and related compounds.

III. *Classes of drugs subject to certain restrictions*

A. Alcohol

Alcohol is not prohibited. However, breath or blood alcohol levels may be determined at the request of an International Federation. The Medical Committee of both FINA and LEN discourage the ingestion of alcoholic beverages in Dope Control.

B. Marijuana

Marijuana is not prohibited. However, tests may be carried out at the request of an International Federation.

C. Local anaesthetics

Injectable local anaesthetics are permitted under the following conditions:

a   that procaine, xylocaine, carbocaine, etc. are used but not cocaine;

b   only local or intra-articular injections may be administered

c   only when medically justified (i.e. the details including diagnosis; dose and route of administration must be submitted immediately in writing to the Medical Commission).

The use of corticosteroids is banned except for topical use (aural, ophthalmological and dermatological). Inhalational therapy (asthma, allergic rhinitis) and local or intra-articular injections.

Any doctor wishing to administer corticosteroids intra-articularly or locally to a competitor must give written notification to the medical commission.

NOTE: The doping definition of the IOC Medical Commission is based on the banning of pharmacological classes of agents. The definition has the advantage that also new drugs, some of which may be especially designed for doping purposes, are banned.

APPENDIX II. *Agreement for the prevention of Doping in Sport between the International Olympic Committee and the International Summer Sports Federations.*

Aware of the need to establish ever closer co-operation, in order to ensure the success of the fight against doping, and in view of the principles stipulated in the International Olympic Charter against Doping in Sport, and bearing in mind the extensive Doping control programmes carried out at present by International Summer Sports Federations, the International Olympic Committee and their International Summer Sports Federations hereby agree:

1   To harmonize as rapidly as possible their anti-doping rules and procedures, both for controls during, and out of competition (unannounced).

2   To adopt each year as a basic minimum the list of banned classes and methods of doping as established by the IOC Medical Commission and as relevant to each Sport.

3   To harmonize the sanctions for violations to the anti-doping regulations in accordance with the recommendations made by the IOC and to ensure their application at national level.

4   To recognize sanctions given by another International Federation.

5   To use the laboratories accredited by the International Olympic Committee, as well as the IOC's mobile testing laboratory for all major international competitions and out of competition.

6   To co-operate fully with the National Olympic Committees, National Federations and Governmental organizations in order to fight against the trafficking of doping substances in Sport.

APPENDIX III. *General Association of International Sports Federations 1988*

The International Sports Federations, Members of GAISF recognize the serious threat to fair competition and competitors' health posed by the use of substances or by practices aimed at artificially enhancing performance:
and pledge themselves to oppose such practices by all the means available to them through their legalisation, management and influence on their National Member Associations.

GAISF News, No. 12, 1988

Part 7
Training

35. The Effects of Fluid and Protein Intake on Muscle Damage during Exercise

N. HOMMEN, R. CADE and M. PRIVETTE

DURING HIGH INTENSITY TRAINING for athletic competition, muscle damage (Davies and White, 1981; Hikida et al., 1983) may result, causing soreness and limiting performance. Serum enzymes, such as creatine phosphokinase (CPK) (Newham et al., 1983; Vaananan et al., 1986) and lactic dehydrogenase (LDH), have been used as an index of muscle "damage". Previous studies from our laboratory have shown that swimmers in high intensity training can have CPK levels elevated two to five times above normal.

Our studies were designed to determine whether or not fluid or dietary manipulation would both protect muscles from damage and accelerate the rate of healing, allowing intensified training as assessed by CPK levels.

In our first study (Fig. 1) measurement of CPK was performed on blood collected at weekly intervals immediately before the afternoon training session for swimmers ($n = 40$) doing two-a-day workouts. Initially all swimmers drank 16 oz of water immediately before and twice during the workouts. As indicated by the double bar in Fig. 1, half of the swimmers were then given an isotonic glucose-electrolyte (GE) solution (Gatorade distributed by Stokely-Van Camp, Inc., Chicago, IL.) before and during the workouts while half continued to drink water. When exercise intensity was increased by about 10%, CPK rose markedly in the water-drinking group, but declined modestly in the group drinking the GE solution. Rectal temperature of the water-drinking group rose to 39°C after only 25 min of swimming. Rectal temperature of the group drinking GE solution reached that level after approximately 60 min. We assume that maintenance of vascular volume, and therefore, of cardiac output was responsible for a protective effect afforded by the GE solution.

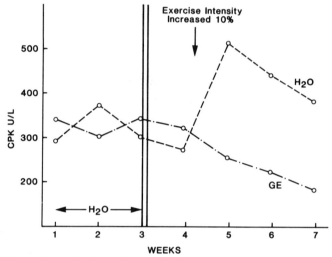

FIG. 1. Effect of exercise intensity and fluid replacement in male swimmers.

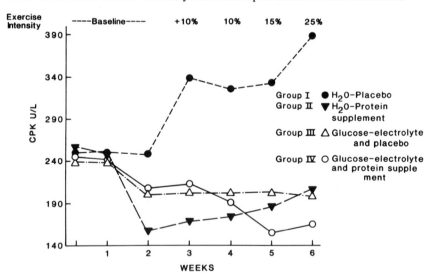

FIG. 2. Change in CPK with increasing exercise intensity with glucose-electrolyte and with protein supplement-men.

For our second series of observations (Fig. 2) we assumed as a working hypothesis that amino acids are used as a source of energy during exercise (Rennie *et al.*, 1981; Dohm *et al.*, 1985). This catabolism depletes the availability of essential amino acids that are used for repairing muscle during the post-exercise period. Supplementation of amino acids immediately post-exercise should therefore allow muscle repair to begin at an optimal rate immediately after exercise. CPK would then be lowered before the next workout session.

Athletes ($n= 40$) swam at a constant intensity for 4 weeks to achieve a baseline, and were then divided into four groups matched for event and ability. Group I ingested 16 oz of water before and during exercise. Immediately post-exercise, they consumed an orange-flavored placebo drink containing 16 g of sucrose. Group II drank water before and during exercise and ingested a fluid high in essential amino acids post-exercise. This fluid was milk-based, containing 15 g of lactoalbumin and 16 g of sugar per 8 oz (Tm) distributed by Nutri-Products, Inc., Gainesville, FL. Group III consumed 16 oz. of GE both before and during exercise, and drank the placebo drink post-exercise. Group IV ingested GE both before and during exercise, and drank the protein supplement post-exercise. When intensity was increased by 10%, the CPK of Group I increased 25%, the CPK of Groups II and III decreased 15%, and the CPK of Group IV fell 23%. At the end of 6 weeks Group I differed significantly ($p < 0.05$) from Groups II, III, and IV. The combination of GE and protein supplement had the greatest effect in reducing CPK levels.

For our last study we monitored CPK and LDH over a 24 h period before and following a workout session. Eight world class swimmers participated in the final phase of the study (Fig. 3). Blood for control CPK and LDH measurements was obtained at 07:30 h. each Saturday, approximately 14 h after conclusion of the second Friday workout. A standard 2.5 h workout followed. The swimmers consumed 16 oz of water before and *ad lib* during the workout. Blood was drawn immediately after the workout, and again 3, 8 and 22 h after completion of the workout.

During the second week, the first week's workout was repeated, with the exception being 16 oz of GE was ingested immediately before the workout and *ad lib* during exercise. No supplement was given afterwards and the subjects' usual training table diet was consumed.

During the third week's workout session, similar in intensity, 16 oz of water was given both before and *ad lib* during the workout. Protein supplement (8 or 16 oz.) was given immediately after and again twice later in the day. The subjects' diet was otherwise unchanged.

The fourth study was performed as described for the previous three, except GE was ingested before and during exercise, and the protein supplement was ingested immediately afterward. In Fig. 3 it is apparent that CPK and LDH, measured immediately after the workout, rose far less when the GE solution was used than when water was ingested. It is also apparent that CPR and LDH fell more rapidly post-exercise when the protein supplement was used than when only the training table diet was ingested. Finally, the data show that when the GE solution and the protein supplement were both used, CPK and LDH were below control values 8 h after the workout ended, while during the control trial both enzymes were still significantly elevated at 8 h.

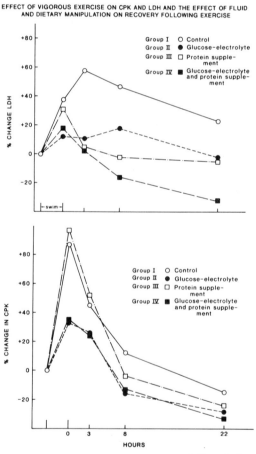

FIG. 3. Effect of vigorous exercise on CPK and LDH and the effect of fluid and dietary manipulatlon on recovery following exercise.

The data suggest that GE, ingested before and during exercise, limits muscle damage as assessed by changes in the concentration of CPK and LDH in plasma. This may be accomplished by maintaining perfusion of both skin and muscle, and attenuating the rise in body temperature (Hommen, 1985; Hommen et al., 1988). In addition, by maintaining availability of carbohydrate, it ameliorates catabolism of protein (Millward et al., 1982) during prolonged exercise. Thus, with less muscle damage, maximal muscle repair occurs before the next training session. Use of the protein supplement immediately after exercise supplies all of the essential amino acids which are catabolized during exercise, and thus allows muscle repair to proceed rapidly immediately after exercise. Use of a GE solution during exercise, and the protein supplement immediately after, both limits muscle damage and hastens repair to allow maximal recovery before the next training session. This allows the athlete to work harder without incurring cumulative damage. Improvement in training and performance is thereby accelerated.

References

Davies, C. T. M and White, M. J. (1981). Muscle weakness following eccentric work in man. *Pflugers Archiv*, 392,168-171.

Dohm, G. L., Kasparek, G. J., Tapscott, E, B and Barakat, H. A. (1985). Protein metabolism during endurance exercise. *Federal Proceedings*, 44, 348-352.

Hikida, R. S., Staron, R. S., Hagerman, F. C., Sherman, W. M and Costill, D. L. (1983). Muscle fiber necrosis associated with human marathon runners. *Journal of Neurological Science*, 95, 185-203.

Hommen, N. M. (1985). Effect of volume depletion on the thermoregulatory system during exercise. Masters Thesis presented to the University of Florida Graduate School, May.

Hommen, N. M., Cade, J. R., Privette, R. M. and Dippy, J.H. (1988). Effect of PO_4 and various fluid replacement regimen on blood volume, cardiac output, and endurance during bicycle exercise. Presented at the 1988 Annual Conference of the Southeast Chapter of the ACSM, January, 1988. Wake Forest University, Winston-Salem, NC.

Millward, D. J., Davies, C. T. M., Halliday, D., Wolman, S. L., Mathews, D. and Rennie M. (1982). Effect of exercise on protein metabolism in humans as explored with stable isotopes. *Federal Proceedings*, 41, 2688-2691.

Newham D.J, Jones D.A and Edwards R.H.T. (1983). Large delayed plasma creatine kinase changes after stopping exercise. *Muscle Nerve*, 6, 380-385.

Rennie, M. J., Halliday, D., Davies, C. T. M., Edwards, R. H. T., Krynawich, S., Millward, D. J. and Mathews, D.E. (1981). Exercise induced increase in leucine oxidation in man and the effect of glucose. *In* "Metabolism and Clinical Implication of Branch Chain Amino and Keto Acids". (Eds M. Walser, and J.

R. Williamson), pp. 361-366. Elsevier, North-Holland, New York.
Vaananan, H. K., Leppilampi, M., Vouri, J. and Takala, T. E. S. (1986). Liberation of muscle carbonic anhydrase into serum during extensive exercise. *Journal of Applied Physiology*, **61**, 561-564.

36. Description and Water Velocity Characteristics of a New Swimming Treadmill

L.J. D'ACQUISTO, J. TROUP and S. HOLMBERG

Introduction

IN PAST YEARS SWIMMING research has been oriented toward the understanding of a swimmer's functional capacity and movements in the water (Liljestrand and Stenström, 1919; Holmér, I. 1979). Astrand and Englesson (1972) have used a swimming treadmill (Flume) to quantify various physiological and kinesiological variables. Since the late 1960s, Denmark, the German Democratic Republic, the Soviet Union, Canada and Japan have utilized a swimming treadmill to study various aspects of swimming performance. Surprisingly, little information has appeared in the literature concerning the validity and reliability of the flume as a diagnostic tool for evaluating various physiological and biomechanical parameters of swimming. The intent of this paper is to provide a general description of a new flume which has recently been constructed in the United States. A second purpose is to describe water velocity characteristics of the swimming channel.

Description

An illustration of the flume is presented in Fig. 1. The outside dimensions are: length 22.9 m, width 4.9 m, height 10.0 m. The swimming channel is 5.2 m long, 2.4 m wide and 1.5 m deep. Water (180 000/l) is circulated by a centrifugal pump at the base of the flume, which is powered by a 250 horsepower motor. To streamline water flow a series of vanes and honeycomb structures have been placed at the front portion of the swimming channel. A special feature of the flume is a hypobaric chamber which allows the simulation of altitudes from zero-1828 m above sea level. For safety, a net has been fixed at the end of the channel. A stop and abort button stops water flow and depressurizes the chamber, respectively, in case of an emergency. Two large observation windows are located on each side of the channel with a smaller window located on the floor of the channel.

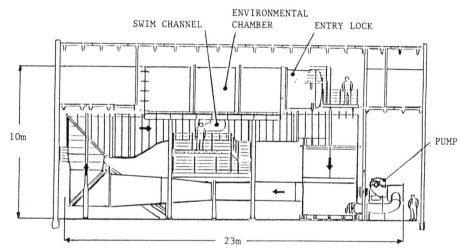

FIG. 1. Schematic illustration of swimming flume.

Flow characteristics

PROCEDURE

A turbine-flow meter was used to monitor water velocity at three different positions in the channel: front corner, back corner, and middle of the swimming channel. The question being addressed is: does water velocity at the front and back of the channel represent water velocity at the center of the channel where the swimming action occurs? This is of practical importance since the probe must either be placed at the front or back corner of the channel to monitor velocity while testing a swimmer. To evaluate the main effect of depth the following points were examined at each position: 0.15 m, 0.30 m, and 0.45 m below the water surface. The range of depths was felt to represent the major body of water that the swimmer's head, trunk and moving limbs would cover during testing.

A potentiometric dial on the control console was used to vary the power output of the motor. The following dial settings were chosen: 2.0, 4.0 and 6.0 (arbitrary units). Preliminary tests showed that these settings represented the range of velocities that are commonly observed in swimming, approximately 0.90, 1.30 and 1.70 m/sec.

To test the reliability of water velocity the following procedure was employed. The turbine was placed at the back corner of the channel at a depth of 0.30 m. The following dial settings were choosen, 2.0, 4.0, and 6.0. Measurements were conducted at two different times: morning (08:00 h, time 1) and afternoon (17:00 h, time 2). For each dial setting and time ten observations of velocity were noted. Each observation consisted of averaging ten velocity measurements (6 sec update of velocity on the digital display).

Statistical analysis

A 3-way Analysis of Variance was performed to examine the main effect of depth, position and dial setting and also to explore interaction between position and setting, and between position and depth. An alpha level of 0.05 was set *apriori*. If significance was noted a Tukey's multiple comparison test was used to find where the significance existed. A Student t-test was used to find any significant difference between time 1 and time 2 measurements of the reliability test ($p < 0.05$).

Results/discussion

The main finding suggests that there is no difference in velocity between the back and center, and between the front and center of the swimming channel, 1.51 m/s vs 1.48 m/s and 1.47 m/s vs 1.48 m/s, respectively ($p < 0.05$). Consequently, the turbine-flow meter can either be placed at the front or back of the swimming channel. No main effect of depth was noted, indicating that water velocity, at a given dial setting, is not statistically different between the tested depths. No significant interaction was found between position and setting, and position and depth. No difference in velocity at the three different dial settings (2, 4, and 6) between time 1 and time 2 was found (Table 1), suggesting within day reproducibility for the velocities tested.

TABLE 1. *Reliability tests for water velocity measurements.*

	Morning			Afternoon		
Dial Setting	2	4	6	2	4	6
Mean	0.91	1.30	1.68	0.90	1.291	0.68
S.D.	0.01	0.02	0.01	0.01	0.02	0.01

The design of the Flume at the International Center for Aquatic Research permits for laminar water flow for velocities ranging from 0.4 to 2.2 m/s with an accuracy of 0.02 m/s. The ability to streamline water flow eliminates turbulence as a confounding variable in both physiological and biomechanical measurements. The viewing windows provide a unique opportunity for the coach and scientist to view the swimmer's movements as they occur below the surface of the water. Furthermore, video cameras have been placed at the bottom of the swimming channel. The swimmer's movements are videotaped and analyzed through standard biomechanical procedures. Future research will focus on exploring those physiological and biomechanical factors which contribute to poor and superior swimming performance.

References

Åstrand, P-O, and S. Englesson. (1972). A Swimming Flume. *Journal of Applied Physiology*, **33**, (4) 514.
Holmér, I. (1979). Physiology of swimming man. *Exercise and Sport Sciences Reviews*. **7**, 87-23. The Franklin Institute Press.
Liljestrand, G. and Stenström, N. (1919). Studien über die Physiologie des Schwimmens. *Skandinavisches Archiv für Physiologie,* **39**, 1-63.

37. Swimming Skill and Stroking Characteristics of Front Crawl Swimmers

J. C. CHATARD, C. COLLOMP, E. MAGLISCHO and C. MAGLISCHO

Introduction

THE PERFORMANCE OVER A 368 METER SWIM, $\dot{V}O_2$ max, stroke pulling pattern and anthropometric data of nine male competitive freestylers were studied to identify aspects of swimming techniques which allow a swimmer to be "more skilled" than another. Performance was mainly related to $\dot{V}O_2$ max, r= 0.80, the incorporation of the hydrostatic lift increased the correlation coefficient to 0.87 at the second stepwise regression. The real performance was compared to the theoretical performance obtained from the results of the stepwise regression. The group of four swimmers whose real performance was higher than that calculated by the regression equation was considered "skilled", when compared to the other group ("less-skilled"). "Skilled" swimmers were characterized by a higher stroke frequency and superposition of both arm actions, a shorter stroke length, downsweep phase and longer upsweep phase. Those two phases were linked together, r = -0.88, $p <$ 0.01, but not related to stroke rate. Entry phase and depth of stroke pattern were related to hydrostatic lift, r = 0.79 and 0.77 respectively, $p < 0.01$. However, there was no relationship between stroke length and anthropometric data. These findings demonstrate the importance of stroke technique on the energy cost of competitive swimming. They also demonstrate that stroke patterns depend, upon technical, economical and anthropometric criteria.

Performance in swimming is governed by the maximal energy output and technical ability. Many authors have found a high correlation between VO_2 max and performance over 400 yards or meters (Montpetit, 1983; Nomura, 1983; Chatard et al., 1985; Costill et al., 1985). Pendergast et al. (1977) showed that swimming economy (SE), i.e. the energy cost to move the body at a given velocity, was a good quantitative measure of technical ability. Van Handel et al. (1988) demonstrated that SE is a prerequisite for success in swimming performance. Thus, the measurement of SE provides a useful means for evaluating the development of swimming technique and of comparing different swimmers with each other. However, the interpretation of SE is not easy because there are many interacting factors. The relative importance of the leg kick (two or six beats) influences the whole SE stroke (Holmér, 1974). Factors related to the swimmer's growth, such as body height and weight increase SE (Montpetit et al., 1983; Chatard et al., 1985) whereas buoyancy decreases it (Pendergast et al., 1977; Chatard et al., 1985; Costill et al., 1985; Montpetit et al., 1988). Costill et al. (1987) have found a link between swimming economy and swimming biomechanics in breaststroke. In freestyle, the arm technique of elite middle distance swimmers has be shown to vary considerably (Schleihauf et al., 1986; Maglischo et al., 1988). However the question whether one style is more efficient than another stlll remains unanswered.

The present study was designed to examine relationships between the swimmers' biomechanical arm pulling pattern and technical ability. In this comparison specific attention was given to anthropometric varia- tions among swimmers. The secondary purpose was to observe whether in freestyle swimming the evaluation of the technlcal ability of the swimmers by the coaches concorded with metabolic and anthropometric analysis.

Materials and methods

The study was conducted in two parts.

Part I was designed to separate nine male competitive freestylers, using a six-beat leg kick, into "skilled" and "less-skilled" groups. The subjects, 21 + 1.9 years old, swam in division 11 of the United States of America, and trained on average 2.5 h, 6-8 km daily. Their best 460-m performance realized in competition was 1.58 ± 0.10 m.s^{-1} They participated in the study on a voluntary basis. Their main characteristics are summarized in Table 1.

Part II examines selected biomechanical aspects of swimming in order to characterize differences between the two groups selected in Part I.

TABLE 1. *Individual and group means, SD values, statistical significance for the main characteristics of the nine swimmers velocity measured during the 360 m test (V), 460 m competition (Vcp) and calculated from the regression equation (Vth), hydrostatic lift (HL), height (H), arm span (AS).*

	n-	V m.s^{-1}	Vcp m.s^{-1}	AGE years	$\dot{V}O_2$Max l.min^{-1}	HL kg	H cm	AS cm	Vth m.s^{-1}
'SK'	1	1.4	1.53	22	4	3.1	173	171.5	1.39
Group	2	1.49	1.53	20	4	0.9	183	190.6	1.44
	3	1.52	1.69	22	4.2	0.3	180	183.3	1.5
	4	1.57	1.68	23	4.8	4	181	187.7	1.52
	X	1.5	1.61	22	4.25	2.1	179	183	1.46
	SD	0.07	0.09	1.3	0.38	1.8	4	8	0.06
'L-SK'	5	1.53	1.67	19	4.9	3.5	188	197	1.55
Group	6	1.56	1.65	21	4.8	1.3	167	176.5	1.58
	7	1.35	1.43	25	3.9	1.8	178	1 86	1.41
	8	1.49	1.5	19	4.4	2.3	185	190.5	1.49
	9	1.47	1.52	21	4.5	2.3	183	193.5	1.5
	X	1.48	1.55	21	4.5	2.2	180	189	1.51
	SD	0.08	0.1	2.4	0.39	0.8	8	8	0.07
TOTAL	X	1.49	1.61	21	4.4	2.2	180	186.3	1.49
	SD	0.07	0.09	1.9	0.4	1.2	6	8.1	0.06
	p	NS	NS	NS	NS	NS	NS	NS	NS

PART I

After measurements of standing height (H) and arm span (AS), buoyancy was evaluated by the hydrostatic lift (HL). HL is the maximal weight just necessary to maintain the swimmer in a balanced position under the water. HL was measured at the end of maximal inspiration. This method was reliable (r = 0.98 for eight swimmers) and easy to apply. Maximum oxygen uptake ($\dot{V}O_2$ max, 1.min^{-1}) was measured from the expired air collected during 20 sec after the completion of a maximal 368 m front crawl swim. The method has been described elsewhere (Montpetit *et al.*, 1981; Nomura, 1983; Daly *et al.*, 1988). Water temperature was 26-26.5°C. Swimmers were free of equipment. Expired gases were collected in a Douglas bag using a Daniels breathing valve. Oxygen and carbon dioxide fractions were determined using Beckman OM 11 and LB 2 gas analyzers, which were calibrated with gases of known concentrations. Volumes were measured in a Tissot spirometer.

Stepwise regressions were computed from performance and anthropometric data. The real performance was compared to the theoretical performance obtained from the results of the stepwise regression. The group of swimmers whose real performance was higher than that calculated by the regression equation was considered "skilled" (SK), when compared to the other group who swam slower. Thus, the second group was defined "less-skilled" (L-SK). It must be emphasized that this method may not be completely justified. Unfortunately, there was no time planned for estimating swimming economy also from a constant swimming velocity for all subjects. Therefore, separation of the swimmers in two groups by regression analysis was considered as a first attempt to assess the relative technical ability of a group of swimmers swimming at their maximal velocity.

PART II

The nine swimmers were filmed during the 368 m swim. The video camera, operated at 30 frames.s^{-1} was fixed at 9 m and pendicular to the direction of swimming in a coach scope at approximately 20 cm underwater. The video camera recorded the lateral view of at least one complete arm cycle. A yardstick was used as reference for distance measurements and it was placed on the bottom of the swimming pool 1.2 m deep. The arm movement of the swimmers and the yardstick could always be seen simultaneously in the same video frame. Stroke patterns for both hands were determined from the frame analysis recorded between the 250th to the 273rd meter. The duration of the five phases (entry, downsweep, insweep, outsweep and upsweep) was calculated in milliseconds and corresponded to the sum of the left and right arm phases for one cycle (Montpetit et al., 1983) (Fig. 1). Because of the lateral view the exact beginning and end of the insweep was somewhat difficult to evaluate and a careful observation of the hand and elbow orientation was done both from frame-by-frame and slow motion analysis. Swimmers were instructed to keep as constant a pace as possible. The pace was checked by an outdoor camera which filmed the swimmers during all the 368 m swim. Stroke rate (SR) was expressed as the number of complete arm cycles per minute. It was measured for each 45 m. The mean SR was compared to SR measured between the 250th to the 273rd meter. When they differed by more than one cycle per minute the test was repeated another day. This was necessary in two cases only. Stroke length (SL, m.cycle^{-1}) was calculated from SR and swimming speed (V). Most of the time, when one hand began the entry phase, the other was finishing the outsweep or upsweep phase. The time when the two arms could be seen together was calculated and called superposition (SP) of both arm actions. It was expressed in percentage of one cycle. Mean pulling length (PL) and depth (PD) of left and right hand patterns were calculated (Schleihauf *et al.*, 1986), (Fig. 1).

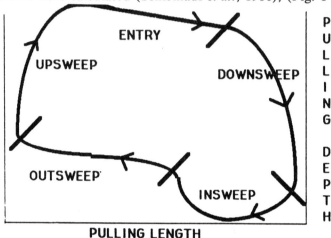

FIG. 1. Conventions used in the definitions of pulling length and depth and stroke phases viewed from the side.

The three usual coaches of the team were required to evaluate the swimmers' apparent technical ability and to divide swimmers into two groups (four skilled and five less-skilled). The two groups were then compared with the first classification established by regression analysis.

Statistical analysis
Means and standard deviations were computed for all variables. Anova comparisons were used to test for significant differences between the two groups (SK and L-SK). Pearson "r" correlation coefficients were calculated between performances, $\dot{V}O_2$ max and anthropometric data and between anthropometric data and stroking characteristics. Because of the low number of subjects, Spearman "r^1" correlation coefficients were also calculated. Multiple and stepwise regressions were used between performance, anthropometric data, stroke rate and stroke length,assuming the variables to be normally distributed. Stat View

512+ and Cricket Graph programs were used. In all statistical analyses, the 0.05 level of significance was taken. In the stepwise regression only the variables which added significantly to prediction, $p < 0.05$, were included in the final regression equation. Thus, coefficient values of all these variables were calculated and related to their standard error of estimate (SEE) to calculate the critical "p" values.

Results

PART I

The mean 368 m performance was swum at 94% of the 460 m performed in competition. The first stepwise regression between performance, VO_2 max and anthropometric factors indicated that the performance was mainly related to $\dot{V}O_2$ max ($r = 0.80$, $p < 0.0\,1$, $r^1 = 0.79$, $p < 0.02$). Inclusion of a second variable, HL, improved the accuracy of the regression up to 0.87, ($p < 0.02$), resulting in the following equation 1:

$$y = 0.\,183\ VO_2 - 0.023\ HL + 0.733$$
$$SEE = 0.043\ 0.009$$
$$p < 0.0\,1\ 0.02$$

The theoretical performance calculated from equation 1 was compared to the real performance. The four swimmers who swam faster than predicted by the equation, were considered as "skilled" compared to the five others who were defined as "less skilled". There was no statistical difference between the two groups with regard to performance realised during the test or in competition, height, arm span, hydrostatic lift and V_2 max, (Table 1), whereas biomechanical differences were found (Part II).

PART II

The results of biomechanical measurements are presented in Table 2. The duration of each phase was very different from one swimmer to another varying up to four times for entry and outsweep phases and to twice the time for downsweep, insweep and upsweep phases. Stroke rate appeared to strongly influence the relationship found in equation 1 between the performance, $\dot{V}O_2$ max and HL. It improved the accuracy of the regression up to 0.96, $p < 0.02$, but slightly better than SL ($r = 0.93$). Inclusion of SR in the regression analysis resulted in the following equation 2:

$y = 0.16\ \dot{V}O_2 - 0.027HL + 0.006\ SR + 0.541$
$SEE = 0.029\ 0.009\ 0.002$
$p < 0.01\quad 0.02\quad 0.02$

SR was negatively related to SL (r= 0.90, $p < 0.01$, $r^1 = 0.91$, $p < 0.01$). "Skilled" swimmers were characterized by higher SR (50.4 ± 4.2 vs 44 ± 3.5 cycles per minute, $p < 0.04$) and superposition of both arm actions (56–7.1vs 40.6 ± 11.3%, $p < 0.05$).They were also characterised by shorter SL (1.79 ± 0.14 vs 2.12 ± 0.08 m.cycle-1, $p < 0.01$), downsweep phase, (0.483 ± 0.114 vs 0.667 ± 0.124 ms, $p < 0.05$), longer upsweep phase (0.366 ± 0.086 vs 0.253 ± 0.056 ms, $p < 0.05$). These two phases were correlated to each other (r= -0.88, $p < 0.01$, $r^1 = -0.89$, $p < 0.01$) (Fig. 2), but not with SR (r = -0.44 and + 0.48, significant level= 0.63).

TABLE 2. *Individual and group means, ± SD values, statistical significance for the biomechanical measurements, superposition (SP) of both arm actions, pulling length (PL) and depth (PD), stroke rate (SR) and length (SL).*

	No	Entry ms	Down ms	In ms	Out ms	Up ms	SP %.c^{-1}	PL cm	PD cm	SR c.min^{-1}	SL m.c^{-1}
'SK'	1	266	534	466	266	266	50	58.4	68.6	49.5	1.7
group	2	400	600	333	266	333	50	69.1	56.9	45	1.99
	3	534	333	400	266	466	63	81.7	43	52.1	1.75
	4	266	466	333	266	400	61	74.3	68.5	55	1.71
	X	367	483	383	266	367	56	70.9	59.3	50.4	1.79
	SD	128	114	64	0	86	7.1	9.8	12.1	4.2	0.14
'L-SK'	5	133	734	266	466	266	50	66.5	68.8	47.1	1.95
group	6	333	734	400	133	200	50	65	49.6	45	2.08
	7	266	534	400	534	333	23	53.4	62.9	38.1	2.13
	8	266	534	466	266	266	36	57.3	60.6	45	1.99
	9	400	800	400	266	200	45	94.1	77.7	45	1.96
	X	280	667	387	333	253	40.6	67.3	63.9	44	2.02
	SD	99	125	73	163	56	11.3	15.9	10.4	3.5	0.08
Total	X	319	585	385	304	304	20	68.9	61.8	46.9	1.91
	SD	114	148	65	121	89	3.7	12.9	10.7	4.9	0.16
	p	NS	0.05	NS	NS	0.05	0.05	NS	NS	0.04	0.01

Some biomechanical measurements were related to anthropometric data. Entry phase and depth of stroke pattern were related to hydrostatic lift (r = -0.79 and 0.77 respectively, $p < 0.01$, $r^1 = -0.78$ and 0.78, p

<0.02) (Figs 3 and 4). However, there was no relationship between SL and anthropometric data.

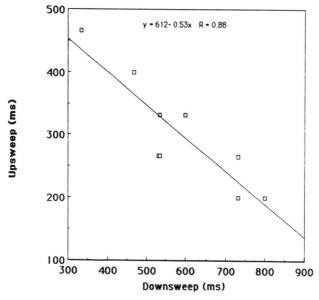

FIG. 2. Relationship between the duration of the up and downsweep phases, expressed in milliseconds.

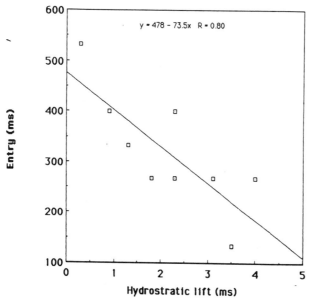

FIG. 3. Relationship between hydrostatic lift and the duration of the entry phase expressed in milliseconds.

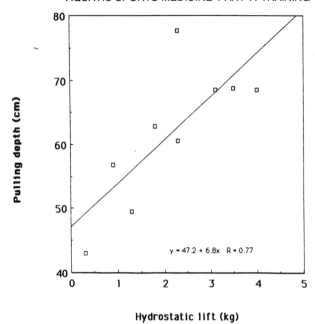

Hydrostatic lift (kg)

FIG. 4. Relationship between hydrostatic lift and depth of stroke pattern.

The technical classificatlon established by coaches concorded for seven swimmers among nine. For coaches, the "skilled" group was characterized by higher performances during the test (1.54 ± 0.04 vs 1.45 ± 0.07 m.s-1, $p < 0.06$) or in competition (1.67 ± 0.02 s 1.50 ± 0.04 m.s^{-1}, $p < 0.0$ 1) and superposition of both arm actions ($56 \pm 7\%$ vs $41 \pm 11\%$, $p < 0.04$). Others comparison values were close to the first classification but not statistically significant: SR (49.3 ± 5.1 vs 44.9 ± 4.3 cycles per minute), SL (1.88 ± 0.18 vs 1.94 ± 0.16 m.cycle^{-1}) downsweep phase, (0.533 ± 0.172 vs 0.627 ± 0.130 ms) upsweep phase (0.350 ± 0.1 10 vs 0.266 ± 0.044 ms).

Discussion

The major finding of the present study was that $\dot{V}O_2$ max was the best indicator of the swimming performance explaining 64% of the variance. It confirms many other studies (Montpetit *et al.*, 1983; Nomura, 1983; Chatard *et al.*, 1985; Costill *et al.*, 1985) where the correlation coefficient between $\dot{V}O_2$ max and performance varied from 0.47 to 0.86 (Table 3). Although these studies demonstrated the strong relationship between performance and $\dot{V}O_2$ max, they also showed a great variation in $\dot{V}O_2$

max for a given performance. This variation depended on the practice level of the swimmers (Montpetit *et al.*, 1983; Nomura, 1983; Costill *et al.*, 1985). For elite or college swimmers (Montpetit *et al.*, 1983; Costill *et al.*, 1985), the variation was twice to six times less than for younger potential swimmers (Nomura, 1983) (Table 4). This variation depended also on the anthropometric differences in height, weight, arm span (Grimston and Hay, 1986; Daly *et al.*, 1988; Huijing *et al.*, 1988; Montpetit *et al.*, 1988) and buoyancy (Montpetit *et al.*, 1983; Costill *et al.*, 1987). In the present study, buoyancy accounted for 10% of the variance of the performance, thus confirming earlier findings (Montpetit *et al.*, 1983; Costill *et al.*, 1987). However, height and arm span were not related to the performance, thereby contradicting previous observations (Grimston and Hay, 1986; Daly *et al.*, 1988; Huijing *et al.*, 1988; Montpetit *et al.*, 1988). This may be due to the difference in the swimmers' growth. In most of the studied populations, growth and maturation has a relationship with VO_2 max, whereas in this study there was no relationship between height and VO_2 max, ($r = 0.10$). Another reason is the smaller range of anthropometric values in the present study in which the subjects were more homogeneous.

TABLE 3. *Extreme values of performances, $m.s.^{-1}$, $\dot{V}O_2$ max, $1.min^{-1}$ and correlation between performance and $\dot{V}O_2$ max of male competitive swimmers studied by different authors.*

Authors	Number of swimmers	Performance Mini	Maxi	$\dot{V}O_2$ Max Mini	Maxi	Correlation Coefficient
Monpetit *et al.*, 1983	39	0.9	1.5	1.9	5	0.86
Nomura 1983	36	1.3	1.6	2	4.5	0.75
Costill *et al.*, 1985	25	1	1.4	2	5	0.47
Present Study	9	1.35	1.57	3.9	4.9	0.80

An important finding of this study was that the swimmer classification established by coaches was close to the first classification. However, in their classification the "skilled" group swam faster than the "less-skilled" group. Thus the coaches tend, perhaps, to judge skill also from the speed. However, after knowing the results of the regression classification, coaches agreed with the rationale for dividing into groups. In this study, SR was a better indicator of swimming technique than SL because it explained a greater part of the variability of the swimming performance (14% vs 10%). In other studies, SL has been preferred as the general indicator of swimming technique (Craig and Pendergast, 1979; Costill et al., 1985; Grimston and Hay, 1986). Costill et al. (1987) demonstrated that SL was the best single independent predictor of performance with r = 0.88. Although the stroke index (SI = SL*V) increased the correlation between performance and $\dot{V}O_2$ max up to 0.97, he specified that SI could not be considered as an independent predictor because the derivation of SI included speed.

TABLE 4. *Extreme values and variations in percentage of $\dot{V}O_2$ max (1.min⁻¹) of male competitive swimmers studied by different authors at the given speed of 1.4ms⁻¹.*

Authors	$\dot{V}O_2$ max Mini	Maxi	Variation percentage	Category
Montpetit et al., 1983	4.2	5.0	19	Elite
Nomura, 1983	2.5	4.5	80	Potential
Costill et al., 1985	4.4	5.1	16	Elite
Present Study	3.7	4.2	14	Elite

Stroke pattern varies to a large extent from one swimmer to another. Almost all combinations are possible in the relative duration of the entry, downsweep, insweep, outsweep and upsweep (Schleihauf et al., 1986; Maglischo et al., 1988). However, this study demonstrated that these phases are not due to chance. They are related to anthropometric, technical and stroke rate criteria. Both entry and depth of the stroke pattern were related to hydrostatic lift. Downsweep phase was inversely related to the upsweep phase. The outsweep phase was found to be the one which varies the most. Maglischo et al. (1988) thought that the swimmers tend to favor either lateral (with longer in and outsweep phases) or vertical stroking motion. The latter is characterized by shorter in and outsweep phases. Furthermore, Maglischo et al. (1988) and Schleihauf et al. (1986) have shown that the upsweep phase often was the phase where elite swimmers generated their maximal peak force. Thus, the longer duration of this phase as well as the higher superposition of both arm actions could explain a better swimming efficiency.

In summary, this study demonstrates the importance of stroke technique in the variations of the energy cost of the performance during competitive swimming. It also demonstrates that stroke pattern depends on individual's anthropometric data, technique and swimming economy.

It is therefore suggested that further efforts should be made to evaluate swimming economy during various levels including constant swimming speeds.

References

Chatard, J.C., Padilla, S., Cazorla, G. and Lacour J.R. (1985). Influence of body height, weight, hydrostatic lift and training on the energy cost of the front crawl. *New Zealand Journal of Sports Medicine, 13*, (3), 82-84.

Costill, D.L., Kovaliski, J., Porter, D., Fielding R. and King, D.(1985). Energy expenditure during front crawl swimmmg predicting success in middle distance events. *International Journal of Sports Medicine, 6,* 266-270.

Costill, D.L., Lee, G. and d'Alquisto, L. (1987). Video- computer assisted analysis of swimmlng technnique. *Journal of Swimming Research, 3*, (2), 5-9.

Craig, B.A. and Pendergast, D.R. (1979). Relationships of stroke rate, distance per stroke and velocity in competitive swimming. *Medical Science of Sports and Exercise, 11*, 278-283.

Daly, D., Persyn, U., van Tilborgh, L. and Riemaker, D. (1988). Estimation of sprint performances in the breaststoke from body characteristics. *In* "Swimming Science V". (Eds B.E. Ungerechts, K.Wilke and K. Reischle), pp. 101-108. Human Kinetics, Champain.

Grimston, S.K. and Hay, J.G. (1986). Relationships among anthropometric and stroking characteristics of college swlmmers. *Medical Science of Sports Exercise, 18*, 160-68.

Holmér, 1.(1974). Physiology of swimming man. *Acta Physiologica Scandinavica,* Suppl. 407.

Huijing, P.A., Toussaint, H., Mackay, R., Vervoorn, K., Clarys, J.P., G. de Groot. and Hollander, A.P. (1988). Active drag related to body dimensions. *In* "Swimming Science V". (Eds B.E. Ungerechts, K. Wilke and K. Reischle). pp. 31-38. Champain.

Lavoie, J.M., Léger, L.A, Montpetit, R.R. and Chabot, S. (1983). Backward extrapolation of VO_2 from the O_2 recovery curve after a voluntary maximal 400m swim. *In* "Biomechanics and Medicine in Swimming". (Eds Hollander A.P. and P.A.Huijing, and G. de Groot), pp. 222-227. Champain.

Maglischo, E.W. (1982). "Swimming Faster". p. 53. Mayfield Publishing Co, Palo Alto.

Maglischo, C.W., Maglischo, E.W., Higgins, J., Hinricks, R., Luedtke, D., Schleihauf, R.E. and Thayer, A. (1988). A biomechanical analysis of the U.S. Olympic freestyle distance swimmers. *In* "Swimmlng Science V". (Eds B.E. Ungerechts, K.Wilke and K. Reischle), pp. 351-359. Champain.

Montpetit, R., Léger, L.A., Lavoie, J.M. and Cazorla, G. (1981). $\dot{V}O_2$ peak during free swimming using the backward extrapolation of the O_2 recovery curve. *European Journal of Applied Physiology, 47*, 385-391.

Montpetit, R., Lavoie, J.M. and Cazorla, G. (1983). Aerobic energy cost of the front crawl at high velocity in International class and adolescent swimmers. *In*

"Biomechanics and Medicine in Swimming". (Eds A.P. Hollander, P.A. Huijing, and G. de Groot). pp. 228-234. Champain.

Montpetit, R., Cazorla, G. and Lavole, J.M. (1988). Energy expenditure during front crawl swimming: a comparison between males and females. *Human Kinetics*, **18**, 229-236.

Nomura, T. (1983). The influence of training and age on $\dot{V}O_2$ during swimming in Japanese elite age group and Olympic swimmers. *In* "Biomechanics and Medicine in Swimming". (Eds A. P. Hollander, P.A. Huijing, and G. de Groot), pp. 251-257, Champain.

Pendergast, D.R., di Prampero, P.E., Craig, A.B., Wilson, D.R. and Rennie, D.W. (1977). Quantitative analysis of the front crawl in men and women. *Journal of Applied Physiology*, **43**, 475-479.

Schleihauf, R.E., Higgins, J., Hinricks, R., Luedtke, D., Maglischo, C.W., Maglischo, E.W. and Thayer, A. (1986). Models of aquatic skill sprint front crawlstroke. *New Zealand Journal on Sports Medicine*, **14**, (1), 7-12.

Van Handel, P.J., Katz, A., Troup, J.P. and Bradley, P.W. (1988). Aerobic economy and competitive performance of U.S. elite swimmers. *In* "Swimming Science V". (Eds B.E. Ungerechts, K. Wilbe and K. Reischle), pp. 219-220. Champain.

38. Training, Stress and Reverse T₃

A.W. GOODE and J.S. ORR

A FUNDAMENTAL PROBLEM facing doctors, coaches and indeed competition swimmers themselves is the understanding and management of progressive deterioration in performance. In some swimmers this may be simply diagnosed and managed as damage to a body mechanism be it joint, tendon or muscle. However, a significant number of swimmers and those associated with day to day training is aware that, in the absence of specific damage, performance may decline: indeed anecdotally the problem seems to be increasing with higher competitive standards to be achieved. Such a decrement and its diagnosis may be associated with insidious infection either bacterial or viral. There is, however, a remaining group that has no obvious stigmata except declining performance and it is to that group that the described studies may be of diagnostic value.

In athletes with a failing performance in the absence of disease or injury it remains uncertain as to whether they are stressed because of a physical cause related to over training or psychologically stressed because of attendant competitive pressures. The distinction is of importance as the first is more open to cure allowing a return to previous competitive achievements, whereas the management of the latter may be protracted and complicated.

Rapid progress in technology since 1970 has resulted in significant revision of our knowledge of thyroid physiology. The thyroid hormones thyroxine (T$_4$) and triiodothyronine (T$_3$) have been extensively studied. In normal man all of T$_4$ comes from thyroid secretion and under steady state conditions 70-90 µg of T$_4$ are secreted and disposed of each day. By contrast T$_3$ production from the thyroid is only 12-20% of the total production of a daily turn over of 26-30 µg/day while at least 80 per cent of the remainder is derived from T$_4$ through loss of one iodine atom from the molecule by monodeiodination in peripheral tissues Pitman et al. (1971). The calorogenic activity of thyroid secretion is principally exerted by T$_3$ being three to five times more potent in regulating body energy metabolism than T$_4$. Recent studies have however identified a third thyroid hormone-reverse T$_3$ (Chopra, 1974). Approximately 95% of this hormone is produced in the peripheral tissues by monodeiodination of T$_4$ but with loss of the opposite iodine atom to that occurring in T$_3$. Thus an almost identical molecule is produced but reverse T$_3$ has one important characteristic: it is essentially devoid of activity in complete contrast to the particularly active T$_3$ molecule. The turnover rate in the plasma of reverse T$_3$ has not been established and the plasma concentration is in the range 20-60 µg/100ml.

Thyroid hormones are distributed in all body tissues and the free unbound form is assumed to be in equilibrium with the unbound form in tissue cells, liver, kidney and skeletal muscle. The administration of small quantities of thyroid hormone is associated with tissue synthesis but in larger quantities it is a stimulus to tissue breakdown and energy release and increased activity and stimulation. Since T$_3$ is the most active and potent hormone, this is the principal effect on mechanism for the well known changes associated with thyroid hormones. However, it has become apparent that in situations of chronic stress which is known to involve a thyroid hormone response there is a change in the peripheral tissue thyroid hormone production converting T$_4$ away from the particularly active T$_3$ to the inactive form, reverse T$_3$. This differential production is found in several conditions, in neonates, old age, hepatic cirrhosis, renal failure, starvation and wasting, the use of steroids in acute and chronic systemic disease (Carter *et al.*, 1975) and following surgical procedures (Goode *et al.*, 1981).

Organic stress, as opposed to psychological stress, has been most thoroughly investigated in previously fit post-operative surgical patients. Among many factors, the thyroid gland may play a considerable role in the response to stress. Our studies of such patients have shown that in the post-operative period the peripheral metabolism of the hormone thyroxine (T_4) including monodeiodination is disturbed in skeletal muscle and there is a diminution in the production of the hormone T_3 in favour of the negative component reverse T_3. Further studies have shown the organically stressed post-operative surgical patient to be unique. A means of discriminating between the organic stress of surgery and the other clinical causes of reverse T_3 production is that a carbohydrate load will abolish reverse T_3 production in disease or starvation conditions but it is not able to alter reserve T_3 production which is relentless in the organically stressed subject.

Consider the swimmer in the absence of organic disease with a deteriorating performance. If one cause is a progressive organic or excessive physical stress then the post-operative situation may be analogous and of value. Measurement of serum T_3 and reverse T_3 in an organically stressed athlete rested for an hour may show levels of both hormones. Excessive reverse T_3 levels as a manifestation of starvation, disease or psychological stress may be abolished by carbohydrate ingestion. In complete contrast, organic stress may not result in such a change after carbohydrate ingestion. The management could then consist of limiting and adapting the training regime to ameliorate the stress condition.

Thus our preliminary studies of post operative organic stress suggest that studies of athletic subjects subject to deteriorating performance be carried out to test this hypothesis. If confirmed this may indicate the possible role of measuring and using reverse T_3 levels of production as a clinical aid to optimal training.

References

Carter, J.N. Corcoran, J.M. and Eastman, C.J. (1975). Effect of severe chronic illness on thyroid function. *Lancet*, 2.

Chopra, I. (1974). A radioimmunoassay for the measurement of reverse T_3. *Journal of Clinical Investigation*, **54**, 583-590.

Goode, A.W., Orr, J.S., Radcliffe, W.A. and Dudlevy, H.A.F. (1981). The effect of surgery with carbohydrate infusion on circulating T$_3$ and reverse T$_3$. *Annals of the Royal College of Surgeons England*, **63**, 168-172.

Pitman, C.J., Chambers, T.B. and Reed, V.H. (1971). The extrathyroidal conversion rate of thyroxine to triiodothyronine in normal man. *Journal of Clinical Investigation*, **50**, 1187-1196.

Part 8
Water polo

39. Medical Aspects of Water Polo

Ä. BODNÁR and G. PAVLIK

ONE PAPER CANNOT cover all the medical aspects of water polo.

Why? Water polo is a game for different ages groups, both men and women, from 10 to 70 years of age.

Figure 1 puts it in the centre of the different medical concerns. It is related to the clinical and theoretical medical sciences, sport sociology,

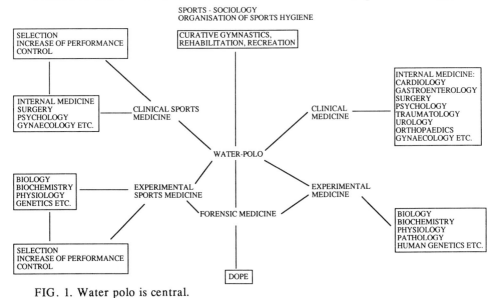

FIG. 1. Water polo is central.

coordination of sport. Three elements are of concern to participants (players, trainers, and the public) in water polo: selection, increase of achievement, and control.

In discussing these requirements, (not peculiar to water polo) I would like to emphasize the medical aspects of the game. The characteristic features of water polo are: it is in the water and it is a team game.

A good water polo player should be well equipped: morphologically, psychically, functionally.

Morphological characteristics

1   Height is essential, but not the most important factor. So many times one has heard that "the water reaches to everybody's neck."

2   The function of specific gravity is different. A light specific gravity enables a competitor to emerge from the water easily with equal muscular power. In the case of equal bodies the physical performance of body is more when the active body-mass is greater. According to Archimedes' principle of specific gravity, the body weight in water can be calculated. We can use the thickness of the skinplica for calculating the fat content of body. A caliper can measure the fat-thickness of body at 22 points and the fat content can be read out. For each sportsman, or water polo player, there is an optimal ratio between the content and active body-mass. The value of the body-mass is the so-called competition weight. Among water polo players in the past, the wet conditions, the heat economy and the thickened subcutaneous fat were well studied. The rules of FINA and LEN standardize the water temperature between 24-26°C. I will deal with the heat economy along with the functional aspects.

Psychological chacteristics

Important in a group game are:

attention to personal concerns; group disciplines; group-mentality; tactical maturity; concentration and knowing the limits of ones individual ability.

Psychological strength can be raised by physical and psychical training.

Functional characteristics

The heat produced by physical work is dispersed easily in 24-26°C water temperature. There is no "high" warming up. Exhaustion arises later on. The circulation-equilibrium is different, the skin vessels do not dilate, but constrict and the characteristic point of the sportsman is that, the armpower and thus the produced weight, the horizontal body-position is accompanied with an increase of peripheral resistance; this brings a increase in blood-pressure. The water resistance decreases the amplitude of movement in water. The water decreases the possibilities of injuries.

From the functional point of view the player needs:

power; speed; performance; endurance.

These can be developed individually; for the sportsman the optimal mix is needed.

The performance itself is generally connected with the muscular work. Approximately 40-45 % of the human body is built up of striated muscle.

Each human activity means some muscle work. The neuroendocrine organizing system regulates muscle work between the two extremes of performance – from total rest to maximum activity, from oxygen uptake to the changes of fluid-electrolyte and energy.

Recent research has divided muscle fibres into two main groups, according to their histochemical, biochemical and physiological characters:

Type I. Slow fibres: these are highly oxidized with low glycolytical activity.

Type II. Rapid fibres with low oxidation and high glycolitical activity. The second type is again divided into more subgroups, according to their ATP-activity.

According to the quantity and quality of load/work-training, changes go into the muscle fibres; the results of these are:

hyperthrophy or atrophy; increase or decrease of the capacity of metabolizing, and tiredness; the change of concentration and relaxation time.

The number of simultaneously activated rapid and slow fibres changes due to the intensity and duration of vegetative work. Rapid work brings changes in the rapid fibres (anaerobic energy) and in the case of slow work the changes go on into the slow fibres (aerobic energy).

The so-called "cross-innervation" experiments prove that, in the case of genetically determined fibres, the command of the nervous system prevails. The performance of human musculature can be increased with training from the view points of speed, endurance and strength.

Experiments with fibres prove that the speed increase of the fibres is most difficult to achieve; speediness is genetically determined.

Endurance has an effect on the performance. The object is to gain energy.

Energy gaining of muscles goes on the three-stairs theory. The fusion of high energy content /macroerg/

ATP – into ADP and phosphor;
ATP resynthesis from creatinin phosphate;
and the glycolysis.

The above mentioned processes are anaerobic. Beside the carbohydrates, the fats and the protein are also of high significance. They participate in the assurance of the muscle work energy needed. It is important to fill up the glycogen stores of muscle glycogenesis, glyconeogenesis. The muscle glycogen is able to move most rapidly and effectively. The restorative processes in the muscle go on under aerobic conditions. In water polo both the factors have their own roles. The processes are dependent on the oxygen circulation.

The oxygen circulation and oxygen uptake determine the capacity of the lung respiratory movement, transportation, cardiovascular system, usage, muscle, oxydo-reductive processes – this system puts limits on the performances of the water polo player.

The vital capacity of a water polo player's lungs is high.

Age is not so important, because it is possible to optimize with training the formation of I and II type fibres.

The circulation in ideal circumstances; rapid muscle + good circulation makes good muscle function and quick restoration.

What does the trained circulation mean? Morphologically it means increased heart muscle fibre, good heart cavities, good coronary flow, better muscle capillarisation, both centrally and peripherally.

We can say that the ideal water polo player is peripherally rapid, and centrally enduranced (i.e. staying power).

How can a player gain these ideal characteristics? By training, and by the correct selection.

I will not discuss the theory of training methods, only how to increase power. You can increase force.

Static – narrow movements against high resistance. The importance of solid ground training with individual maxima of 70-80% occasionally 100% of full effort.

Dynamic – repeated the quick movements against resistance. The load needed for 50% of the maximum power can be applied for approximately 1-2 minutes, while for 15 % there is no limit.

Quickness (is inherited; it can be enhanced by the development of dynamic force. This is done by destimulating coordination by technical exercises and by the acceleration of these. Quickness can be developed only minimally.

Endurance (the best chance for increased of performance) can be increased by the training of the aerobic system and circulation by steady work, and interval training.

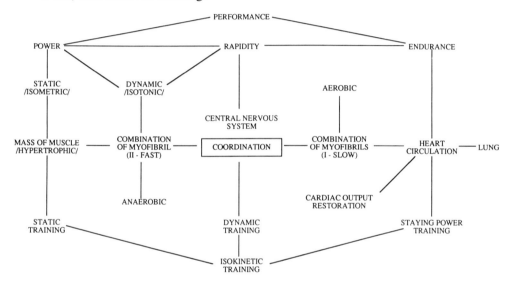

FIG. 2. The elements of performance.

The water polo player must strengthen his force, endurance, quickness in an optimal ratio.

Modern isokinetical training ensures this. Its advantages are: it never overloads the muscle, being strengthened; it can be applied to the whole of the body; it affords continuous loading; it does not contain eccentric muscle contraction; by training the muscle it need not be restrained.

The results of training should be examined at determined times by complex methods, which should themselves be checked.

Such examination is not easy because of the two main characteristics of the game (it is in the water and a group game). The strength and quickness (on solid ground also) can be controlled easily.

Tensiometry, dinamometry, different electrotechnical, isokinetic methods are all used.

The requirement is to determine and relate the different physiological indexes to the high level performance characteristic the sport demands.

To determinate oxygen circulation, spiroergometrical tests can be performed under "solid ground" circumstances, in water there is no ergometer. The Kayak-ergometer can be used otherwise.

Anaerobic performance is measured fron pH, and from lactic acid acid before and after quick anaerobic work.

These are tested twice a year. The specification of circulation due to loading such as changing in the pulse-rate, blood pressure, ECG, can be easily measured. The pulse-measurement can give sufficient answers for practical purposes as to whether the circulating endurance changed or not and what amount how intensive a dynamic load can be applied to the player's circulation.

In the past 8 years the conditional water polo players was investigated by (one of us (GP)) using the main parameter of circulation this to assess how effectively; the restorational mechanism in reverting the steady state of circulation after loading is.

"Pavlik's Test"

This is a simple test of pulse-rate changing and restoration (recovery) after traditional loading.

The player swims 6×30 m between the goals flat out with 15 min rests.

We measure the traditional pulse-counting under load, while playing we did not count the maximum load. We only measure the heart-frequency under restoration.

Under test we measure the following parameters: the mean time of 6×30 m rapid swimming and the time of 30 m swimming at maximum speed. Then we examined the ratio of the two T max.

We also counted the total-pulse beat for 4 min during restoration, which is of two components: the basic-pulse-beat (P), and the excess coming out during the load, which is equal to the difference of 4 minutes total pulse-beat (P_4) and the four times the pulse-beat (P+), we also counted the difference of pulse-beat in the first and the second half-minute – which is the index of rapid restoration. With the help of it, it is possible to give advice to the trainer to change the tired player.

Performance - Age

The sprint-performance develops constantly after 15 years. Maximum performance is at the age of 21-22 years. After that the performance seems to go down. For endurance in $6 \times 30\,m$ rapid swimming the same development is seen in the young age, in between 22 and 30 years there is no special change and in the older ages little change is observed.

PULSE: P-4 AND IN THE AGE OF DELTA

The total pulse-beat decreases in relation to the age during the 4 min recovery. The improvement of restoration is characterised with the linear regression. In case of rapid restoration, improvement is found with increase of age. The pulse-beat difference in the first and second half minute is significantly increased with age. This increase is lower than in the case of 4 min pulse-beat.

REST-PULSE (P) AND RESTORATION (±) IN AGES

Figure 3 contains the two components of total pulse during the 4 min restoration. As the pulse does not change in different ages of life the decrease of 4 min value is explained by the rapid restoration.

$$\frac{(X - \bar{X}) * 10}{S}$$

$$T_{max} = \frac{17.2 - t_{max}}{0.06}$$

$$\bar{T} = \frac{19 - \bar{t}}{0.1}$$

$$P_4 = \frac{430 - P_4}{5.7}$$

$$\Delta = \frac{\Delta - 10}{0.4}$$

$$S_wP = \frac{T_{max} + \bar{T}}{2}$$

$$P = \frac{P_4 + \Delta}{2}$$

$$T = \frac{S_wp + P}{2}$$

FIG. 3. Indices.

Indexes

The first step is that we take these indexes of different character dimension which it is possible to add. The common principle is to count the deviation from the normal value and to equalise the variation. We need to divide by the decimal factor. So every index for each sportsman varies between ± 30. The direction of the subtraction was chosen so that the better indexes got into the positive and the weaker into the negative territory. It is advisable to produce indexes with characteristically changing parameters. Further we did not want to use the parameters for many tests, only the 30 m sprint performance. The mean time of 6 × 30 m sprint, the total four minutes pulse rate and the difference of first and the second half minute were counted with the help of the figures. With the help of the first two we count the swimming performance (SwP), with the help of the second two figures the restoration of the pulse-rate (P) and from these two we obtain the index (T).

SwP, P, T, IN AGES

Swimming performance increases constantly up to 20-22 years of age, after this it decrease steeply than the increase. The of the pulse-rate restoration improves constantly so that the combined index shows the constant improvement between 15-21 years of age. After that is does not change.

Summary

Our results show that water polo players, with the training methods used in Hungary, reach their top performance around 21-22 years of age; this can be maintained up to 30 years of age with proper swimming. We note however that, with age, endurance improves. Speed and explosivity decreases. Beyond quickness and endurance there is a need for other attributes such as skill, technique on the ball, hardness etc. And these can be achieved with proper routine. We can conclude that water polo is not the sport of teenagers, the performance can be expected from the older players. This paper relates the medical aspects of the water polo with the physiological. My first figure shows how many medical concerns there are; it is evident there are many possibilities for experimental and clinical sports medicine to help the sport water polo.

Part 9
Anthropometry and Swimmers

40. Flexibility: a Review

L.P. GARRATT

THE MOST INTRIGUING THING about being a coach is that we never really know what we are doing as far as combined fitness is concerned, such as the overall result of strength, endurance and energy levels. What is enough strength work, endurance work (or in the case of the sprint coach, speed work), enough rest? Of course our final result, the performance, does not depend on any one of these things. It depends on our skill and interpretation of certain signs and an accurate evaluation of these signs.

We may ask ourselves, have our swimmers done enough or too much flexibility work? During the early 1970s I became very interested in the Flexibility and Mobility programmes used by swimmers throughout the world, now universally known as "stretching".

It was noticeable that swimmers from the eastern block countries the USSR and East Germany particularly, placed a great deal of importance in their stretching programmes. These swimmers spent a great deal of time on their exercises prior to entering the water before both training and competition.

It was equally noticeable that swimmers from many other countries paid scant or little more than token attention to this aspect of their training and warm up, despite the fact that stretching programmes were advocated by many internationally known coaches and physiologists. Counsilman devoted a complete chapter to the subject in "Competitive Swimming Manual" (1977).

As a coach working with British and English teams for the first time in 1970, it surprised me how few top British swimmers did any flexibility and mobility work despite the efforts of Mr A Power, the then physiotherapist to the GB team, to establish a regime of mobility work. In 1980 I produced a small book, "Flexibility For Swimming", in the hope that it would help to educate British youngsters at grass roots level and make them aware of the importance of having a correct routine of mobility work as an integral part of their swimming programmes, whether they be speed, synchronized swimmers or water polo players. My book was later translated with an extra chapter added by Niels Bouws (FRG Women's Coach) and produced in West Germany. This book is now being up-dated and at least two other books are being written by other national coaches.

Recently this aspect of training has taken on a whole new meaning and speed swimmers have become a great deal more active in this area prior to training and competition. However, this feature of the swimming training programme needs to be developed further, particularly with the younger competitive swimmers, in order to maintain their natural mobility.

Swimmers from the GDR have a very early background of multi sports activities as part of their overall early training, including certain forms of gymnastics as well as track and field athletics. This must play a vital role in their appreciation of flexibility work, when they eventually specialize in swimming, and goes some way towards explaining the outstanding all-round physical development evident in both their male and female swimmers. We should make a mobility programme a vital part in our training plan.

The most important and obvious reason is from the point of view of preserving energy which is required to produce the best possible performance during competition. In order to execute the stroke as efficiently as possible the swimmer is required to be able to hold, reach and maintain specific positions within that stroke, without over-stressing the muscular structure and surrounding tissue of those joints belonging to the active limbs.

Stress requires valuable energy in order to cope, therefore undue stress must be avoided. Muscular relaxation cannot be achieved within the stroke if there is not a great deal of mobility present.

Swinging and stretching exercises have the effect of "warming up" the muscles before training or competition.

When executed in a more controlled manner swinging and stretching will help with the recuperation and recovery of "wear and tear" and other training related injuries by encouraging an increased blood supply to the injured area.

When "swimming down" facilities are limited, swinging and stretching can aid the recovery process by helping to disperse the lactic acid and other waste products produced by muscular activity.

I am certain that many overuse problems will be avoided if a regular and meaningful programme of "stretching" is undertaken throughout a swimmer's career with much time spent on this from an early age – the earlier the better!

Competing at the highest level requires the power and reflexes of a track athlete, the rhythm of a dancer and the grace and agility of a gymnast, all of whom practise a great deal of mobility work in their training programmes. Competitive swimmers should do the same type of exercises in order to produce the same type of mobility. While many swimmers require stretching work in order to increase their range of movement, some (particularly women) require to practise it only in order to maintain their natural mobility although I have noticed that despite a regular stretching programme over the years even females tend gradually to lose some their "natural" mobility).

Some aspects of flexibility need to be questioned. Is it possible that the excessive stretching of the joints could in turn affect the muscles, thus actually impairing the swimming performance? This area requires looking into by the sports scientists and physiologists. Or does the practice of stretching actually improve the swimming performance, or do better swimmers tend to practise stretching more conscientiously?

Most swimmers now have some kind of stretching programme, or seem to have, judging by the pre-race activity displayed during various competitions, including the recent European Championships. Some swimmers may just be mimicking others and producing a routine out of habit, others are may be using the activity to combat nerves, or both. Whatever the psychological reason behind the activity the end result is obviously a necessary feeling of being loose. During the last two years some nations have done some stretching work on the physiotherapist's table, where the usual "rubbing down" routine is augmented by joint stretching techniques. The most active in this area seem once again to be eastern block countries, particularly the GDR. These stretching techniques are not to be confused with the usual manipulative practices executed by team physiotherapists: these exercises are closer to the "passive resistance" partner work – but in many cases are less than passive!

Finally, perhaps the importance that some swimmers now place on stretching can be best illustrated by the action of the world class sprinter who took his personal "stretching man" to the European Championships in Bonn this year.

---

41.   Proportionality   and   Anthropometric Fractionation of Body Mass in South American Swimmers

J.C. MAZZA, N. ALARCON, C. GALASSO, C. BERMUDEZ, P. COSOLITO and F. GRIBAUDO

Introduction

IN THE LAST 20 YEARS, MUCH attention has been focused on the application of kinanthropometry methodologies in athletes of different sports; and particularly during the Summer Olympic Games, Mexico (1968) (De Garay and Carter, 1974) and Montreal (1976) (Carter, 1982). Consequently kinanthropometry has developed as a basic science applied to Sports and Physical Education.

Kinanthropometry has been very well defined by Ross et al. (1982) as the quantitative link between structure and function or the interface between anatomy and physiology. Also, as a scientific specialization which is concerned with the application of measurements to determine human size, shape, proportion, composition, maturation and gross function in relationship to growth, exercise, performance and nutrition (Ross et al., 1982). It puts the individual athlete into objective focus and provides a clear appraisal of his structure through growth development or modifications generated for training influences (Ross et al., 1981).

Particularly, kinanthropometric measurements applied to swimmers give approximate information about anthropometric factors that might contribute to success in this sport, developed in an environment more resistant than the air/water.

Previous important and controversial studies, relating to aquatic drag, buoyancy and somatic or body measurements, have been conducted (Huijing *et al.*, 1988; Van Tilborgh *et al.*, 1983). Several workers have established relationships between performances or events and physique (Tittel and Wutscherk, 1972; Araujo *et al.*, 1978; Vervaeke and Persyn, 1981; Stager *et al.*, 1984; Blanksby *et al.*, 1986; Bloomfield *et al.*, 1986).

In general, the findings of these studies showed that swimmers have well defined physical characteristics and that there exist differences according to the level of competition. Differences by styles, strokes and distance events are not clear, although tendencies appear to be. There are previous studies applying kinanthropometric methods in South American swimmers (Araujo, 1976; Perez, 1977; Rocha *et al.*, 1977; Araujo *et al.*, 1978; Perez, 1981), but there are no published research methods involving proportionality and fractionation of body mass, at least in a representative multinational sample.

The purpose of the present study is to describe body mass profiles by geographical area, and compare body characteristics of South American swimmers in general (SAS), with South American Swimming Championships finalists (SACHS) in the last continental competition (Medellin, Colombia, March 1988). Additionally, it is our interest to compare anthropometric measurements between the finalists group in the above event with those who were measured during Montreal Olympic Games Anthropological Project – HOGAP 1976 (Carter, 1982; Carter and Yuhasz, 1984).

Material and methods

The sample includes 295 South American swimmers (180 males and 115 females), divided in two groups: 236 South American swimmers in general (SAS: 150 males and 86 females) and 59 South American Swimming Championship finalists (30 males and 29 females).

Proportionality method described by Ross and Wilson (1974) and later revised by Ross and Ward (1981), and the anthropometric fractionation of body mass, by Drinkwater and Ross (1980), were used to check both samples. The landmarks, technical specifications and kinanthropometry instruments are vastly and conventionally described (Ross *et al.*, 1982; Lohman *et al.*, 1988).

Mean (x) and standard deviation (sd) values were calculated for by all the variables; significant differences (SD), applying test for two independent samples, are set on 0.05 level of statistical significance: (1) between SAS and SACHS male and female for all the variables (Tables 1-5); (2a) between SACHS males and MOGAP males for the anthropometric variables measured but not for the mass components; between SACHS (Van Tilborgh et al., 1983) females and MOGAP females (Tables 6-7). Additionally, we developed proportionality profiles presenting z values. Variables are shown as bargraphs with ending set at $\pm$ SEM of z scores (sd/square root of n). Although not a strict test of statistical significance, a useful inspectional of the graphics may be applied by observing if standard error bars overlap (Ross and Ward, 1984). We compared proportionality profiles: (a) SACHS males vs. SAS males; (b) SACHS females vs. SAS females; (c) SACHS males vs. females; (d) SAS males vs. females; (e) SACHS vs. MOGAP males (6) ; (f) SACHS vs. MOGAP females (6).

Results

Statistical analysis and comparison between SACHS and SAS males are described in Table 1.

TABLE 1. *Statistical comparison for anthropometric fractionation of body mass SACHS vs SAS male swimmers.*

Variables	South American championships swimmers (SACHS) n = 30		South American swimmers (SAS) n = 150		Statistical conclusion
	$\bar{x}$	sd	$\bar{x}$	sd	p
Age	19.10	2.84	16.19	3.38	0.01
Weight	73.54	7.10	65.16	10.55	0.01
Height	181.26	6.28	172.67	8.93	0.01
% Residual mass	28.30	1.07	25.21	1.58	0.01
% Fat mass	9.32	1.59	11.08	2.47	0.01
% Muscle mass	47.97	1.14	48.01	2.35	0.01
% Bone mass	8.40	1.05	17.72	2.03	0.01

SACHS males are older, heavier and taller than SAS males ($p < 0.01$); when we compare mass %, SACHS males have more muscular and residual mass, and less fat and bone mass than SAS males ($p < 0.01$). The same variables are compared for SACHS and SAS female groups in Table 2.

TABLE 2. *Statistical comparison for anthropometric fractionation of body mass SACHS vs SAS female swimmers.*

Variables	South American championships swimmers (SACHS) n = 29		South American swimmers (SAS) n = 88		Statistical conclusion
	$\bar{x}$	sd	$\bar{x}$	sd	p
Age	17.48	3.42	15.49	2.07	< 0.01
Weight	58.67	7.15	57.15	7.70	NS
Height	167.08	5.81	165.01	7.09	NS
% Residual mass	26.69	0.94	25.72	1.45	< 0.01
% Fat mass	13.59	2.49	16.10	3.38	< 0.01
% Muscle mass	44.57	1.96	42.30	2.30	< 0.01
% Bone mass	15.14	1.44	15.87	1.47	< 0.05

TABLE 3. *Variables measured males, SACHS vs SAS.*

Variables	SACHS (n = 30)		SAS (n = 150)		Statistical conclusion
	$\bar{x}$	sd	$\bar{x}$	sd	p
Biacromial breadth	41.31	2.08	38.73	2.89	< 0.01
Transverse chest br.	29.31	1.81	27.08	2.38	< 0.01
A-p chest br.	20.85	2.35	19.29	2.01	< 0.01
Biiliocristal br.	28.09	4.13	25.64	1.99	NS
Triceps skinfold	7.46	1.85	9.07	3.03	< 0.01
Subscapular sk.	8.82	2.55	9.00	2.87	NS
Suprailiac sk.	7.97	2.97	9.42	5.18	NS
Abdominal sk.	8.37	2.70	10.42	4.93	< 0.01
Thigh sk.	9.47	2.74	12.58	4.63	< 0.01
Mid Calf sk.	6.30	1.70	8.84	3.11	< 0.01
Arm girth	31.20	1.50	28.89	2.83	< 0.01
Chest girth	97.68	4.31	91.43	7.58	< 0.01
Thigh girth	54.92	2.48	53.43	4.27	< 0.05
Calf girth	36.21	1.87	35.51	2.39	NS
Wrist girth	16.98	0.93	16.34	0.86	< 0.01
Ankle girth	22.03	1.18	22.68	1.74	< 0.05
Humerus breadth	7.07	0.34	6.86	0.38	< 0.01
Femur breadth	9.91	0.48	9.77	0.48	NS

SACHS females are older ($p < 0.01$), but no SD was established in weight and height. Similarly to males, SACHS females have, more muscular and residual mass and less fat and bone mass than SAS females ($p < 0.01$ for the first three variables, and $p < 0.05$ for the last one).

In Table 3, we compare the measurement values between SACHS and SAS males groups: the SD obtained are probably, influencing the SD presented previously.

It is interesting to observe that SD obtained in bone mass (SACHS males less than SAS males), would be strongly influenced by the lesser value of ankle girth, rather than higher values of wrist girth and humerus breadth.

In Table 4, we present the same data, which correspond to SACHS and SAS females.

TABLE 4. *Variables measures females, SACHS vs SAS.*

Variables	SACHS (n = 29)		SAS (n = 86)		Statistical conclusion	
	$\bar{x}$	sd	$\bar{x}$	sd	sd	p
Biacromial breadth	37.12	2.12	38.51	2.19	NS	
Transverse chest br.	28.75	1.61	28.45	2.27	NS	
A-p chest br.	18.60	1.55	17.80	1.84	< 0.05	
Biiliocristal br.	26.54	1.68	26.34	1.73	NS	
Triceps skinfold	11.97	3.34	14.88	5.00	< 0.01	
Subscapular sk.	9.89	3.15	11.30	4.48	< 0.05	
Suprailiac sk.	9.05	3.93	12.35	5.92	< 0.01	
Abdominal sk.	12.08	5.12	13.87	5.75	NS	
Thigh sk.	18.18	5.18	23.20	6.12	< 0.01	
Mid Calf sk.	11.66	3.82	14.62	4.62	< 0.01	
Arm girth	27.66	2.30	27.71	2.25	NS	
Chest girth	85.07	5.49	82.05	5.49	< 0.05	
Thigh girth	53.65	3.45	54.17	3.73	NS	
Calf girth	33.53	1.73	33.91	2.15	NS	
Wrist girth	15.03	0.91	15.00	1.11	NS	
Ankle girth	20.45	1.12	21.37	2.05	< 0.01	
Humerus breadth	8.22	0.33	8.10	0.31	NS	
Femur breadth	8.97	0.38	9.10	0.43	NS	

When we analyze age, weight and height according to styles, SD ($p < 0.01$) are established in SACHS freestylers, who are older, heavier and taller than SAS freestylers. This does not occur with the other styles, except that SACHS backstrokers are heavier ($p < 0.05$) than SAS backstrokers. Sprague (1974), also found that greater height was a significant performance level factor in freestyle, and not significant in the other styles of competition. Similar comparison for the female samples, demonstrates that only in the freestyle group, are SACHS older ($p < 0.05$) than SAS, not registering SD in any other style for age, weight and height.

If we consider mass % by styles, between the two groups, the conclusions (show in Table 5), are: (a) In males, only the freestylers SACHS present SD for all the fractions compared with SAS males (higher % in muscular and residual mass, $p < 0.01$, and less fat and bone mass, $p < 0.01$). No SD are detected for the other style groups. (b) In females, SD are established in freestylers (SACHS have less fat and higher muscular mass than SAS group, $p < 0.01$), in backstrokers (SACHS have less bone and higher muscular and residual mass than SAS, $p < 0.05$), and in the combined group of butterflyers and I.M. swimmers (SACHS have higher muscular mass than SAS, $p < 0.05$). Probably, some of these results are affected by the small n in non freestyler groups.

TABLE 5. *Summary of SD in age, weight, height and % mass by styles, SACHS high (+) or less (–) than SAS.*

Males			Females		
Freestyle			*Freestyle*		
Age	+	$p < 0.01$	Age	+	$p < .01$
Weight	+	$p < 0.01$	% Fat mass	-	$p < .01$
Height	+	$p < 0.01$	% Muscle mass	+	$p < .01$
% Fat mass	–	$p < 0.01$			
% Residual mass	+	$p < 0.01$			
% Muscle mass	+	$p < 0.01$			
% Bone mass	-	$p < 0.01$			
Backstroke			*Backstroke*		
Weight	+	$p < 0.05$	% Residual mass +		$p < .05$
			% Muscle mass	+	$p < .05$
			% Bone mass	–	$p < .05$
			Butterfly and I.M.		
			% Muscle mass	+	$p < .05$

TABLE 6. *Varibles measured MOGAP vs SACHS.*

Variables	MOGAP (n = 33)		SACHS (n = 30)		Statistical conclusion
	x̄	sd	x̄	sd	p
Males					
Age	19.30	2.37	19.10	2.84	NS
Weight	73.00	8.04	73.54	7.10	NS
Height	178.60	4.73	181.26	6.28	NS
Sitting height	84.50	2.69	95.54	3.58	NS
Biacromial breadth	40.80	1.78	41.31	2.08	NS
Transverse chest br.	29.40	1.68	29.31	1.81	NS
A-P chest br.	20.70	1.68	20.65	2.35	NS
Biiliocristal br.	27.90	2.20	26.09	4.13	$p < 0.05$
Triceps skinfold	7.40	2.30	7.46	1.85	NS
Subscapular sk.	8.10	1.80	0.82	2.55	NS
Suprailiac sk.	6.00	1.80	7.97	2.97	$p < 0.01$
Abdominal sk.	9.00	4.00	8.37	2.70	NS
Thigh sk.	9.50	2.90	9.47	2.74	NS
Mid calf sk.	7.20	2.40	6.30	1.70	NS
Arm girth	30.60	2.27	31.20	1.50	NS
Chest girth	98.80	5.00	97.88	4.31	NS
Thigh girth	55.40	3.88	54.92	2.48	NS
Calf girth	30.90	2.48	36.21	1.97	NS
Wrist girth	17.10	1.00	16.98	0.93	NS
Humerus breadth	7.30	0.33	7.07	0.34	$p < 0.01$
Femur breadth	9.80	0.47	9.91	0.48	NS
Females					
Age	16.60	2.81	17.48	3.42	NS
Weight	57.80	8.83	58.87	7.15	NS
Height	168.90	5.70	107.08	5.81	NS
Sitting height	88.90	3.46	88.68	3.25	NS
Biacromial breadth	37.10	1.45	37.12	2.12	NS
Transverse chest br.	26.20	1.37	26.75	1.61	NS
A-P chest br.	18.40	1.89	18.60	1.55	NS
Biiliocristal br.	28.70	1.85	26.54	1.68	NS
Triceps skinfold.	14.30	3.80	11.97	3.34	NS
Subscapular sk.	8.90	2.20	9.63	3.15	NS
Suprailiac sk.	7.70	2.60	9.05	3.99	NS
Abdominal sk.	12.00	4.10	12.08	5.12	NS
Thigh sk.	20.30	5.50	18.18	5.19	NS
Mid calf sk.	13.70	3.60	11.68	3.62	NS
Arm girth	27.30	1.91	27.66	2.30	NS
Chest girth	88.00	4.69	85.07	5.49	$p < 0.05$
Thigh girth	52.80	3.35	53.65	3.45	NS
Calf girth	34.00	2.03	33.53	1.73	NS
Wrist girth	15.40	0.81	15.03	0.91	NS
Humerus breadth	6.40	0.33	6.22	0.33	$p < 0.05$
Femur breadth	9.00	0.48	8.97	0.38	NS

It is interesting to compare the variables measured, between SACHS and MOGAP groups (males and females). The results are presented in Table 6 and Table 7.

Considering males, we observed that SACHS have less biiliocristal and biepicondylar humerus breadths ($p < 0.05$ and $p < 0.01$ respectively) and higher suprailiac skinfold ($p < 0.01$) than MOGAP swimmers. Considering females, SACHS present less biepicondylar humerus breadth ($p < 0.05$) and less chest girth ($p < 0.05$) than MOGAP swimmers. In reference to skinfolds, SACHS have less triceps and mid-calf sk. ($p < 0.05$) than MOGAP swimmers.

Finally, we present proportionality profiles (x of z values and $\pm$ SEM) comparing: (1) SACHS vs. SAS males (Fig. 1); (2) SACHS vs. SAS females (Fig. 2); (3) SACHS vs MOGAP males (Fig. 3); (4) SACHS vs. MOGAP females (Fig. 4). In addition, to define sexual dimorphism, we describe proportionality profiles between males and females (SACHS in Fig. 5 and SAS in Fig. 6).

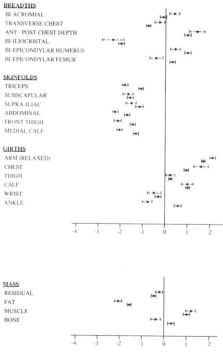

FIG. 1. Proportionality profile of z values for SAS males (-, $n = 150$) vs SACHS males (- -, $n = 30$).

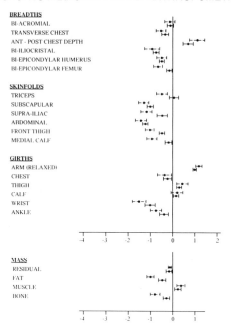

FIG. 2. Proportionality profile of z values for SAS females (-, n = 86) vs SACHS females (- -, n = 29).

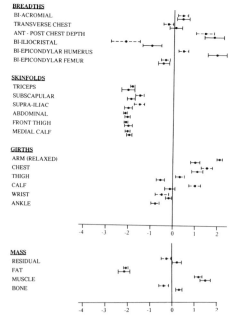

FIG. 3. Proportionality profile of z values for MOGAP males (-, n = 33) vs SACHS males (- -, n = 30).

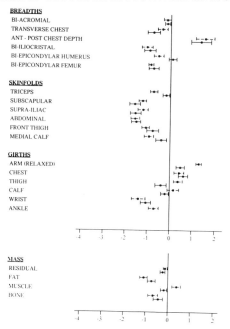

FIG. 4. Proportionality profile of z values for MOGAP females (-, $n = 32$) vs SACHS females (- -, $n = 29$).

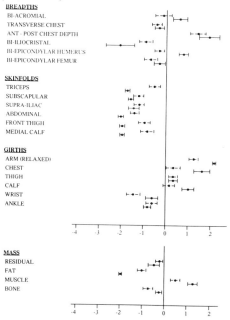

FIG. 5. Proportionality profile of z values for SACHS males (- , $n = 30$) vs SACHS females (- -, $n = 29$).

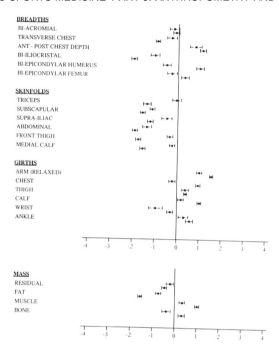

FIG. 6. Proportionality profile of *z* values for SAS males (-, *n* = 50) vs SAS females
(- -, *n* = 86)

Discussion

Considering age, weight and height, it will be seen that while SACHS
males are older, heavier and taller than SAS, SACHS males are older
but do not differ in weight and height from SAS. These results agree
with typical individual height and weight-attained curves presented by
William Stini (1984). While males continue to grow, increasing height
and weight between 15 and 19 years period, females stabilize the
mentioned variables for the same period of age (Stini, 1984). In
reference to body composition, anthropometric fractionation of body
mass method, allows one to observe that both male and female SACHS,
have less fat and bone mass but higher muscular and residual mass than
respective SAS groups.

This could probably be related to a higher level of performance
reached by SACHS groups, because they present less fat/muscle mass
ratio and a higher muscle/bone mass ratio. Also, SACHS males and
females groups have a higher lean body mass (or fat-free mass) than

respective SAS groups (both SD = $p < 0.01$). Our data coincide with others reported previously, which relate positively lean body mass and performance level (Stager *et al.*, 1984; Blanksby *et al.*, 1986). Also, these findings are consistent with the same conclusions informed referring to different sports (Parizkova, 1972). The relationship between fat mass and performance in swimming, is still controversial. Some assumptions were made relating to fat mass and buoyancy (Brozek *et al.*, 1983), in order to explain that individuals with more fat mass float better and reduce drag coefficient and energy expenditure during swimming (Von Dobein and Hamer, 1979); on the other hand, previous studies have reported increased drag coefficient relating to body shape. A swimmer with a large body fat mass, although less dense, will present a high cross-sectional area to the water (Stager *et al.*, 1984; Blanksby *et al.*, 1986). Additionally, and not less important, if the swimmer has a high fat/muscle mass ratio (overall in the limbs) this would affect his/her muscle power rates and, in consequence, the performance level. For example, less triceps skinfold (among others) in SACHS male and female-groups, compared with SAS groups ($p < 0.01$), would support this idea, and agrees with previous reports, which indicated that thicker triceps sk. correlates significantly with poor performance (Blanksby *et al.*, 1986). The same conclusions were demonstrated, correlating high fat values associated to slower performance times (Blanksby *et al.*, 1986). Although body fat assists floating the detrimental effect would appear to outweigh the advantage, particularly in short distance events (Sprague, 1974; Jensen and McIlwain, 1979). Although we could not relate bone mass % with body density, it appears that high level performance swimmers have less bone mass and this has a beneficial effect, a better level of buoyancy. Further studies understand, more deeply, the relationship between muscle/bone mass ratio and density, buoyancy, aquatic drag and performance. The observation of proportionality profiles provides us with the idea that common anthropometric characteristics and body mass tendencies in MOGAP and SACHS groups are associated with optimal performance in swimming. On the other hand, it is strongly evident that different proportionality profiles between SACHS and SAS groups both males and females, are reflected in the present study. Particular and more consistent conclusions of anthropometric measurements and body composition by style and/or distance events, must be developed using larger samples of international swimmers at a high level of competition.

Conclusions

In conclusion, SACHS groups (both male and female), revealed SD in proportionality and fractionation of mass components (less lean body weight, fat and bone mass and higher values of muscular and residual mass). This would probably explain greater muscle power rates, which are related to a higher level of performance. The present conclusion is coincident with Carter, who reports: "when adiposity is low in athletes, fat-free mass is probably of greater functional significance than fat mass (Carter and Yuhasz, 1984)." Finally, similar characteristics in body shape and composition of MOGAP and SACHS groups, suggest that there are body models associated with optimal performance in swimming.

References

Araujo, C.G.S. (1976). Somatotyping of top swimmers by the Heath-Carter method. *In* "Swimming Medicine IV" (Eds N. O. Ericksson and B. Furberg), pp. 188-189. University Park Press, Baltimore.

Araujo, C.G.S., Pavel, R.C. and Gomez, P.S.C. (1978). Comparison of somatotype and speed in competitive swimming at different phases of training. *In* "Swimming III" (Eds J. Terauds and E.W. Beddingfield), pp. 329-337. University Park, Baltimore.

Blanksby, B.A., Bloomfield, J., Ponchard, M. and Ackland, T.R. (1986). The relationship between anatomical characteristics and swimming performance in a state age group championship competitors. *Journal of Swimming Research,* **2**, (2), 30-36

Bloomfield, J., Blanksby, B.A., Ackland, T.R. and Elliott, B.C. (1986). The anatomical and psychological characteristics of preadolescent swimmers. *In* "Perspectives in Kinanthropometry". (Ed. J.A.P. Day), pp. 165-170, Champaign, Il.

Brozek, J., Grande, F., Anderson, J.T. and Keys, A. (1983). Densitometric analysis of body composition: Revision of some quantitative assumptions. *Annals of the New York Academy of Science,* **110**, 113-140.

Carter, J.E.L. (1982). "Physical Structure of Olympic Athletes. Part I: The Montreal Olympic Games Anthropoligical Project". Karger, New York.

Carter, J.E.L. and Yuhasz. (1984). Skinfolds and body composition of Olympic athletes. Physical structure of the Olympic athletes. Part II: Kinanthropometry of the Olympic athletes. *Medicine Sport Science,* **18**, 144-182, Karger, Basel.

De Garay, A.L. and Carter, J.E.L. (1974). "Genetic and Anthropological Studies of Olympic Athletes". Academic Press, New York.

Drinkwater, D.T. and Ross, W.D. (1980). Anthropometric fractionation of body mass. *In* "Kinanthropometry II". (Eds M. Ostyn, G. Beunen and J. Simmons). pp. 177-188. Academic Press, Baltimore.

Huijing, P.A., Toussaint, H.M., Mackay, R., Vervoorn, K., Clarys, J.P., De Groot, G. and Hollander, A.P. (1988). Active drug related to body dimensions. *In* "Swimming Science V". (Eds B.E. Ungerechts, K. Reischle and K. Wilke), pp. 31-38, Champaign Il.

Jensen, R.K. and McIlwain, J. (1979). Modelling of low extremity forces - the dolphin kick. *In* "Swimming III". (Eds J. Terauds and E.W. Beddingfield). University Park Press, Baltimore.

Lohman, T.G., Roche, A.F. and Martorell, R. (1988). "Anthropometric Standarization Reference Manuel". Human Kinetics, Champaign, Il.

Parizkova, J. (1972). Body composition and exercise during growth and development. *In* "Physical Activity, Human Growth and Development". (Ed. G.L. Rorick), pp. 97-124. Academic Press, New York.

Perez, B. (1981). "Los Atletas Venezolanos, su Tipo Fisico". Univer sidad Central de Venezuela, Caracas.

Rocha, M.L., Araujo, C.G.S., de Freitas, J. and Villasboas, L.F.P. (1977). Anthropometria Dinamica de Natacao. *Revista de Educacion Fisica, Brasil*. **102**, 46-54.

Ross, W.D. and Wilson, N.C. (1974). A stratagem for proportional growth assessment. *In* "Children and Exercise". (Eds J. Borms and M. Hebbelinck). *Acta Paediatrica Belgica*, Supple. 28, pp. 169-182.

Ross, W.D. and Ward, R. (1981). Sexual dimorphism and human proportionality. *In* "Human Dimorphism in 'Homo Sapiens'". (Ed. Hall), Chapter 7, Praeger, New York.

Ross, W.D. and Ward, R. (1984). Proportionality of Olympic Athletes. *In* "Physical Structure of Olympic Athletes Part II: Kinanthropometry of Olympic Athletes". (Ed. J.E.L. Cater). *Medicine Sport Science*, **18**, 100-143.

Ross, W.D., Harfell-Jones, H.J. and Stirling, D.R. (1981). Prospects in kinanthropometry. *In* "The Sport Sciences". (Eds J.T. Jackson and H.A. Wenger), University of Victoria, Physical Education Series 4.

Ross, W.D., Harfell-Jones, H.J., Ward, R. and Kerr, D.A. (1982). Kinanthropometry, *In* "Physiological Testing of Elite Athlete". (Eds J.D. Macdougall, H.A. Wenger and H.J. Green). pp. 75-117. Movement Publications, Ithaca, New York.

Sprague, H.A. (1974). The relationship of certain physical measurements to swimming speed in male age-group swimmers. Doctoral Dissertation, George Peabody College of Teachers.

Stager, J.M., Cordain, L. and Beoker, T.J., (1984). Relationship of body composition to swimming performance in female swimmers. *Journal of Swimming Research*, **1**, (1), 21-28.

Stimi, W.A. (1984). Kinanthropometry: An anthropological focus. *In* "Perspectives in Kinanthropometry". Vol. 1. (Ed. J.A.P. Day), pp. 5-23. The Olympic Scientific Congress Proceedings. Human Kinetics, Champaign, Il.

Tittel, K. and Wutscherk, H. (1972). "Sportanthropometic". Barth, Leipzig.

Van Tilborgh, L., Daly, D. and Persyn, U. (1983). Influence of some somatic factors on passive drag, gravity and buoyancy forces in competitive swimmers. *In* "Biomechanics and Medicine in Swimming". (Eds A.P. Hollander, P.A. Huiging and G. de Groot). pp. 207-214. Champaign, Il.

Vervaeke, H. and Persyn, U. (1981). Some differences between men and women in various factors determining swimming performance. *In* "The Female Athlete". (Eds J. Borms, M. Hebbelinck and A. Venerando). pp. 150-158.

Von Dobein, W. and Hamer, I. (1979). Body composition, sinking force and oxygen uptake of man treading water. *Journal of Applied Physiology*, **37**, 55-59.

---

42. Adaptation Rachi's Curves of Selected Female Olympic Breast and Backstroke Swimmers

CZ. WIELKI

Introduction

THE STUDY OF THE ANATOMICAL rachi's curve of swimmers of different major stroke practice was reported at the VII FINA Congress at Orlando (1987).

It was observed that the rachi's curves of high performance swimmers change enormously, especially in breast (BR) and back (BA) strokes. In order to interpret the changes according to the sex of the swimmers a Normative Typology for each sex was established.

Methodology

Applying the "Improved Radius Method with Intersection Point" to 190 female and 286 male subjects, the relation between the length of the dorsal curve to that of the lumbar was 2 to 1 (2.1 to 1 for females and 2.2 to 1 for males), but the relation of the height of the dorsal curve to that of the lumbar was 1.7 to 1 for females (F) and 2.4 to 1 for males (M).

Statistical analysis indicates that 82.6% of females and 80.3.% of males grouped in this sample, presented approximatively the same relation between lengths of the curves, and between their heights as in the "Normative group" (190 F and 286 M). Therefore the curves with these characteristics were named "Type A - Normal" of the biological development of the rachi's curve.

On the other hand, for 7.9% of the F and 11.5% of the M, the relation between the lengths of the curves was 1 to 1 (1.1 to 1 for F, 1.2 to 1 for M). The relation between the heights of the curves was 0.7 to 1 for F and 1.04 to 1 for M. The curves with these characteristics were named "Type B Lordotic". Moreover, for 9.5% of F and 9.6% of M, the relation between the lengths of the curves was about 4 to 1 (3.9 for F, and 4.6 for M). The relation between the heights of the curves was 3.6 to 1 for F, and 8.03 to 1 for M The curves with these characteristics were named "Type C Kyphotics".

This classification called "Normative typology" is a statement of fact and not a speculation, it permits an analysis of the rachi curve evolution for each sex if we take into consideration the following:

A. FOUR INDEXES FOR THE WHOLE CURVE OF THE RACHIS

1 Dorso-lumbar index: relation between lengths of dorsal and lumbar parts, $DLII(1) = (AC : CB) \times 100$.

2 Curve relative index: relation between heights of dorsal and lumbar parts, $CRI(2) = (h_1 : h_2) \times 100$.

3 Relative Summation index : ratio of sum of both heights to the total length of the rachis, $RSI(3) = (h_1 + h_2) : AC \times 100$.

4 Inclination index: inclination of the rachis to the vertical, $II(4) = (BI : AI) \times 100$.

B. THREE INDEXES FOR THE DORSAL PART

5 Dorsal top index: position of the top (D) of the dorsal curve. $DII(5) = (AF : FC) \times 100$.

6 Dorsal curve index: relation between height and length of the dorsal curve, $DCI(6) = (h_1 : AC) \times 100$.

7 Radius dorsal curve: size of the radius of the dorsal curve, $RDC(7) = (h_1^2 + S_1^2) : 2 h_1$.

C. THREE INDEXES FOR THE LUMBAR PART

8 Lumbar top index: position of the top (E) of the lumbar curve. $LTI(8) = (CG : GB) \times 100$.

9   Lumbar curve index: relation between height and length of the lumbar curve, $LCI(9) = (h_1 : CB) \times 100$.

10 Radius lumbar curve: size of the radius of the lumbar curve, $RLC(10) = (h_2^2 + s_2^2) : 2h_2$.

Results

When one considers the X of the anatomical rachi's curves in the Normative group, the indexes for the lengths of the curves show their respective similarities for the two sexes: DLI is 209 for F and 222 for M; RDC(7) is 462 mm for F and 459 for M.

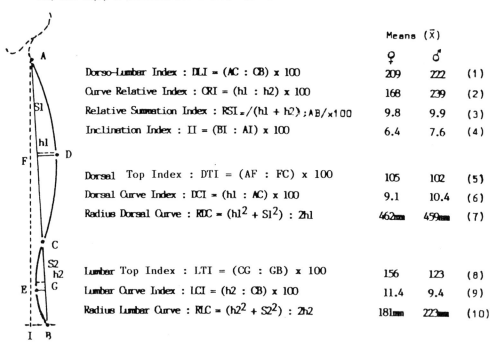

	Means ($\bar{x}$)		
	♀	♂	
Dorso-Lumbar Index : DLI = (AC : CB) x 100	209	222	(1)
Curve Relative Index : CRI = (h1 : h2) x 100	168	239	(2)
Relative Summation Index : RSI=/(h1 + h2) ; AB/x100	9.8	9.9	(3)
Inclination Index : II = (BI : AI) x 100	6.4	7.6	(4)
Dorsal Top Index : DTI = (AF : FC) x 100	105	102	(5)
Dorsal Curve Index : DCI = (h1 : AC) x 100	9.1	10.4	(6)
Radius Dorsal Curve : RDC = (h1^2 + S1^2) : 2h1	462mm	459mm	(7)
Lumbar Top Index : LTI = (CG : GB) x 100	156	123	(8)
Lumbar Curve Index : LCI = (h2 : CB) x 100	11.4	9.4	(9)
Radius Lumbar Curve : RLC = (h2^2 + S2^2) : 2h2	181mm	223mm	(10)

FIG. 1. Profiles and means of spinal curves – normative group (190 F and 286 M).

Important differences appear in the indexes for the heights of the curves. The relation of the height of dorsal curve to the lumbar height CRI (2) is 168 for F., and 239 for M. This is because the DCI(6) of F (9.1) is smaller than for the M (10.4) in the dorsal curve. In the lumbar curve on the contrary, the LCI(g) is greater in F (11.4) than in M (9.4).

The difference between females and males is confirmed by the size of the Radius Lumbar Curve. RLC(10) is only 181 mm for F and 223 mm for M. The differences between F and M in the profiles of the curve of the lumbar parts of the rachis could be explained by the child bearing function of women.

To give a better visual demonstration of the differences and similarities of the normative typology of rachi's curves of F and M we present, in the Fig. 2. profiles and means of their indexes according to the results obtained in the following order: Type "B" – Lordotic; Type "A" – Normal; and Type "C" - Kyphotic, characterized by ten indexes.

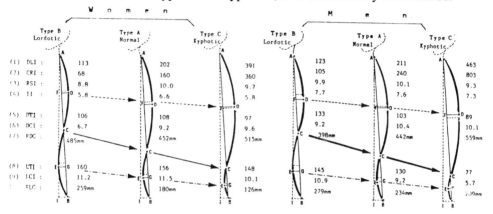

FIG. 2. Normative typology of anatomical rachi's curves and their indexes.

In Fig. 3, we present the profiles and means of four indexes of selected Olympic swimmers specialist in one major stroke in the order: breast (BR), butterfly (BU), crawl (C) and backstroke (BA).

The means of the ratio of the length of the curves DLI(1) was 141 for the group BR showing a strong prevalence toward Type "B" Lordotic (F = 113, M = 123), 224 for BU and 264 for C, close to the DLI(1) of Normative group (F = 209, M = 222). For BA, the DLI (1) is 315 between Type "A" Normal and Type "C" Kyphotic (F = 391, M = 463).

As far as the ratio of the heights of the curves CRI(2) is concerned, BR have a CRI of 105, less than the Normative group (F = 168, M = 23), which is situated between 9 of Type "A" Normal and Type "B" Lordotic. It was 173 for BU and 266 for C, close to the CRI(2) X of Normative group (F = 168, M = 231). For the BA. the CRI(2) is 266, more than the X of Normative group (F = 168, M = 239). The slight difference between X of BU and C seems to be caused by the technique of propulsion with undulating movements.

Concerning size of the dorsal radius : breaststroke swimmers with RDC(7) = 407 mm and BA swimmers with 396 mm, present a radius

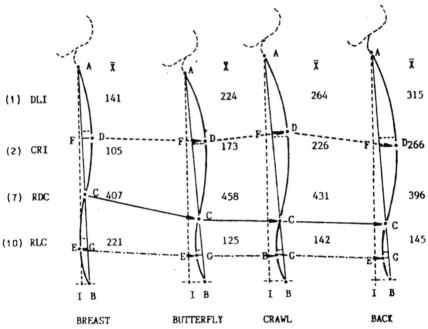

FIG. 3. Profiles and means of spine of swimmers according to major stroke practice.

smaller than the Normative group (F = 462 mm, M = 459 mm) while Bu and C swimmers with 458 mm and 431 mm are very close to the Normative group. For the radius of the lumbar part : BR. swimmers with 221 mm are close to the Normative group (F = 181 mm, M = 223 mm). For the other strokes, the radius is a little smaller than the Normative group (BU = 125 mm, C = 142 mm, BA = 145 mm). It means that the curvature for these three strokes is greater than for the BR stroke, and the X of Normative group.

Spherosomatograms (Fig. 4) of the rachis of four selected female Olympic swimmers permit analysis of the characteristics the spine in the sagital plane (side view) and the frontal plane (back side deviation). Two of the swimmers use BR as their major stroke. two use BA, all are identified thus: 1 BR: age 15.5 years, size: 156 cm weight : 48.5 kg; 2BR: age 13 years, size: 155 cm, weight: 37.5 kg; 1 BA: age 16 years, size: 167 cm, weight: 61 kg; 2BA: age 15 years, size: 164 cm, weight: 53 kg.

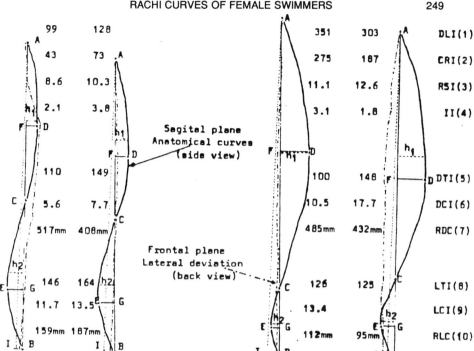

FIG.4. Spherosomatograms of spines of BR and BA female swimmers.

Sagital plane

1BR and 2BR belong to Normative Type "B"-Lordotic. DLI(1) of 1BR is 99 but it is 122 for 2BR. For both swimmers the ratio between the lengths of the dorsal and lumbar curves is lower than X of the group of BR swimmers (141).

CRI(2) of 1BR is only 43 but it is 73 for 2BR. This ratio, between the heights of the curves is for 1BR lower than X of the group of BR swimmers (105) and of Normative Type "B" Lordotic (68). 2BR with 73 is a little higher than Type "B".

RSI(3) sum of the heights to sum of the lengths of the curves is 8.6 for BR1, less than X of the group BR (10.1), but close to Type B - Lordotic (88), while 2BR with 10.3 is the highest of her swimming group and a little higher than Type A - Normal (10.0).

II(4) is 2.1 for 1BR but 3.8 for 2BR. The inclination of the Rachis of 1BR is low compared with X BR group (4.0) and with Type B - Lordotic (5.8). 2BR is close to the X of BR swimmers group.

Dorsal part

DII(5) of 1BR is 110 and 149 for 2BR. The position of the top D of the dorsal curve of 1BR is a little higher than X BR (117) but a little lower than Normative Type "B" Lordotic (106) while with 149 2BR has a top D much lower.

DCI(6) which shows the relation between the height of the dorsal curve to its length is 5.6 for 1BR much less than X of BR (8.7) and than Normative Type "B" - Lordotic (6.7). 2BR with 7.7 is between X BR and Type "B" - Lordotic.

RDC(7) size of the radius of the dorsal curve is 517 mm for 1BR compared with 407 mm in X BR and 485 in Type "B" Lordotic. It means that the dorsal curve is rather flat because of the effects of the elevation of the upper part of the body in order to inhale. For 2BR the size of the radius is 408 equal to X BR and closer to Type "A" - Normal than Type "B" - Lordotic.

Lumbar part

LTI(8): this index concerns the position of the top E of the lumbar curve. 1BR with 146 has a top E in the same position as the X BR but higher than Type "B" - Lordotic (160). 2BR with 164 has a top E lower than X BR but very close to Type "B" - Lordotic.

LCI(9): relation height to length of the lumbar curve is 11.7 for 1BR, but 13.5 for 2BR. 1BR is the same as X BR and close to the Type E - Lordotic (11.2). On the other hand 2BR has more than X BR and than Type "B" - Lordotic.

RLC (10): the radius of the lumbar curve of 1BR is 159 mm, less than X BR (221 mm) and closer to Type "A" - Normal (188 mm) than to Type "B" - Lordotic (259 mm). 2BR with 187 mm is the same as Type "A" -Normal.

1BA belongs to Type "C" - Kyphotic while 2BA is rather on the edge of Type "C" - Kyphotic and Type "A" - Normal.

DLI(1) of 1BA is 351 while it is 315 for X of BA swimmers, but 391 for Normative Type "C" - Kyphotic. 2BA has DLI of 303, a little less than X BA.

CRI(2) of 1BA is 275, and compares well with X BA 266, but it is much lower than Type "C" - Kyphotic (360). 2BA with 187 is much lower than X BA and close to Type "A" - Normal (160).

RSI(3) of 1BA is 11.1, the same as X BA, but higher than all

Normative Types. Type "A" - Normal (10.0). 2BA with 12.6 has a very great RSI.

II(4) is 3.1 for 1BA but only 1.B for 2BA. It is a very low inclination compared with X BA (9.2) and Normative Type "C" - Kyphotic (5.8).

Dorsal part

DII(5) of 1BA is 100 but for 2BA it is 148. The top D is higher in 1BA than in X BA (116) but lower than in Normative Type "C" - Kyphotic (97) and Type "A" - Normal (108) while the top of the curve is much lower for 2BA.

DCI(6) 1BA is 10.5, equivalent to X BA (10.7), but more than Normative Type "C" - Kyphotic (9.6). For 2BA the value is 17.7, considerably more than all other means.

RDC(7) is 485 mm for 1BA and 432 mm for 2BA. The radius of the dorsal curve is in each case greater than X BA (396 mm) but smaller than in Type "C" - Kyphotic (515 mm). Note that when the radius is great, the curvature is small.

Lumbar part

LTI(8) of 1BA is 126 and 125 for 2BA. The position of the top D is the same for both swimmers, it is lower than in X BA but higher than in Normative Type "C" - Kyphotic.

LCI(9): 13.4 for 1 BA and 17.7 for 2 BA. whilst it is 12.7 in X BA and 10.1 for Type "C" - Kyphotic, or 11.5 for Type "A" - Normal. The LCI of 2BA is enormous, outside all our means.

RLC(10): with 112 mm for 1BA and 95 mm for 2BA, less than 145 mm of X BA and 125 mm of Type "C" - Kyphotic, both swimmers present great curvature, especially 2BA.

Frontal plane

BR and 2BR have spines with lateral deviation to the right side (scoliosis).

For 1BR, the deviation grows gradually from the upper quarter of the dorsal curve up to a maximum at about top "D" of the dorsal curve then it diminishes progressively and crosses the cord of lumbar curve quite low to the end between lower point B and "I" (projection of upper point A L_5 ± 4CM) on the right side of the vertical.

For 2BR, the lateral deviation to the right is smaller than for 1BR but has the same appearance, it crosses the cord about the middle of the lumbar curve and ends like 1BR but closer to point B.

1BR is the best of the swimmers, and had longer training in 25 m swimming pool. The deviation is caused, according to us, by constant turning on the left side. In both 1BR and 2BR the maximal deviation was at the level of top "D" dorsal curve, and it is about double for 1BR than for 2BR. The lateral deviation for 2BR is smaller because the training time was shorter.

For 1BA the lateral deviation from the cord of the rachi's is extremely small, the line is regular but a little on the right of the vertical (rotation of spine).

For 2BA the lateral deviation is great, irregular and the difference with the cord is great, reaching its maximal value at level of top "D" and occurs on the left of vertical. In this case, one can speak of deformation because it is far from the anatomical position of the spine. The efficiency of the spine is reduced with an effect on performance.

The performance of 1BA is incomparably better than that of 2BA, who not being able to progress, has now abandoned swimming.

Conclusions

1   Normative typology by sexes with 10 Indexes permits the analysis of individual spherosomatograms.

2   The difference in Normative typology between males and females is small but differences in the lumbar parts are large, reflecting the child bearing function of women.

3   Many top swimmers have abnormal changes in their spinal curvature.

4   The shape of the spine of swimmers changes according to their major stroke practice. It is functional adaptation namely:

i   BR stroke specialists tend towards Type "B" -Lordotic or even Hyperlordoctic;

ii   BA stroke specialists tend towards Type "C" -Kyphotic or even Hyperkyphotic;

iii   C and BU swimmers are mainly close the Type "A" Normal.

5   Early specialization in BR or BA could cause deviation or even deformation and it is not profitable for overall long range results.

6   Spherosomatography of the rachis curve and Interpretation by Normative typology with 10 Indexes show the hight complexity of the

spine – the most dynamic part of the body.

7   We are convinced that there is a relationship between the shape of the body and performance. Further study is necessary with a spherosomatograph connected to a computer.

ACKNOWLEDGEMENT

Thanks are given to the Faculty of Medicine at UCL for financial support for the study.

References

Wielki, Cz. (1979). Vers une méthode électronique des mesures des courbes de la colonne vertébrale. Lyon Méditerranée Médical Médecine du Sud-Est, Paris, XV: 1223-1227.

Wielki, Cz. (1983). Method for measuring the curve of the spine by "Electronic Spherosomatograph". "Biomechanics VIII B". Vol. 4B, 1190-1197, Human Kinetic Publishers Inc, Champaign.

Wielki, D., Sturbois, X. and Wielki, Cz. (1985). Classification of the anatomical spinal curves of female students in standing position. "Biomechanics IX A", Vol. 5A, 263-268, Human Kinetic Publishers Inc, Champaign.

Wielki, Cz. (1986). Anatomical functional deviation of the rachis in aquatic sports. *New Zealand Journal of Sports Medicine,* **14** (1), 28-29.

Wielki, Cz. and Adrian, M. (1987). Aspect of spinal curve measurement of athletes. "Biomechanics in Sport", III and IV, Research Center for Sports Del Mar, California, 397-408.

Wielki, Cz. (1987). Anatomical functional deviation of the spinal curves of athletes. "Biomechanics X A", Vol. 6A, 567-573, Human Kinetic Publishers Inc, Champaign.

43. The Female and Competitive Swimming

C. A. HARDY

FOR HISTORICAL, CULTURAL AND pedogogical reasons, many females are discouraged from taking part or continuing in competitive swimming.

During the Roman and Viking eras of early Britain swimming held high status as a healthy and useful activity for men. To swim was part of the prowess of a hero and, frequently, the expert swimmer was singled out for special attention (Orme, 1983). Occasionally a female swimmer was cited in Norse literature but such a female would be regarded as unusual, viz. Thorgerd Brak, the slavewoman of Skallagrim and the fostermother of his son Egil was "a big woman, as strong as a man and a great sorceress who, when chased by Skallagrim to a cliffe, is able to jump down it and to swim away" (Orme, 1983 p.15).

Swimming was still a manly pursuit during the Middle Ages, albeit without the status of earlier times. Although the Tudor swimmer was able to perform various tricks in water (Orme, 1983) he did not compete publicly. With a society obsessed with a hierarchy of social ranks, defeat in competitions could have tarnished his social position. However, with swimming being regarded as a "boyish" activity, water for females was for ablution only, and rivers and ponds were for bathing and not for swimming (Orme, 1983) .

In William Percey's (Orme, 1983) "The Compleat Swimmer" (1658) swimming was presented as an activity for both males and females, although Percey assumed that the practitioners would be males (Orme, 1983, pp. 103-105). In fact, until the middle of the nineteenth century, it could be said that swimming was a male domain. In the early part of the nineteenth century Britain appeared to be lagging behind in promoting swimming for females and Clias, a well known physical educationalist and an author of a treatise on swimming, asked in 1825, "Why should the English females not learn to swim?" and said they "... remain inferior ... to the women of other countries" (Thomas, 1904, p. 162). It was not until 1859 that females started making efforts in London to promote swimming among themselves and to ask the question, "Why do not women swim?" (Thomas, 1904, p. 284). However, by the turn of the century, and just over 40 years after the opening of a bath for females in London (1858), there were 60 baths that could be used by females in the capital city.

Sergeant Leahy in his book "The Art of Swimming in the Eton Style", had emphasized the importance of teaching girls to swim. However, his comments reflect some of the prejudices of the day (Leahy, 1875, p. 52).

> I have heard people say that there is very little use in teaching girls to swim, as their clothes would prevent their swimming any distance, if they fell overboard. But I say differently, and I offer myself as a test. Clothe me in a woman's dress, and I will emerge to swim two hundred or three hundred

yards in it. It is very seldom that a woman would have more than fifty or sixty yards to swim to shore if capsized. If she knew anything about swimming she would not be in one-fiftieth of the danger which a woman who was quite ignorant of the art would incur. Even the being accustomed to the shock of suddenly entering cold water might save her life, as not unfrequently such a shock to the nerves would prove fatal to a woman.

Nevertheless, even in 1875 there were some females who, far from fainting on entering cold water, were performing feats of endurance.

On September 1, 1875, Miss Agnes Beckwith, then only fourteen years of age, swam from London Bridge to Greenwich, a distance of five miles, for a wager of £100. Commencing her journey at eight minutes to five with a steady breast stroke, Miss Beckwith covered the first mile and a half in 18 minutes. Limehouse Church – a trifle over half-way – was passed in 33 minutes, and Greenwich Pier was reached in 1 hr. 7 min. 45 sec. (Holbein, 1914, p. 102).

With regard to competitive swimming it was not until 1861 that females were allowed to watch a swimming "entertainment" given by males, and this was presented by the Ilex Swimming Club at Lambeth Baths. However, it took another 40 years (1901) before the ASA, having agreed to a female costume for galas, allowed a "ladies' championship" to be swum "in the presence of men or ladies only as they choose" (Thomas, 1904). Nevertheless very few females were involved in competitive swimming and Sachs (1912) puts this down to the ordeal of swimming in front of mixed audiences. Sachs felt "the present tendency to exploit females in a swimming bath in order that a gate may be attracted is a retrograde step in connection with amateur sport. These public exhibitions in baths are moreover prone to confine the sport to a certain class of swimmer – the class that has no qualms about being stared at when attired in a wet University costume ... It has been said that the ASA is not a society for the protection of public morals, and this is literally correct, but one of its manifold duties is to see to it that the amateur sport it governs is kept clean and decent." With the opening up of swimming facilities, the development of swimming as a school activity, the work of such institutions as the London Schools' Swimming Association, the formation of ladies' clubs (Kay, 1901, p.52) and the declared support of such authors as Sinclair and Henry (1893), Kay (1901) and Austin (1914), females would undoubtedly be given the opportunity to learn to swim in the twentieth century. Nevertheless attitudes do not change so easily and some swimming authors emphasized the differences between males and females by writing books for females only (Hedges, 1927); Bassett-Lowke, (1940) and the ASA did not illustrate "Swimming Instruction" (there were some female illustrations in the 1922 edition of Swimming Instruction) and "Swimming and Swimming Strokes" with females until 1937 and 1935 respectively.

Accepting that there is hardly any opposition to females learning to swim nowadays, why is it that competitive swimming for females is still regarded with some reservation by twentieth century society? Scott (1975; in Boutilier and San Giovanni, 1983, pp. 101-103) says that sport is our "civilized" society's most prominent masculinity rite and "it is in their games that boys assert their difference from girls and their superiority over them. It is in sport that they learn to compete, to control, to take risks, to be strong and to achieve mastery over self and others." Such a statement may seem very much out of line in modern society with the demands for equal opportunities for all, but Boutilier (1983) sees it as a reaction to the shift from rural to urban lifestyles, the growth of bureaucracy and technology and changes in the nature of work. With less opportunity for males to show physical strength, to take risks and to innovate in the workplace there has been an increased involvement by males in sport (General Household Survey, 1983). Also, for some males "to allow women into sport would be an ultimate threat to one of the last strongholds of male security and supremacy." (Boutilier, 1983). Although more females than ever compete in such festivals as the Summer Olympic Games, the sporting female may upset the gender role stereotype by bringing into question the social evaluation of gender roles that has ranked males higher than females. Although such activities as swimming, tennis and gymnastics are sometimes regarded as "female activities" compared with such contact sports as water polo, rugby and soccer, competitive sport is still a masculine domain. Water polo has only been accepted as a serious female game in Britain since 1982 and, even then, males have been quick to emphasize the differences between the male and female game. At present the women's water polo team is ranked higher in Europe than the men's team, but it is only the men's team that is being sent to the European Championships! Swimming as an activity is very popular among females (Evans, 1983; Ikulayo, 1983; Cockerill, 1987), and, in a recent report based on a scheme to stop school leavers dropping out of sport, swimming was listed at the top (Wade, 1987). However, although such an activity as swimming "may complement the supposedly 'natural' grace and charm of the female performer, the demonstration of the traditionally masculine traits of aggression ... competitiveness ...

strength is likely to lead to loss of femininity" (Cockerill and Hardy, 1987). As pressures for females to conform to gender norms increase during adolescence, many females are deterred from becoming seriously involved in highly competitive situations (Hendry, 1968; Schiltz and Rabe, 1979). Some researchers have noted the similarities between the personalities of male and female swimmers (Hendry, 1968) whereas others have noted the differences (Schiltz and Rabe, 1969). In addition, the stresses of training up to 25 hours per week and competing (Mugno, 1983; Tierney, 1988) increase the drop-out rate of female swimmers. Whereas the number of female registered swimmers is similar to that of boys between the ages of 11 and 17 years, females make up only 32.0% of the 10 258 registered swimmers over 18 years (Jan., 1989)(Table 1).

TABLE 1. *Census listing date: 30/01/89.*

Born year of	Age	Male	Female	Total
1979	10 and under	991	916	1907
1978	11	2233	2193	4426
1977	12	2684	2798	5482
1976	13	2578	2870	5448
1975	14	2177	2545	4722
1974	15	1911	2199	4110
1973	16	1610	1690	3300
1972	17	1286	1231	2517
1971	Over 18	6976	3282	10258

(Amateur Swimming Association)

According to Leaman (1985) working class girls are less likely to be attracted by the new sporting media image of the strong athletic woman, as they are still restricted by the ideal image of femininity as perpetuated by working class boys, i.e. the "page 3" model. Also, even if a girl is physically capable of taking part in a vigorous activity, she may not feel that it is a desirable thing to do (Scraton, 1985). Once females have made the decision to opt out of sport, they may find it difficult to return at a later date as gender is a structuring division in leisure (McInnes, 1989). According to Green et al. (1987) adult females have less time available for leisure than males and they have less time that is unambiguously free. (This may also account for the dearth of female swimming coaches.)

In spite of these gender constraints on females becoming involved in competitive sport, some females do train and compete at club, county, national and international level. However, by training and competing, females have to cope with the further problem of how to respond to a male dominated coaching environment (Cox and Noble, 1989). Very little research has been done on the interaction between the coach and the female swimmer during the actual coaching sessions. Although authors (Hastings, 1987) may list the qualities of an effective coach, mainly based on male data, many questions have yet to be asked, and answered, about the coaching process. How does the female swimmer perceive the coach? Is the female motivated by the coach's instructional style? Does the amount of training reflect the quality of that training? Do females respond more positively to male coaches?

Scraton (1989) has reported that in mixed-sex teaching boys take up a disproportionate amount of the teacher's time and attention, and that boys controlled the setting verbally and practically. Does this happen in swimming coaching? Undoubtedly, there are mediating processes (Doyle, 1977) that influence the female's responses in the training and competitive settings, and such processes need to be studied in our search for coaching effectiveness.

In concluding, I feel that progress has been made, and that females have become an integral part of the competitive scene. However, the emphasis placed on the performance gap at the highest level between males and females in the Olympic type events by the media only highlights the differences and superiority of the males, and minimizes the advances made by females in competition. Although males may be 12% faster at 100 m and 6% faster at 800 m (Hardy, 1989) (Figs 1 and 2; App. A), the feats of females in lake and swimming cross-channel is often more impressive than those of males.

"Alison Streeter, aged 23, swam from Ireland to Scotland, 20 miles across the North Channel, in nine hours and 53 minutes. She endured intense cold, multiple jellyfish stings and arrived in Port Patrick, Scotland, to cheering crowds and beat the world record, held by a man. Six days later she was off to swim 42 miles around Jersey. She also holds the British Double Channel record, a distance of 50 miles and the Round the Isle of Wight record, 62 miles." Hanson, 1988 p. 19 .

"Canadian Vicki Keith completed the first crossing of the English Channel last month using butterfly all the way. The 28-year-old swimmer made the crossing to France in 23 hours and 33 minutes." Swimming Times, p.1.

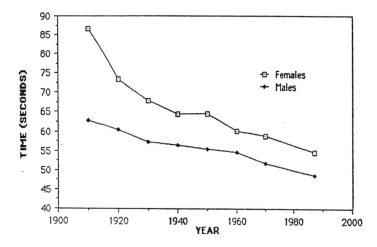

FIG. 1 Male and female world swimming records: 100 m freestyle.

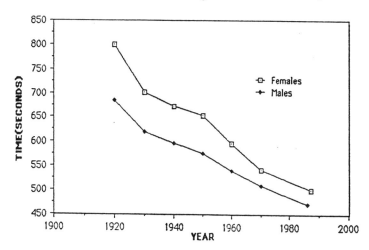

FIG. 2 Male and female world swimming records: 800 m freestyle.

However, such events are not exciting enough for media coverage and perhaps the females involved do not conform to the image portrayed in leisure advertising. The historical traditions placed females at an early disadvantage, the positive influences at the turn of the century improved their position, and female feats since have helped to break down many physiological myths about females and training. Nevertheless the gender stereotype is a very powerful "hidden" force that discourages many females from competing. "The socalization of girls and boys, men and women, leads to social role expectations and related behaviours that result in gender differences in achievement and in related motivation." (Farmer, 1987). As some occupations are seen as more suitable for men, others for women, and some are regarded as gender neutral, it is hardly surprising that competitive sport is often categorized in such a way.

According to Hall (1972), participation in sport among females could be increased if the image associated with "athletic women" was somehow changed so that it became more congruent with the stereotype associated with "feminine women". However, this would also involve "the concomitant change in the feminine image toward a direction more consonant with athleticism." In addition, the effects of the male dominated coaching environment on female competitive swimmers is unclear, and the mediating mechanisms that affect the coaching relationship need to be understood. The argument that females have the opportunity to compete assumes that free choice exists and denies the existence of social pressures and conditions. Perhaps fully to comprehend the issues and problems of the female in competitive swimming, we must not only study the female competitor, but also those females who have rejected competitive sport.

References

Amateur Swimming Association. (1941). "Swimming Instruction". Simpkin Marshall, London.

Amateur Swimming Association. (1935). "Swimming and Swimming Strokes". Simpkin Marshall, London.

Austin, H.R. (1914). "How to Swim". Methuen, London.

Bassett-Lowke. J. (1940). "Swimming and Diving for Women and Children". Sir Isaac Pitman and Sons, London.

Boutilier, M.A. and San Giovanni, L. C. (1983). "The Sporting Woman". Human Kinetics, Champaign.

Cockerill, S.A. (1987). The attitude of fourth year girls to physical activity. Unpublished M.Phil. thesis, Loughborough University of Technology, Loughborough.

Cockerill, S.A. and Hardy, C.A. (1987). The concept of femininity and its implications for physical education. *British Journal of Physical Education*, **18** (4), 149-151.

Cox, R.H. and Noble, L. (1989). Preparation and attitudes of Kansas high school head coaches. *Journal of Teaching in Physical Education,* **8** (4) 329-341.

Doyle, W. (1977). Paradigms for research on teacher effectiveness. *In* "Review of

Research in Education". Vol. 5, (Ed. L.S. Shulman). Itasca, Illinois.

Evans, D. (1983). Methods of gaining feedback from senior girl pupils in school. *British Journal of Physical Education*, **14** (1), 20-21.

Farmer, H.S. (1987). A multivariate model for explaining gender differences in career and achievement motivation. *Educational Researcher*, **16** (2), 5-9.

Green, E., Hebron, S. and Woodward, D. (1987). Leisure and gender. *In* "A Report to the Joint Panel on Leisure and Recreation Research". Sports Council and Economic and Social Research Council, London.

Hall, M.A. (1972). A "feminine woman" and an "athletic woman" as viewed by female participants and non-participants in sport. *British Journal of Physical Education*, **3** (6), 43-46.

Hanson, M. (1988). Sport for All, *The Guardian*, September 26th, 1988.

Hardy, C. A. (1989). "The Development of Female Competitive Swimming in Great Britain". Department of Physical Education and Sports Science, Loughborough University.

Hastings, D.W. (1987). "College Swimming Coach". University Press of America, New York.

Hedges, S. G. (1927). "The Girls' Book of Swimming". Brown, Son and Ferguson, Glasgow.

Hendry, L.B. (1969). A personality study of highly successful and ideal swimming coaches, *Research Quarterly*, **40** (2), 299-304.

Holbein, M.A. (1914). "Swimming". C. Arthur Pearson Limited, London.

Ikulayo, P.E. (1983). Attitudes of girls towards physical education. *Physical Education Review* **6** (1), 24-25.

Kay, J. (1901). "How to Teach Swimming in Schools and Colleges". Croneen and Company, New Brompton.

Leahy, "Sergeant", (1875). "The Art of Swimming in the Eton style". MacMillan, London.

Leaman, O. (1985). "Class and the Female Body". Workshop in the Sociology of Physical Education and Sport, Sheffield City Polytechnic, September 18th.

McInnes, H.A. (1989). Life Styles and Leisure Participation. Unpublished Doctoral dissertation, Loughborough University of Technology, Loughborough, England.

Mugno, D.A. (1983). Why are young swimmers dropping out? *Swimming World*, **24** (4), 29-30.

Orme, N. (1983). "Early British Swimming". University of Exeter, Exeter.

Office of Population Censuses and Surveys, (1983). General Household Survey, H.M.S.O., London.

Sachs, F. (1912). "The Complete Swimmer". Methuen, London.

Scraton, S. J. (1985). "Gender and Schooling". Workshop in the Sociology of Physical Education and Sport, Sheffield City Polytechnic, September 18th.

Scraton, S. J. (1989). "Issues in Mixed Physical Education". Sheffield City Polytechnic, June 17th.

Schiltz, J. and Rabe, K. (1979). Personality traits of state-level swimmers. *Swimming Technique*, **15** (4), 98-101.

Sinclair, A. and Henry, W. (1893). "Swimming". Longmans, Green, London.

Swimming Times, (1989). "Reported in the Swimming Times". **66** 8,1.

Thomas, R. (1904). "Swimming". Sampson Low, Marston, London.

Tierney, J. (1988). Stress in age-group swimmers. *Swimming Technique*, **24** (4), 9-14.

Wade, E. (1987). "Bridging the Gap". Research Working Paper 22, Sports Council, London.

Appendix

Percentage differences in world record performances between males and females from the early part of the twentieth century to the present day (1987).

Distance (metres)	Year	Time (minutes and seconds) Female	Male	Percentage Difference
50 freestyle	1987	00.25.28 (1986)	00.22.32 (1987)	13.261
100 freestyle	1910	01.26.60	01.02.80	37.898
	1987	00.54.73 (1986)	00.48.74 (1986)	12.289
200 freestyle	1920	02.56.00	02.19.80	25.894
	1987	01.57.55 (1986)	01.47.44 (1984)	09.409
400 freestyle	1920	06.30.20	05.14.60	24.030
	1987	04.05.45 (1987)	03.47.80 (1985)	07.748
800 freestyle	1920	13.19.00	11.24.20	16.778
	1987	08.19.53 (1987)	07.50.64 (1986)	06.138
1500 freestyle	1930	23.44.60	19.07.20	24.180
	1987	16.00.73 (1987)	14.54.76 (1983)	07.372
100 breaststroke	1930	01.26.30	01.14.00	16.621
	1987	01.07.91 (1987)	01.01.65 (1984)	
200 breaststroke	1930	03.11.20	02.45.00	15.878
	1987	02.27.40 (1986)	02.13.34 (1984)	10.154
100 backstroke	1930	01.20.60	01.08.20	18.181
	1987	01.00.59 (1984)	00.55.19 (1983)	09.784
200 backstroke	1930	02.58.20	02.32.20	17.082
	1987	02.08.60 (1986)	01.58.14 (1985)	08.853
100 butterfly	1960	01.09.10	00.58.70	17.717
	1987	00.57.93 (1981)	00.52.84 (1986)	09.632
200 butterfly	1960	02.34.40	02.12.80	16.265
	1987	02.05.96 (1981)	01.56.24 (1985)	08.853
200 individual medley	1970	02.23.50	02.09.30	10.982
	1987	02.11.73 (1981)	02.00.56 (1987)	09.265
400 individual medley	1970	05.04.70	04.31.00	12.435
	1987	04.36.10 (1982)	04.15.42 (1987)	08.096

Note: Dates were selected only where comparisons could be made.

Part 10
Psychological Factors

44. The Psychology of Learning to Swim

L. E. COOKE

Where do our international swimmers come from?

THE OBVIOUS AND SEEMINGLY simple answer to this question is, that they come from amongst the thousands of youngsters who learn to swim in the early years of their life. The problem hidden by this simple answer is that if the number of children learning to swim is not the full number who might be able to learn, then the field of potential Internationals is correspondingly reduced. Sufficient restraints already operate to reduce the "base" numbers swimming (lack of opportunity, lack of uptake, reduced school swimming and so on), without adding to the problem by making "learning to swim" a negative experience.

The importance of it being a positive experience is that it will become the foundation to a lifetime's activity and can underpin many other aquatic activities. This is well summarized by Hardy (1987).

How is "learning to swim" to be a positive experience?

The answer is obviously, because the child learns to swim, and enjoys him or herself in the process.

But again, a simple answer masks a complexity of factors. For example, the way in which the child comes to view him or herself as a success, a failure, a conscientious swimmer or as a "skiver", is to a large extent the result of interactions between him/herself and the teacher. These attributions and self evaluations can stay with the child throughout his/her swimming life and have dramatic effects on training attitudes, competition performance, and his/her psychological strength and health.

It is very easy to make swimming a negative experience.

How to ensure dropout

1 If the child is nervous, make a big effort to frighten him or her more.
2 Make the lesson as boring as possible.
3 Make the lesson too long, so that the child gets thoroughly chilled.
4 Make sure that the session hurts.
5 Keep individual attention to the minimum. Make sure that you forget the child's name.
6 Never speak in a kindly way, never smile, never joke and above all, *never* praise the child.
7 Keep the child standing on the side, especially if he or she is already wet. If possible, make sure that there is an open door nearby.
8 Always use the best swimmer for demonstrations. Make sure everyone else knows how hopeless they are.
9 Have a word with the technicians at the pool and ensure that there is too much chlorine in the water (adapted from an idea by Richardson, 1976).

What are the main foci of psychological interest and/or research in swimming?

Stress/Anxiety and management (e.g. Berger and Owen 1987; and for a summary: Cooke, 1985).
Motivation (e.g. Gould *et al.*, 1982, Nideffer, 1982)
Personality characteristics (e.g. Furst and Hardman, 1988)
Attribution (e.g. Houghton, 1986).

Whilst there is a real paucity of specifically swim-oriented literature, most of the aforementioned areas are well researched through a wide range of other sports (e.g. the wealth of research work from Roberts and his students at Illinois University).

Why, despite the clear recognition of the value of psychological strength in competitive swimming and an awareness of the implications of psychological damage in youth sports, is there so little published about the youngest ages/stages in learning to swim?

I suggest that there are three major reasons. Firstly; there is no real evidence of a linear relationship between what occurs whilst the child is learning to swim and whether that child stays in swimming. However, anecdotal evidence from, *inter alia,* my own students makes it very clear that there is a strong link. Secondly, there are difficulties in carrying out psychological research with young children which do not occur in the "hard" sciences. For example, the need to consider the child's intellectual and/or cognitive level and to work within the child's language frame. These mean that interactions with the children tend to be simplistic, and this in turn can throw some doubt on to the validity of the experiential data. Thirdly, longitudinal research, such as would be needed to monitor the progress of young swimmers over a period of years, needs financial and academic resources that are inevitably at a premium.

What does psychological research tell us about "learning to swim"? Surprisingly little, although there is much published material concerned with psychological aspects of skill acquisition, training adherence, performance enhancement (especially under stress) in other sports. However, by searching for material specifically looking at developmental aspects of skill acquisition, cognitive stage, competitive ability and perception of control, it is possible to identify factors that explain what is going on during the process of learning to swim. More general material about psychological processes in youths (12 years plus) gives further indication of what might be occurring in the later stages of childhood (8-12 years), and why. This in turn can help us look more closely at early stages of the swimming career.

What aspects of psychology are particularly relevant to a child learning to swim? In answer to this question, here is a flow diagram looking at the psychological dimension of coaching, followed by one of teaching (see Fig. 1) (modified from Fox, 1988a). It is clear that if the child is to have a positive orientation towards swimming, at whatever level, he/she must have a positive experience of swimming. There are many areas of psychological content to consider, but the focus here will be on four of these: readiness to learn, interpersonal relationships of communication, and perceived controllability. These four overlap and interrelate strongly.

Swimming Teacher

Teaching style   Teaching content

Swimming experience
↓
Child's perception in/of swimming
↓
Psychological orientation to swimming
↓
Future activity patterns

FIG. 1. Adapted from Fox (1988a).

Readiness to learn

Defined by Malina (1984) as "the match between a child's level of growth, maturity and development on the one hand, and the tasks/demands presented by competitive sport on the other", it applies to the beginner in the sense that the child's individual capacity (his/her physiological and psychological competency) must balance the demands of the swimming lesson. These latter include the skill level, language level, cognitive capacity, level of fear and anxiety, past experience of the child and the quality and attitude of the teacher. Should a mismatch occur, learning will be hampered. This will occur whether the mismatch is due to the lesson demands being too great (child cannot cope) or too low (child is bored).

The motivation of the child affects the effort he/she is prepared to put into the lesson. Besides the well known work by McClelland, Horner and others on Achievement Motivation (e.g. need for success, need to avoid failure, the need to avoid success), the research generated by Marty Maehr and John Nicholls during the 1980s has some relevance. These latter suggest three Universal Achievement Orientations, common to all cultures and ages: Ability orientation; Task orientation; Social approval orientation.

Robert's (e.g.1984,1982) research with children and adolescents, retitles these as Sport Competence (outcome oriented); Sport Mastery (performance oriented); Social Approval.

It is believed that children move through these orientations as a function of age, although it is clear that the goals are not mutually exclusive. Maehr and Nicholls (1980), and Roberts (1984 and personal communication) argue the notion that sport mastery comes first, chronologically. This is supported by the fact that the concept of ability affecting success seems to arise around late childhood/early adolescence. Further research has suggested that the greatest number of dropouts from sport appear to be from the children strongest in competence orientation. This could be because they come to believe that they cannot win (discovering that effort alone is insufficient for success) and therefore choose to drop out rather than "fail" (Roberts, 1984). Recognizing that besides being split by the same language, we might also be split by the same motives Whitehead (1986) looked at British sports children (X ages: 9, 12, 15 years). She found that there was a non-significant dropout from the competence group, compared to the others. However, she found, in parallel to the American research, that the children most likely to stay in sport were those whose strongest motivation was for social approval. In a sport such as swimming, where the teacher/coach works so closely with the swimmers, once the child is able to understand and articulate, these goals are open to discussion and possible modification. In the meantime, recognition of the fact that most young children find pleasure in mastering skill and being alert for the moment that his/her swimmer's main achievement goal moves towards competence and/or social approval, means that the teacher can plan accordingly

Interpersonal relationships

The relationship between the swimming teacher and the child is of enormous significance to the child's perception of the entire "swimming experience" modifying Fox's (1988*b*) work, this can be shown thus:

Swimming teacher
Teaching style, teaching content
Swimming experience
Child's perception in/of swimming
Psychological orientation to swimming
Future activity patterns (adapted from Fox, 1988*b*).

It is clear that a child's statement that "I don't like swimming" can hide a multitude of reasons, and most parents of swimming children will have experienced the need to sift out the "true" reason behind such a statement, at some stage. Deffner (1987) points out that "people may not appear to others, as they imagine themselves to appear, and thus there is a possibility of profound differences between intended and received messages". In other words: the teacher who sees herself as caring, considerate and sensitive might be seen by the child as overbearing, "nosey" or even as threatening. However, as Fox (1988) points out, teachers who are sensitive, willing to show respect and an ability to listen to children are those teachers most likely to have a positive effect on a child's self esteem, which in turn leads to a positive attitude. It would seem that an ability to be critically aware of one's teaching style; one's interactive style as well as of one's material is an important part of the teaching experience. Equally, being sensitive to the child's perceptions is an important part of the success of the learning process. Kagan *et al.* (1957) claim that childhood traits, of cautiousness and shyness, and of fearlessness and uninhibited behaviour which are present in the second year of life are carried through to the sixth year of life. Having identified physiological differences, mainly in the limbic and hypothalamic structures, they point out the value of combined psychological and physiological investigations. From the teacher's point of view, the research is of value because it reminds us that behaviour of children in new, unfamiliar or challenging situations or with unfamiliar adults is a complex of many factors. Clearly the establishment of mutually positive interpersonal relationships, so important to the child's progress, is a fascinating and complex process.

Communication

In 1983 Hopper highlighted the importance of an interactive flow of information between coach and swimmer. In this case he was referring to masters swimmers. But it is equally important that there is good communication between young swimmers and their teacher. This does not mean that the lesson needs to degenerate into a verbal "free for all".

One particular aspect of communication that deserves attention is that of Non Verbal Communication (NVC), which makes up about 70% of the communication. For successful interaction, both teacher and swimmer need to know each other's "codes" of NVC. The "good" teacher often is one who instinctively knows and registers the child-specific NVC pattern: for example whether a smile indicates happiness, nervousness or mischief (Cooke, 1989). Equally the teacher must ensure the child understands his/her own code, remembering that if NVC and the verbal message do not tally, the child will pay far more attention to the NVC.

Perceived controllability

Over recent years there has been considerable interest in the reasons that children (and adults!) give for their successes and failures. Early work by Heider and Weiner in the 1950s produced a model to show the four main attributions.

A model of attribution locus of causality, internal/external.
Stable/ability task/difficulty.
Unstable/effort/luck.

Deriving from this fairly simplistically, it is possible to state that the child who attributes his/her success in swimming to luck, will take little responsibility for this. Equally, a child who attributes his/her failure to lack of ability, may drop out of the sport, since s/he will see little hope of progress. Roberts (1984, 1986) points out that children over the age of 12 years begin to see that effort is not a sufficient compensation for lack of ability, which tends to hasten the dropout. A pilot study by Redfern (1989) suggested that children begin to make differential attributions to effort/ability at a slightly earlier age than the American studies suggest. Obviously, if this is so, it has some implications for the teacher of swimming.

Johnson and Biddle's (1989) report on the behaviour of nonpersisters in sport suggests that they make more negative self statements and more negative attributions than those who persist in the face of failure. Since attributions have such a significant effect on the future behaviour of children (and adults), it is clear that the teacher at the initial stages of learning has an enormous part to play, he/she needs to structure the swimming demands so that the child successfully moves from stage to stage, but he/she must recognize that, as the learner moves into competitive swimming, the child must also experience "failure" at times. The way in which the teacher/coach helps the child to attribute these successes and failures will lay a pattern of perceived control which will become an intrinsic part of that swimmer's behaviour.

References

Berger, B. and Owen, D. (1987). Anxiety reduction with swimming. *International Journal of Sport Psychology*, **18**, 286-302.
Cooke, L. (1989). Learning to swim, psychological aspects. *Swimming*, **5**, 17-20.
Cooke, L. and Alderson, J. (1986). "Stress and Anxiety in Sport". Pavic, Des.

Deffner, G. (1987). Looking at self or others – Differences in facial expression. *British Journal of Sports Psychology*, **4**, 341-343.

Fox, K. (1988*a*). The psychological dimension in PE. *British Journal of Physical Education*, **19**, 34-38.

Fox, K. (1988*b*) The child's perspective in physical education: The self-esteem complex. *British Journal of Physical Education*, **19**, 247-252.

Furst, O. and Hardman, J. (1988). The iceberg profile and young competitive swimmers, *PMS*, **67**, 478.

Gould, D., Feltz, D., Weiss, M. and Petlichkoff, L. (1982). Participation motives in competitive youth swimmers. *In* "Mental Training for Coaches and Athletes". (Eds T. Orlick, J. Partington and J. Salmela). Canada Coaching Association of Canada, Ottawa.

Hopper, R. (1983). Let your swimmers do the talking. *Swimming Technique,* May-July 11-19.

Houghton, D. (1986). Winning and losing: an attributional perspective. (unpublished) University of Liverpool/Chester College.

Johnson, L. and Biddle, S. (1989). Persistence after failure: an exploratory look at "learned helplessness" in motor performance. *BJPE Research Supplement,* **5**, 7-10.

Kagan, J., Reznick, S. and Snidman, N. (1987). The physiology and psychology of behavioral inhibition in children. *Child Development*, **58**, 1459-1473.

Malina, M. (1986). Readiness for competitive sport. *In* "Sport for Children and Youths Human Kinetics". (Eds M. Weiss and D. Gould).

Nideffer, R. (1982). Aiming the mind swimming. *Technique*, **18**, 4 (Feb/April) 12-15.

Roberts, G. (1984). Towards a new theory of motivation in sport. *In* "Psychological Foundations of Sport Human Kinetics". (Eds J. Silva and R. Weinberg).

Roberts, G. (1986). The growing child and the perception of competitive stress in sport, *In* "The Growing Child in Competitive Sport". (Ed. G Gleeson). Hodder and Stoughton.

Whitehead, J. (1986). Achievement goals and dropout in youth sport. *In* "The Growing Child in Competitive Sport". (Ed. G Gleeson). Hodder and Stoughton.